'DAS BOOTY is a bewitching linguistic confection. Every sentence sparks with invention.'

Lee Brackstone, *Faber and Faber*

'DAS BOOTY is fascinating. A remarkable and weird book. It feels a bit like Genet, Kerouac and Henry Miller having a particularly strong smoke together. It could outsell Burroughs. More readable but equally strange.'

Michael Schmidt, *Carcanet Press*

'The writing is full of energy and the story is very strong.'

Ailah Ahmed, *Canongate*

'DAS BOOTY is a very funny, rueful, uproarious book. The events it depicts are largely incredible and all true. It is written in a wonderfully rich, louche style. It is so *sui generis* that I believe it might indeed have considerable critical and popular success. It has film written all over it.'

Chris Miller, *Critic*

D1513111

SIMON PRINGLE

DAS BOOTY

In Memoriam
Bruno Lúcio de Carvalho Tolentino
1940-2007

'Shipwrecked in flesh
as a final remark.'
'Se non è vero, è ben trovato.'

Published in 2013
by FeedARead.com Publishing – Arts Council funded
Copyright © Simon Pringle.

A CIP catalogue record for this title is available from the British Library.

THE PLAYERS

LUCIO – Brazilian poet, wizard, astrologer. The Brains
SHYNO – Lucio's partner and Muse. The Skipper
MONA GORDA – 40 foot concrete hulled bare boat
BIG NEV – youth crippled by polio. Crew member. Mascot
DAVE JEEKS aka YAYA – DJ, cult member. The Fall Guy
ALAN ARMSTRONG aka THE MECHANIC . The Muscle
RICH LEE BAZAAR aka ESCARGOTS – Coke dealer. Driver.
JADE – Irish Tarot Card reader. Psychic Controller
LARRY – East End car dealer and breaker
WILHELM – Danish boat builder in PUERTO ANDRATX
MUSTAPHA aka THE CUCUMBER – Moroccan hashish farmer
CAPTAIN ALI MANSOUR – Commander of the Moroccan
coastguard cutter
TIO ENRIQUE aka EL COJO – Colombian emerald dealer
GLORIA – Enrique's Transsexual nephew
MAYA – Cuban Santeria Priestess and Medium

PRESS-GANG

It was YaYa who floated the idea of a boat.

YaYa was actually Dave Jeeks, a lanky, somewhat mournful youth who could have passed for a young Clint Eastwood. This likeness had given rise to a second nickname, Rowdy, which amused the gang since he hardly ever spoke a word. Dave worked part-time as a bookie's assistant and as if to make up for his apparent aphasia had become adept at tic-tac. He was also an occasional DJ and it suited him, as he could let the music do most of the talking. In his spare time he was a member of some specious cult known as *The Divine Lighters*. He was a recent recruit, a *premmie*, or neophyte. 'Dimly lit', as Lúcio once remarked.

True, Dave was no bright spark. He was in thrall to a teenage Guru who operated out of Malaga by way of Bangkok. Four times a year, along with several thousand other benighted followers, they would congregate in a southern Spanish bullring where their Master, a fat little crook, gave *satsang* from a raised dais garlanded with flowers. Prayer over he would hose them all down with jets of coloured water using a Franco-era fire engine hired for the occasion. Meanwhile his acolytes wandered among them collecting up offerings of a more metallic hue. He was called Gugugajuju or something similar. A true holy roller with a small fleet of that marque which he employed to ferry about his retinue.

None of the gang had ever heard Dave utter more than one or two syllables at a time. Da. Damn! Ya? Ta... So the effect of his outburst was immediate. Lúcio stopped reading, closed the Ephemeris in which he had been calculating the effects of his outer planetary transits, put down the book, looked up over his gold rimmed half-moon reading glasses and with customary politeness enquired,

'What was that again, Dave?'

'Ya ya, yuse shud do ah boot run, down tae Maroccoh.'

YaYa was neither German nor braying hooray. He was Scots but he hailed from Milton Keynes. Somewhere along the way he had contrived to reduce his vocabulary to this surprisingly expressive duo-syllabic format. To hear him holding forth quite so expansively was as compelling as a cat farting *a cappella*.

His chum Alan, who styled himself The Mechanic, was a mechanic, which meant he carried tools, in his off-white van, which he used for motor repairs and inflicting wounds that would also require repairs.

'Goodun, Dave.'

Alan Armstrong was not entirely the caricature he pretended to be. Certainly the close-cropped simian skull, swart forearms festooned with lurid tattoos and casually contrived air of menace were enough to warn off many who strayed into his environs. But he liked poetry and especially Larkin. The Old Wanker he called him, with some affection.

'*Something is pushing them
To the side of their own lives*' he would intone.

'And it's probably me.'

Big Nev, Neville Black, who was both big but not big, sat folded in an antique armchair, his scruffy NHS boots poised on a brocaded footstool.

'Any one fancy a number? Got a decent bit of Leb.'

The question was rhetorical as he had been furnishing

joints to the assembled tea party for the better part of the afternoon and they were drinking tea, not builders' brew, but Lapsang Souchong out of Lúcio's delicately patterned fine bone china. Given the array of mitts on display it was salutary that nothing had been broken.

Take Nev's hands for a moment. Winged and powerful, they operated at an angle from his wrists that recalled nothing so much as the flippers on a seal. That he was quite so adroit with a couple of skins and a hank of draw was a matter of quiet wonder. It was his crutches, set like two I-Ching picking sticks alongside his chair which had brought this odd alignment about. Crutches for his Polio. And a decade of dragging around the cast-iron braces that bracketed his wasted limbs from heel to thigh. Which was why he was big, with the upper torso of a front row rucker; and not big, with the truncated and collapsible pins of a marionette. He stood, when he did, just short of five feet nothing.

A snuffle followed by a sniff was the familiar prologue to any contribution from Rich Lee Bazaar. He did not really require a sobriquet as his folks had furnished him with one at birth.

'Sounds over-complicated, if you ask me.'

'I am not sure that anyone was asking.'

Rich shifted uneasily before Lúcio's mild rebuke. He never felt quite comfortable in the man's presence, veering between some kind of obsequious fawning and a bluff bonhomie that in his more cogent moments he ascribed to the fact that he was born Californian and what's more, a bit of a bore. In restaurants he would invariably order snails in garlic, so the gang referred to him as Escargots.

Whereas Lúcio had history. A solid five hundred years of inscribed, framed and traceable lineage. Antecedents. Those who had fallen before. You would have to make it up. Prize-winning multi-lingual poet, philosopher, aristocrat, mathematician, voodoo practitioner, member of the Papal court. A Renaissance mind settled in distinctly dark-age Little England. His family portraits hung in national museums across Europe. His great-great-grandfather had, he claimed, built an opera house in the jungles of Brazil and sent his laundry back home by clipper ship to his estate in Tuscany. Lúcio, a dapper little *guinea* exile with a golden tongue and a quick-silver mind. The genuine DD. A double diamond. A dope dealer. And a queer's queer. He said,

'Have some more tea Dave, and tell me your idea.'

'Okies, ya ya.'

Why is it criminals, even amateur ones, adorn themselves with nick-names, monikers? Perhaps it helps foster the gang mentality. Elevates them out of their mundane sphere.

The one remaining bum in the room had so far kept *schtum* and was wondering when Neville would eventually spark up his number and how he could secure a berth on the guest list to Tetouan.

A former beauty and Lúcio's catamite, he was known variously as Shyno, Dr Know and the Official Opposition. All these were terms of endearment. He was a feckless, genial chancer and a budding minstrel. Wastrel was more like it. Besides he didn't have a dime to his name and his only immodest claim to fame was as Lúcio's muse,

'*Per cui tant'alto il ver discerno.*'

And a few loose leaves of his own somewhat recherché poetry.

Sure, there had been the odd menial job. In no particular order, short order chef, labourer, record shop assistant. And yet despite a reasonable Eng. Lit. degree he had let himself devolve into some sort of parody of the reluctant wife, a Rupert Brooke manqué,

'*Dreaming on the verge of strife,*
Magnificently unprepared
For the long littleness of life'.

As Lúcio was fond of reminding him.

Still, if this boat business had any legs, they were going to need a Skipper. And since Lúcio disdained to drive a car, relied on Shyno as his chauffeur and could barely swim; while Neville could hardly stand even on dry land, let alone perch on some pitching ocean deck, he spied a vacancy. One benefit of being brought up on boats in the Caribbean. Besides, he had some inkling of what it meant to put out to sea.

'Any good, Nev? How much are we talking about?'

Neville was all set to elaborate on his lump of resin when Alan pre-empted him.

'Just under three hundredweight mate, first shake, top quality press. Go on Dave, tell 'em.'

Which Dave then did with a fluency and concision that even Lúcio had to admire.

'Yaya, yuse guys ya buy a boot in Majorca, take it doon tae Ceuta. It's still Spanish territory, so nae Roccy stamp in yer passports. We ken this farmer ya? So come harvest we poot the bales onnie beach an yuse guys cruise by ya, an ah get loaded up yup, anna head on back ya? The rest is by mo'ah.'

A look of defeated bliss settled across YaYa's features. Nev rocked forward from his waist, snapped straight the hinge of first the left and then the right calliper of his braces, plucked up his crutches and with two swings stood swaying over the beatific Dave.

'Have a suck on this mate, it's blinding shit.'

And to the assembled crew,

'Excuse us, gotta take a creak.'

Richly Bizarre looked like his nose was out of joint, which in truth it was. Some trick of genes had gifted him an almost pert beak of a proboscis, Roman-lite. But at the last minute it swerved off like an inverted ski jump down and to the left. An inveterate tooter, the constant rifling and tweaking of this pink-tipped set of tubes set him apart.

'Uh yeah, well, wad do you reckon?'

Reckon. Recce. Recon. Re: con. Wrecked on. Rocks. Right.

'Sounds intriguing,' said Lúcio, languidly.

Rich nodded. YaYa's gambit made him feel like he had been doubled on his own slam bid. He was the one who had first finessed Neville as a cripple dope mule to the border patrol at LAX, long before it was fashionable. Taped a bundle of *perrica* to his parrot legs in the bogs at *El Dorado*, Bogota, and watched him swing sweating through customs control.

Rich had a talent for spotting talent in matters of transport. So when Nev introduced him to Lúcio it was love at first sniff. The man was of another order. A Latin-American lecturer in languages with a diplomatic passport, almost untouchable. A top Top Trump. What's more he was nerveless, deemed the Law negligible, and was broke.

On his first run Rich duct-taped a kilo of flake to Lúcio's waist and he waltzed it, but for a paltry commission. Lúcio spoke fluent Spanish and had charm, whereas Rich didn't. So Lúcio turned himself into the Capo and Rich the capon. Thus and thus he made 'the business' *his* business.

Bruno Lúcio dalla Quercia [meaning oak] di Tolentino. You can see a portrait of his ancestor Niccolò in the Duomo, Florence. *Il Condottiere*, a mercenary from the 15th century. Or view him in action at the battle of San Romano, in the

National Gallery. Tuscan, soldier, seer, sage.

'No, we do not run in circles. We follow
the one straight line, provided
its ends never meet an end. Given that
movement but disproves itself.'

A man not of this Age.

So how did it come to this? A gang of misfits gaming to get rich quick.

A brief back history should give you the gist of it.

ADDENDA

In 1970, while living in London, Lúcio took a lectureship in languages at Bristol University and in the autumn of his first year there made a serious mistake. He fell for one of his students. The affair was conducted in public and created a scandal, not only for the impropriety but because it was illegal. Had he chosen a female and been discreet he might have got away with it. He chose the opposite and the youth was underage. It cost him his job, wife, reputation and later seven years at Her Majesty's pleasure. There is a price to pay for passion and for poetry.

Word got about. Sam 'The Beak' Beckett had some sympathy. As did Bacon and Adrien de Menasce, a painter of exquisite abstract figures few have yet heard of. Lúcio might have thought he could count on the artistic *confrérie*, but in the end they were also his wife's friends and they settled for the orthodox; took neither the side of the betrayer nor the wounded bride, lovely Marcia. She was the original *Girl from Ipanema*.

As for Lúcio, it proved both social and professorial suicide. Shunned, impoverished, he and Shyno rented a modest two-up two-down in North Oxford and set out a salon of sorts, where those few who knew but didn't care came to pay court. Lúcio was a virtuoso entertainer, Catholic in his audience and incautious about his guests. He crossed paths with Neville one day outside the benefits office and the rest would be, if not inevitable, some kind of history.

A late July sun basked the sitting room. Nev clanked back in. There was a perfumed air of part-refined degeneracy. Two lags, a cripple, a pair of sodomites and one West Coast wannabe. Lúcio rose and unlatched a small sash window to clear the fumes. A pact had been made. It was the damp midsummer of 1978.

After all their guests had gone Lúcio turned to his friend and said,

'I think we had better have a word with Jade.'

JADE

Lúcio never undertook any enterprise, legitimate or otherwise, without first consulting the invisible realm. He called the visible *the untrue* and subscribed to the adage that as far as the physical world was concerned, whatever *can* go wrong, will. He preferred to rely on insights he derived from the motions of the planets and when pressed would explain it thus:

'Astrology has nothing to do with cause and effect. It's a map of probabilities, a symbolic language. Of course if you can't read or speak it, it's the purest mumbo-jumbo.'

His second source of intelligence was *Candomblé,* an animist religion brought over to Brazil by African slaves, commonly and mistakenly demonised in the popular press as voodoo. True, it did entail spirit possession, magic and blood sacrifice (not human but animal), especially if you wished to influence the natural order of things and curry favour with its gods.

The third was a small coterie of mediums and clairvoyants of whom Jade was the seeress of choice. Head of Psychic Air Command, as Lúcio called her. A peerless reader of Tarot. Of Irish ancestry. The seventh daughter of a seventh daughter, born with a caul over her face. First class academic mind, mediaeval scholar. Matriarchist. Lucid and accurate.

'Simply the best card reader I have come across. No psychic gossip, she gets straight to the point.'

Lúcio rarely made comment or passed judgement about anyone's peculiarities or appearance. He was too much a gentleman or he thought it irrelevant.

'Mind you, she is somewhat unusual.'

Shyno met her for the first time when they went to enquire about the boat. Jade operated out of a third floor flat in St. John's Street, Oxford. Lúcio rang the bell, the lock buzzed open and a disembodied voice full of static hissed down to the street.

'Mind the stars.'

Did she mean stairs? Maybe. Stares? No, but she might as well have. They were shown in by a short plump girl wearing a head shawl with a thick rope of hair down to her waist which gave her the look of a Thelwell pony. She had a prodigious rump and pneumatic breasts, Shyno couldn't help noticing. She never raised her thick-lashed eyes and seemed almost somnambulant, as though she were high on some other-world drug.

Then Jade appeared. Shyno stared and tried not to, so he fixed on her eyes. They were the colour of the stone she was named after and had a faraway gaze that was entirely focused. When she looked back it was not through but into him as if a torch-beam was probing the cellar of his soul. He shivered and shifted his attention to her hands, which she didn't offer in greeting but kept clasped on her chest. They were a work in living ivory: bluish-green prominent veins tinged by the rose of blood, long tapered fingers with plain nails and quarter moon lunulas. Ideal for dealing cards. He wanted to look away but was compelled to complete the picture. Shoulder-length, lank mousey hair parted in the middle. A nose that looked broken and un-repaired. An obvious hare lip, decently sutured, camouflaged with a thick application of makeup, which accounted for her lisp. A small but prominent pot belly, like the pregnant looking bride in Van Eyck's marriage portrait, though as Lúcio later informed him, no man had ever crossed her desire.

'Please her Dea, cumminy in.'

Shyno was having difficulty making sense of her words. A lilting chant, part nasal, part sibilant. He put it down to her impediments, nodded and forced a smile.

There were two adjoining sitting rooms, one a kind of antechamber, the other a studio with a green baize card table where Jade did her readings. There was a small kitchen off to one side. Shyno settled into an armchair as Lúcio went through.

As with most waiting rooms there was an eclectic mix of reading material to while away the hour. Pamphlets, magazines and periodicals, many out of date. He selected one at random, *Lux Madriana*, and flicked through the pages. It was intriguing stuff, with references to a few names he had come across, Guénon, Schuon, Kumaraswamy, Lings, the Great Tradition, the pre-Sumerian matriarchal culture, the Goddess, that sort of thing. He was only half paying attention to the words as he tuned in to the duet in the adjacent parlour. It was hard to make out, what with Jade's speech patterns and Lúcio's cryptic interjections. He could hear the shuffling of the cards, the snap of the spread, but most of it was a foreign language which he didn't speak. All the same he grasped the headlines which read something like this.

A journey across water. Difficulty in the beginning. An authority figure who comes to your aid. A chance encounter. The influence of a Fool. Danger. The tower. Revolution. A new beginning. Conflict. Success.

Back out on Walton street, passing by Sunshine Records where he used to work, *Riders on the Storm* hissing from the turntable, he turned to Lúcio.

'You're not really serious about this boat business, are you?'

MONA GORDA

Puerto Andratx is a classic Spanish *cala* which opens as a long, deep coral-cliffed throat on the south-western coast of Mallorca. It forms a natural harbour, not too narrow-mouthed to make the approach difficult and not so wide as to be vulnerable to any incoming swell.

A smattering of white lego like blocks of low-rise apartments dotted the western shore. This was before the boom and the blitzkrieg of mass German tourism. But the port was prepared and in anticipation of what was to come a dozen pale finger piers formed the skeleton of a rudimentary marina. Fuel dock, chandlery, dry hoist, running water, power points, ramp. The basic basics. It was overseen by a toothy Dane called Wilhelm, whose nautical ineptitude made a mockery of the Viking nation.

An example: for three years Wilhelm had been hand-building a modest wooden fourteen-foot tender with an in-board engine, for an elderly, retired, former civil engineer called Robin. To say that the craft was roughly finished would be true in both senses. Robin had passed beyond the stage of exasperated frustration and incredulity; had transcended rage and now adopted the look and tone of an eager and grateful penitent, whose one remaining hope was that god would eventually forgive whatever sin of omission he had committed and that despite Wilhelm's endlessly inventive talent for botching and bodging and interminable delays, he would, one day, have his reward. So far it had cost him some ten thousand pounds in penances, but he would not give up. Robbing Robin was about the sum of it.

A great day dawned. The engine had been installed and the ugly little craft was at last in the water. Even to an unskilled eye something looked out of kilter. The bow tilted down and the stern angled up. Robin stepped aboard and sat abaft, achieving a kind of level, though the sea still lapped at the splintery gunwales. He knew in his soul that Wilhelm had put the motor in backwards, but like a latter day Thomas, he had to have proof. He turned the key, engaged forward gear, and promptly reversed into a concrete pier.

Apocryphal? There were witnesses who will swear.

At first glance the only thing the boatyard appeared to lack were boats. There were perhaps six in all, excluding the converted PT craft still in its gun-metal grey, idly swinging on her hook in the middle of the bay. Two were for sale. One was a thirty-foot miniature gin-palace, cabined fore and aft, the other was *Laurene*. She was what is known as a bare boat. If she had been a car she would have been a jeep. Just every essential part.

'No great beauty, I grant you, but she's got a fair line. Just under 40 foot and wide-beamed. Single Perkins diesel, does about 10 knots on a good run. Full displacement, holds plenty of water and fuel. Head, shower, small galley, double berth in the bow, brought her over last month from Menton in a force-six gale. You can see a bit of give in the superstructure. All double marine ply, so she's solid, weighs twelve ton, has a ferro-cement hull.'

Larry, the owner, was a middle-aged car breaker from Deptford. He sensed a sale.

'Step on board, see how stable she is.'

So they did and he was right. Laurene was rock stolid.

Lúcio sat down on one of the three benched seats that framed the open stern and turned his gaze to the riveted rectangular panel set square in the centre of the deck.

'Plenty of storage down there, it's a dry bilge. I'll show you, if you like.'

Larry wanted 17k. They settled on seven down and the balance in three months.

'You'll want to register a different name. For the authorities.'

So they called her *Mona Gorda,* which means Pretty Fatty.

THE HIGH RIF

Alan and Dave drove a clapped out, dun-coloured VW camper down south across the several European borders, caught a ferry from Malaga to Ceuta, then toiled up the hopeless Moroccan roads to a remote blue valley that concealed the hashish farm and Mustapha's mountain village.

Neither of the lags had either any Arab or French, but they got there, mostly by grunt and gesture. On board the van they had stowed a small inflatable dinghy and a twenty-five horsepower outboard motor. That was to be YaYa's gig. To make the transfer. Launch by night into the surf, bales of dope aboard, and rendezvous with the *Mona Gorda*.

It's not as simple as it sounds. First off, it would be extremely dark. Images of ink don't do it justice. The twinkling lights of Tétouan may look like illuminating stars out on the ocean, but down at the beach it's just black on black, with this persistent roar of swells crashing against the shore. You need to get your timing absolutely spot on. Best is under a fullish moon, if the sky is clear, as it quite often is in late September.

Besides, the Med is no millpond come autumn and though the bottle-neck of the Gibraltar strait affords some shelter, the Atlantic is never far. You can't afford to get spilled or swamped. It takes practice, but that was what YaYa was there for.

And to get familiar with the coast. Plan was, once he'd delivered, he'd make a swift run back toward Ceuta, hook up with Alan on some designated beach, dump the tender, and like two tourists who'd had their taste of alternative culture, motor discreetly home.

A piece of cake? Or piss-take? Come the said day, YaYa would still be in two minds.

THE WATER IN MAJORCA

'Done any navigation?' asked Larry.

Shyno was ensconced in the plushly veneered saloon of Larry's recent upgrade. A sixty-foot converted Cornish trawler that he'd customised to his own brand of East End taste. Plenty of brass and a small herd's worth of leather.

None, was the short answer. And this was before the advent of GPS.

'Won't matter once you hit the coast. You'll have visual. But the hop to Ibiza can be dicey. There's a current in the Med, people forget, and with a shift of wind, bit of cloud cover, go off course by a couple of degrees, you'll miss it completely. End up going round in circles, won't have a clue where you are. Worse comes to worst, just head west, bound to hit Spain eventually. Unless of course your fuel runs out. I'd carry a can or two of spare. Always call out the coastguard, needs must. Anyway let's have a look at some of these charts. And another G&T, while we're at it.'

Lúcio was blithely indifferent to anything you might call maritime. It bored him, the whole boat business of ropes, knots, mooring up, true north, lookout, bilge pumps, spare battery, hauling anchor, auxiliary power, manoeuvring in and out of confined spaces, weather, rights of way, fixes, shoals, warning buoys, not wasting water in the shower, it just struck him as somehow tedious.

It wasn't the detail as such, because he could spend hours, days even, fine-tuning the intricate rhyme scheme of a *sestina*. He put it down to what Jung called 'the inferior function'.

'Look, Shyno, you asked to be the skipper. Nev's your crew. Just allow me to concentrate on the overall picture.'

What else does a poor boy do? They shipped out on a cool, clear mid-September day, around dawn, course set, bound for Ibiza.

From Puerto Andratx south to the smaller island's north shore was about an eight hour trawl. By mid afternoon there was still blank sea on the horizon. A couple of hours more and it would be dusk, then sundown. Downer. *Mona Gorda* kept on chugging. Just as the last light was settling west off the starboard bow a brown hump hove into view. Have you any idea how sweet a calm bay beckons on your first day out, almost lost at sea? You drop anchor, there is torchlight, music, a beach bar, crackling barbecue, a few friendly yachts swaying in the breeze and all that angst and panic simply ebbs away? Try it and see.

TRAVEL LOG

It seemed odd, looking back, how a near miss, avoided by sheer luck, could gee them up for some greater fall.

'Reckon we could handle a night crossing? You know, get some experience, ready for the real thing.'

Nev was eager to get rolling. Lúcio, absorbed in a Verdi libretto he had brought along to while away the passage, hummed and shrugged. Shyno was certain of only one thing. He was rapidly turning into Dr Not-so-Sure and feeling more than his twenty-six years. It was a good two hundred miles to Alicante, their projected port of call. Sure, as soon as they had rounded by nightfall the rump end of the island it was a straightforward haul over open water, so no big deal. And the Perkins diesel, once it was fired up, would burble on happily, regardless; so no worries there. They had plenty of fuel, water, and the sea beyond the bay looked invitingly calm. The forecast was fair.

Shyno ran through the mental check list that he found he was performing with increasing regularity, looking for the snag, but he couldn't find one. So far he had managed an air of cheerful competence, confidence almost, even when for a spell it had seemed as if Larry's gloomy prophesy was about to be fulfilled.

'Why not. Let's go for it. If we leave soon we can be past the cape by dusk and then it's a clear run southwest. At ten knots we should be there by mid-afternoon.'

There was something reassuring in hearing these words

spoken out loud. Inwardly, Shyno was wondering what could go wrong.

Not a lot really. They left the bay by mid-morning and followed the coast south. Even at top speed it was slow passage. Shyno kept about a mile offshore, far enough out to maintain a straight line, close enough in to decipher the island's contours. Around teatime they passed through the strait north of Formentera and by nightfall they were clear of the land. Shyno reduced speed to five knots and they ate in the wheelhouse, basic provisions and leftovers from the barbecue.

At around 3am, with the other two bods bunked up below, Shyno was trying hard not to nod off at the wheel because the trip was proving so uneventful, almost dull, when all of a sudden *Mona Gorda* ran smack bang into, no, not a whale, but a thick white wall of fog. No cause for alarm. Just slow right, right down to a couple of knots. They had running lights and an impressively loud klaxon. The good thing about foghorns was that they worked. If you heard one go off it was a pretty obvious guess there was another vessel nearby, so Shyno peeled his eyes and got ready for evasive action. The not-so-good thing was when several of them started blaring at once. From not having seen a single light throughout the night, it appeared that *Mona Gorda* had strayed into some sort of shipping lane.

The effect on the two sleepers was pretty immediate. And the melancholy sound of the surrounding horns made *them* seem pretty immediate also. Wide-eyed and groggy they scrambled up into the wheelhouse. Nev could shift when he needed to. One look at the dense white stuff shrouding the boat made any expletive or explanation superfluous.

'Shite!'

'Christu.'

Shyno eased the throttle back into neutral and began his own steady and regular trombone salvo. A radar might have come in handy but there wasn't one and it's not certain it would have helped much in such conditions. Anyway, there suddenly wasn't any more time to think about it, or anything else for that matter.

The curtain of cottony white murk that was swirling around them was abruptly replaced by another even whiter but much more solid one. A vast cruise liner loomed up out of the fogbank like a man-made glacier, fully 500-foot long and dead ahead.

What they heard was the sustained blast of a giant flugel-horn. What they felt in their bones was the immense heart-beat of the turbines pulsing out jolts of sheer power, as the great screws sent judders of current through the water and made *Mona Gorda*'s concrete hull shudder as if under the blows of some jack-hammering drill. The ship cut across their bows a hundred feet in front of them with all the stately indifference of a gigantic swan and they just stood there gawping and then she was gone. It was several moments before they were hit by her wake and the roller-coaster. If she had been doing more than five knots, they would have been swamped within seconds and *Mona Gorda* would have sunk like the lump of stone that she was.

It took another hour for the fog to shift and a couple more for their collective shock. No one was much minded for small talk, or any talk for that matter, so they sat and waited, feeling rather like those fish in the proverbial barrel. There were still the odd mournful blasts from invisible boats, but they appeared at a distance and staying put seemed no more peri-lous than getting under way. Dawn, when it finally broke, was a prolonged low sigh of relief.

Shyno fired up the diesel and set a course. Lúcio acquired a novel interest in compass and chart. Nev sat like some form of human Meccano, chain smoking, butt after butt. The three lost hours had set them back by about thirty miles, plus a bit for drift. There was little chance of making Alicante. With a flourish Lúcio spread out his chart on the saloon floor.

'Listen chaps, I have made a few quick calculations which should cheer you both up. If we simply turn right *here*, we will most likely make landfall approximately *there*. At about lunchtime, all things being equal; which in this instance, I believe they are.'

Lúcio placed one point of the extended compass on a small x he had marked in the middle of the sea and the other on the Spanish mainland shore. Shyno had long learnt not to underestimate him, but he was still annoyed. Lúcio had refused to attend Larry's liquid geometry lesson, so if he knew how to navigate, why not say so? Then the more galling truth occurred. In the first hour of first light, Lúcio had simply worked it out by himself.

'Are we agreed?' he said, with a winning chuckle.

They were. None of them was keen for another night out on the water. Shyno engaged the throttle, put it hard down, and spun the wheel until the compass turned through ninety degrees. West by northwest.

HASTA LA COSTA

By ten in the morning the first hazy outline of the coast appeared as a lightly tanned stain on the horizon. By noon, there was topography. Brownish hills that sloped down steeply to a foreshore studded with what looked like row upon row of squat gleaming headstones. By one o'clock you could tell exactly what kind of graveyard it was. Here the corpses were still pinkly living and in considerable numbers. And out of these high-rise coffins spilled their low-rent occupants. Grockles. Colonies of them. Basking and broiling in the midday sun.

'Mmm, where do reckon we are?' said Nev. 'I mean I know it's Spain, but what bit of it, any idea?'

'I am not absolutely sure,' said Lúcio. 'I more or less guessed our original position.'

'Might as well just ask, don't you think?' said Shyno, as he throttled back the engine some seventy yards from the shore. 'What about him over there?'

A lagerly-looking, shaven-head type was lolling on a Union Jack lilo a little way off. He was dozing, lying on his back, and had floated out beyond the scrum of bathers wallowing in the shallow water. Shyno nudged La Gorda forward and idled within hailing distance.

'I say, excuse me, could we have a word?' he shouted, trying not to. The fellow obviously hadn't heard, or they were being ignored. He tried again, louder. Still no response. *Nada.*

'Perhaps he doesn't speak English,' said Nev, who could be a bit of a wag.

'I'll have to get closer. Hope the bugger doesn't have a heart attack.'

Shyno edged the boat up until the floater was almost alongside, cut the motor, leaned out over the gunwale and as gently as was feasible said,

'Hello mate, would you mind telling us where we are?'

This time the bloke did hear. Rousing from his stupor he did two things at once that perhaps he should not have done. He tried to sit up and turned to look around. The result was his lilo abruptly folded in the middle and gave him a quick smart thwack on his sunburned cheek, then he bellowed and fell off. When he surfaced he was simmering, they could tell, but he managed to compose himself. He gazed up at this unlikely trio, glanced out to sea as if trying to imagine where on earth they might have come from, shook his head and with as much dignity as he could muster, snarled,

'Haven't you got any effing charts, you pillocks?' And then pointing shoreward with a meaty finger to a prominent cone-shaped mount that appears on a million postcards, 'It's only bloody Benidorm. Any twat can see that...' With which he hauled himself back onto his plastic raft and paddled off in the direction of the beach.

How many close encounters could they manage in a single day? If this was their second, the third, though they didn't know it, was just around the bend and heading their way.

OI! GRINGO!

Shyno was knackered from lack of sleep. After eighteen hours at the helm he thought that if he didn't crash soon he would do something stupid, like crash the boat.

'Listen guys, I've got to lie down for a bit, get some kip. Nev, you can drive, there's not much to it: forward, neutral, back. Just stay a decent way out, a quarter mile off and follow the coast. Should be fine but keep a lookout you know, it's flat calm, can't see much traffic. Any probs give me a shout, I'm going below. Right. Oh and see that headland down there, the one sticking out, just head towards that.'

Nev was chuffed. He levered himself up onto the skipper's stool, propped his crutches against the bulkhead and took hold of the wheel. Lúcio was already out on the stern deck in his director's chair, listening to a Sibelius symphony, the 5th probably, on a portable tape machine, catching some sun. He had his headphones on. Shyno signed him, miming sleep. Lúcio gave a thumbs up, turned to see Nev intent on his steering and with thumb and index made a reassuring circle, then picked up his book.

The forward cabin had two separate berths with an insert panel that formed a small double bed. They were cushioned with foam mattresses in dark blue vinyl. Access was by way of a narrow set of stairs which led off from the wheelhouse down past the head and shower on the left and a compact galley with a two ring burner and fridge on the starboard side. Two portholes and a pair of front-facing windows in the shape of reading glasses provided natural light. He couldn't open any of them as they were riveted shut. The ceiling was the underside of the bow deck and low enough that he had to crick his neck if he didn't want to crack his head. It was stiflingly hot. A two-foot square deck hatch was the only possible source of free-flowing air. Shyno slipped the brass latch, propped the lid open as far as it would go on its hinges and fixed it with the short pole provided. What Larry had described as 'your basic air-con-do.' Shyno rolled onto the sticky plastic bunk and fell at once into a fretless sleep.

There are many ways of waking. Some are agreeable. What dragged Shyno from the depths was at first indecipherable. A *sotto voce* chorus in a foreign tongue, *oye, oye*, swelling in unison, like a kind of benison, until it burst into a sudden crescendo of guttural oaths banging on his eardrums.

'Hijo de puta! Coño de tu madre! Descarado, imbécil, carajo!'

Shyno jerked awake and hauled ass from his berth, but it was much too late. A snapshot will have to suffice. Nev frozen at the wheel, his view no longer blocked by the open deck hatch. Lúcio, eyes closed, headphones on, counting bars. And a very large Spanish trawler, nets set, hard on their nose. They were that close. In a *corrida* when the bull and matador embrace it will leave a smear of blood on the cape. In this case the encounter was even more intimate. The fender buoy on *Mona Gorda*'s port bow was flicked up on deck by the passing trawler's flank and the towering rump of the tub smudged a scab of rusty red paint all down her side as it scraped by. Shyno grabbed the wheel and spun it hard to starboard. The thought of ploughing through the Spanish trawler's nets was too much to contemplate, a foul-up too far. Nev was mortified, not pink embarrassed, but with a chalky corpse-like pallor.

'Man, I mean, I never saw her...'

And Lúcio never heard her either. Later, they speculated on the improbability of coming that close while still managing to avoid disaster. Put two boats on collision course a mile apart, deliberately, chances were they would either miss by a margin or crash head on. Even with two expert helmsmen the odds of merely rubbing shoulders struck them as remote. The pass had been so precise they hadn't felt a thing, yet what separated them was less than the thickness of a skin. Shyno felt the time was now right to talk about getting serious. Much more of this mucking about in boats and someone was going to get hurt. Seriously.

OLD MUSTAPHA'S FARM

'You like cucumber, I think so, Dave?'

Mustapha grinned at YaYa as he set down yet another congealing goat tagine on the wooden pallet that served them as their table. Accompaniment was a large earthen dish brimming with chopped cucumber, mint, and curdled yoghurt supplied no doubt by the aforementioned beast. Alan flicked a tie-dyed scarf half-heartedly at the ever present swarm of flies.

Let no one gainsay the delights of Moroccan cuisine, but even he, a committed carnivore, was tiring of the oily fare. YaYa was vegetarian and something in Mustapha's insinuating leer unsettled him. Over the past three weeks he had lost quite a bit of weight.

'Just a few days more mate, and we're out of here. Meet up with Nev and the guys in Ceuta. A couple of beers, decent meal. Do the business. Back on the bus and we're trucking. No more fucking fears, right? I swear that cunt thinks we're a couple of queers.'

YaYa could well imagine it. But between the idea and the reality lay the small matter of being the night ferryman for ten thirty-pound triple-wrapped bales of top grade hashish and something in his gut besides the rankly indigestible stew revolted. In short he was afraid. The thought of having to do the runs with the runs was one thing, a minor issue. Getting caught was another.

Mustapha took a peculiar delight in regaling Dave with

tales of torture, gang rape, harsh gaol sentences of indeterminate nature without reprieve, and other exquisite penalties which he outlined with wide solemn gaze and authoritative gestures, followed by peals of childish laughter.

'Drop you bottle, Dave?' he would mock, as he let slip from his grasp the latest in a long succession of empty Johnny Walker flasks. Not for him the whisky-berbère of sugared mint tea.

Alan offered up 'Ah, piss off, you rag head, go get sucked by one of your skinny goats; or better still your mother, she's even uglier and she's got no teeth.'

Mustapha slapped his thighs with glee. This was what passed as banter *entre amis*. But it was the kind of knockabout for which YaYa was peculiarly unsuited. Although his interior monologues flowed freely his outwards were strictly limited, especially when threatened. So when Mustapha started in with his joshings all he could do was respond in the affirmative. He had yet to convince himself that this repartee would not end up in violence, to which by temper and the guru's teaching he was violently opposed.

Alan had no such qualms. He and Mustapha had been knocking about for a couple of years. They had met during one of Alan's infrequent call-outs, attending to a broken down ride-on floor-scrubbing machine at some megabrasserie in Covent Garden, where Mustapha was the gang master and supervisor of a small army of illegal Africans: kitchen porters and night cleaners. They got chatting over a number in the goods-in bay.

Alan had a nose for these things and in short order realised that profanity was a kind of ping-pong for Mustapha, an expert in search of an opponent. The cursed and cursing Arab. It was a game for which Alan had a natural affinity. A test of your limits, where there are no limits, except in the case of the Moroccan's own personal physiognomy. Unlike many ugly men he was inordinately vain, and any reminder of his various disfigurements would provoke a disproportionate outbreak of furious and uncontrollable rage. As Alan kept telling YaYa,

'Say anything you like, mate, just stay out of his face.'

And like many men Mustapha was subject to male-pattern balding, except in his case there was no discernible pattern. A random scattering of tight black pubic-like curls tufted his gleaming skull. His skin was slick, sebaceous and pockmarked from periodic outbreaks of acne. His nose, a bulbous truffle, was generously black-headed. One ear stuck out, the other lay flat. His teeth were gappy, tar-stained, with the odd flash of gold. Yet his prowess with women and boys was legendary.

'Is my cucumber,' he would boast modestly.

One dull midsummer dawn when the trash truck came round, a sleep-deprived, lardy and underpaid council employee called out to him,

'Oi, mushmash, here for the bins.'

Mustapha fed him to the compactor where they dumped the food slops and once he had been thoroughly soiled and had soiled himself, reversed the motor and, as it were, excreted him.

'How's it going with the pressing?' said Alan.

'Good, yes, is almost finished, maybe two days more.'

It required about six acres of cultivation to produce three hundred pounds of first class resin. Mustapha knew nothing of THC and crystal science. He did what his tribe had done for generations. Cut the crop, dry it in the sun, hang a tarpaulin up on two sides so that the v-shape forms a right angle where it meets the ground; then beat it with the dried fronds of marijuana, three strokes maximum per branch. At intervals, collect the powdery residue which gathered at the fold and compress it into blocks on a hand-screwed press heated by the noonday oven.

Each slab was twelve by six and one inch thick and weighed half a pound. There would be a round six hundred of them by the time Mustapha and his in-laws were done.

CRUISE CONTROL

Sometimes a couple of quick sharp shocks can achieve considerably more than a dozen imprecations. A fresh spirit of collaboration was abroad aboard the *Mona Gorda*. Lúcio had discovered an affinity for knots of both nautical kinds. Distance and speed over water. And hemp loops useful for tying up in a dock.

Daily he would plot a course and had become a dab hand with the log. A cylindrical device laid out on a length of line from the stern, by which they could calculate their progress through the water. An old-fangled boat speedometer by which travel could be accurately plotted. Their advance southward down the Spanish coast lay marked out in pencil lines on a chart, with 'x's denoting various marinas and small ports they had frequented. Dénia, Fuengirola, Almuñecar, Cartagena, Cabo Negro.

Nev soon found his own distinctive brand of sea-legs as he learned to time his swings to the easy sway of *Mona Gorda*'s roll, planting the rubber tips of his crutches as does a skier with his poles on a gentle hill. True he could not negotiate the narrow decks that on both sides of the wheelhouse gave to the bow. He might have wriggled and hauled himself up through the near fatal forward hatch but it would have been a struggle, so he confined himself to cabin, wheelhouse and the stern deck. He and Shyno took turns at the wheel, the one spelling the other as lookout.

Lúcio kept abaft, where he plotted away the hours penning stanzas and fine-tuning the planetary gyres which, he calculated, placed their venture under auspicious stars.

A short wooden ladder at the back of the wheelhouse gave access to a flat upper deck, where Shyno would sprawl like a cat and monitor the sea traffic of which there was surprisingly little.

Breakfast was toast and apricot jam, *café con leche*. Lunch, *a bocadillo* of smoked ham, aged *manchego* cheese and tomato. Then it was watch, steer, sunbathe, listen to music and come dusk moor up in their chosen fishing village. Evenings were spent with a carafe or two of authentic *sangria* and grilled prawns *al ají* at the local taverna. Crash, sleep easy, wake and repeat. The days settled into something resembling routine, almost a holiday. They were making about a hundred miles daily.

THE PINK PANTHER

The 'mo-ah' to which YaYa had referred was a 1974 pink XJ6 four-door Jaguar saloon upholstered in tan leather, with faun carpets and plenty of walnut veneer. *Heather* was the manufacturer's designated colour and it had not proved popular. A hint of lilac, lavender even, raspberry perhaps, but to any layman's eye it was pink and conspicuously so.

Rich often asked himself what had possessed Lúcio to acquire a vehicle quite so outstandingly the opposite of discreet. The prosaic answer was that they needed a Jag quick and it was available and cheap. The owner, a dairy farmer from outside High Wycombe had grown weary of the jibes and ribbing from friend and neighbour. He wanted shot of it. When Rich dropped by to collect the pink cat it was parked up outside a corrugated cow barn, liberally daubed with creamy mud, the interior stubbly with dog hair, dried straw and a lingering air of expensive cigars.

Rich had been tasked to oversee the reconfigurations to the chassis, for the transport, and delivery to a rented villa in the hills north of Malaga. Even tooling about the streets of Oxford he felt faintly queasy.

His sense of self-worth had already been punctured by YaYa's Moroccan coup. Rich was fully alive to the mimicry practised by the rest of the crew and he was still smarting from an episode which occurred shortly before the gang's departure. He came calling at the house one morning, with no more specific intent than mulling over what he described to himself as Tolly's Folly. When Shyno answered the door and called upstairs, saying 'Rich is here to see you', the voice that drifted down was as mellifluous as it was magisterial.

'Tell Richard I am on the throne. And I can only deal with one turd at a time.'

Lúcio thought the pink panther just the ticket for what he had in mind. He subscribed to his own theory of reverse camouflage. If you wish to avoid the attentions of your enemy, draw as much attention to yourself as you possibly can. Rich could not quite grasp this subtlety of argument. His instinct was hide and glide. Poncing around in a puce Jaguar did not sit well with his idea of anonymity. Let alone masculinity. He was becoming neurotic at the idea that everyone would think he was fey, or worse, gay. His gender ID was something he protested and protected assiduously.

There were three cavities in the chassis of an XJ6 you needed to know about if you were going to stuff it with contraband. Two were the sills that ran lengthways, on either side under the doors, from wheel-arch to wheel-arch. The third lay beneath the generously wide rear seats.

Method: unbolt said seats and remove. With solvent, loosen and peel back the carpet there laid. Take an angle grinder and cut two rectangular panels in the steel box cabinets that form the base which supports your bum, just in the area where you might kick your heels. Remove and affix four small flanges to each panel. Drill the relevant holes and screw back in place. Relay carpets with adhesive tabs. Put back the seat.

For the sills: prise out the caps that seal the hollow steel tubes at each end. Fit back and secure with flanges and disguise entry, with blacking and what will pass for road spray. Done. *C'est ça.* Simple. If you packed it properly there was room for some sixty pounds. Which added up to five separate trips, fifteen borders and a lot of driving.

The beauty of the Jag was that it was immensely comfortable and almost completely silent. No motorway roar to spoil your conversation or musical enjoyment. They dubbed it the Monastery of Transport.

MoT for short.

METHODOLOGY

But why so many borders? Good question. The simplest route back home would have been a ferry crossing from some northern Spanish port, Bilbao say, to Southampton. Just two exposures to officialdom. Or St. Malo in France which would entail three sets of scrutiny. Both choices would necessitate a night voyage in Autumn across the Bay of Biscay. Par for that course. But to motor through four countries, Spain, France, Holland, Belgium, then ship from Ostende to the UK, surely the apogee of idiocy? Four clear chances for discovery.

Not according to Lúcio's theorem of counter-psychology. It was the same principle he applied to the purplish Jag, which to most minds was the equivalent of waving a pink rag to every border-patrol and customs- house bull they would cross. Lucia's reasoning flowed quite to the contrary and went something like this.

All smugglers have two things in common. Something to hide and no wish to get caught. Customs officers know this and base their work on profiles, information, common sense and a kind of intuition which boils down to 'too good to be true'. The little old lady who shuffles through nothing-to-declare with her aluminium framed walker, but just a little too awkwardly. The stout pink-cheeked vicar with his dog-collar who is a degree too portly. A myriad of prototypes all employing varying disguises of tireless ingenuity.

Customs and Excise is a kind of All Soul's for qualified twitchers, with flocks of potential jailbirds just waiting to be spotted. Lúcio's own stratagem he named the LAM and can be formulated in three simple words. Look At Me. In my louche, preposterous rose-coloured Jag, puffing, or is that pouffing, on an oversize cigar. With my long fair-haired chauffeur, who is obviously my shag. Please do examine our passports at your leisure, my pleasure. Note the multiple foreign stamps, yes a world traveller, (of course there will not be a Moroccan one will there?) and now dismiss me and speed me on my way as some *outré*, or in your terms, faintly ridiculous, charming but quite harmless little twerp who, whatever he may be, is not a trafficker.

Besides, the itinerary suggested numerous opportunities to savour the provender and hospitality of various Paraderos, Châteaux de Relais, and Haut Bourgeois Inns along the way.

CONDE NICE

Shyno was a reluctant convert to this philosophy. On a visit to Bogotá, Lúcio had introduced him to his associates as Count Shyno. This gave rise to a phrase which stuck. *Es Conde lo que lleva.* He carries the title of Count. *Esconde lo que lleva.* He hides what he carries. The irony was that Lúcio never let him tote anything incriminating. Protecting my *assiette* was how he put it. Shyno was along simply for the ride.

During one of their sojourns in Miami, they had fallen in, then out, with an envious and vindictive *bruja* who practised her own renegade brand of Santería.

This witch was called Maya, a three-tyred Michelin star lesbian exiled from Cuba with her thin-lipped and slimmer-hipped middling age consort Michi. A ratty little minister out of the top drawer of that communistic plague. This was a couple of years before Fidel, 'Ol Faithless', unlocked the doors to various prison camps and asylums and set loose a swarm of degenerates, reprobates, lunatics and term criminals. The Marielitos, whom Jimmy Carter, President and peanut-gleaner, welcomed with flotillas of small craft and gave safe haven in south Florida.

Maya was a reluctant medium, in thrall to more modern media. A middle-class teen-age girl born in classless Cuba. One day she was struck down on a sunny Havana avenue with what several eminent Cuban medicos, and there are many of them, diagnosed as an epileptic seizure. Flung to the ground, she thrashed around speaking in the kind of tongues, a mix of Spanish and African patois, that she could not possibly have learned at school. There were two distinct voices, one female, the other male. The sudden fits became more frequent and unprompted. She was on the verge of being sectioned as a schizophrenic and consigned to an institution for the mentally ill.

As much out of shame as desperation, her mother took her to an old *Santero*, a friend of the family, who lived in the *Campo*. He spelled it out with pierced cowrie shells and chalk dust on his earthen floor.

'*Es Caballa, se tiene que montar.*'

In short, she was the 'mare' for a pair of her African ancestors, both slaves, one called *Calunga Vira Mundo*, the other *Ma Francisca*. She hated it, but there was no way out. Either submit to being ridden and possessed by these entities or be dispossessed of her freedom in some sanatorium without exit. She made the choice. And though her tastes veered towards fashion, food and game-show TV, she became adept at it and gained a reputation as an *Espiritista*.

Ma Francisca was a benevolent old Ghanaian soul. When Maya submitted to be mounted her body would arch and tremble spasmodically as she went into a trance and the spirit as it were 'took the saddle'. Ma's voice was deep and melodious and she liked to receive gifts of perfume, tobacco, alcohol and flowers. Gladioli were her favourites. Sipping and puffing she would dispense healing and advice to the many callers, mostly by brushing down their bodies with bundles of *yerbas,* fresh cuttings of greenery and shrubs. During a sitting she would sup *aguardiente* out of a small dried gourd and work her way through several cigars.

Evidence that this was not some specious mummery on Maya's part was twofold. She was completely teetotal. After a session, during which on average Ma Francisca would consume a good half bottle of 100% proof raw cane liquor and three cigars, Maya would emerge from her trance stone cold sober, her breath smelling faintly of a delicate perfume which might have been violets.

Calunga was another matter. Few had encountered him, as Maya refused to let him mount her unless absolutely forced to. She was disgusted by what she had been told of how he liked to 'canter' on his mare and what he required as propitiation for his services. He was a former plantation slave who had rebelled against his master. Before the authorities managed to put down the revolt, Calunga slaughtered most of the overseer's, then the owner's extended families. He used a machete and his teeth.

Maya confessed to Shyno that when he possessed her he would require a mongrel dog as a sacrifice, whose whimpering breath he then extinguished with her jaws. He would then drink the blood from its torn throat, smearing her delicate dark lips and irregular white teeth. A bit of a brute you might say, but extremely powerful in matters magical. Not someone you wanted to get on the wrong side of.

Shyno fell foul of Maya over money. Michi stole some cash from his locked apartment, several thousand dollars, and denied it – though she was in possession of the one spare key. Maya knew it was Michi but she wasn't going to take sides against her lover. Shyno accused her of being complicit and in a fit of guilty rage Maya cursed him deeply and for several hours. Shortly after they parted on poor terms and went their separate ways.

You did not need to believe in any of this folklore for it to work. Within a matter of weeks Shyno was much the worse for wear. Lúcio, who was himself a practitioner, dispatched him to Brazil for a spot of 'cleaning up'. In that country there is a long tradition of these African shenanigans, loosely covered by the umbrella term of *Candomblé*.

Shyno was sequestered in a jungle compound some fifty miles outside Belem, in the province of Bahia. Three aged black women swathed in white attended to his twice daily baths. They boiled up vats of jungle cuttings, herbs and selected greenery and when it had steeped and cooled, ladled it over his body with calabasha gourds. They sacrificed a white dove and a black cockerel and strapped the bloody little hearts with linen strips to his shaven skull.

Something in this white witches brew must have been mildly narcotic, for he slept almost uninterruptedly, apart from food and bathing, for the better part of a week. He would just conk out on a straw pallet on the concrete floor of his monkish cell, amid the multiple white *Soperas*; covered bowls, which housed the relics and symbols of the household gods. Cowrie shells, beaded necklaces, smooth pebbles, trinkets, all impregnated with honey, dried egg-white, and blood from various sacrificial animals.

And the point of this episode?

After a week of treatment Shyno was feeling much more chipper. On the day of departure, the Sisters of Clarity presented him with three large bin-bags stuffed full of foliage. He was to return to England with this medicine and continue with the baths for two more weeks, or they could not guarantee the lifting of Maya's spell. So, tell pray, how does one manage to carry all this forestry through customs? You will find a way was their farewell word.

Shyno crammed the rustling bags into one large suitcase and on arrival at Heathrow headed for the Red Channel, goods-to-declare. A sleepy Asian customs official was on hand to attend to this rare and eager volunteer.

'I appear to have exceeded my allowance for alcohol and tobacco. How much do I owe?'

Shyno proffered up two cartons of Rothman's and a couple of litres of Imperial Vodka. Gul, that was the name on his badge, clocked the offending items and tapped into his calculator.

"£17 and fifty pence, sir, including VAT."

Shyno paid up and was waved through.

DIRE STRAITS

On a clear day you can easily make out the outline of the Port of Ceuta from within the lee of the Rock of Gibraltar. It's about twelve miles away. A swift crossing in the right type of boat. But the straight acts as a kind of giant plughole for the Med which drains out into the Atlantic, whence the Atlantic funnels it all back in, depending on the tide. The current runs at around six knots and can get up to eight or nine at the equinox. It's not something you can accurately gauge until you are in it.

By slow boat the best bet was to head off at the appropriate angle and slip-slide across. Which is what they did. It took them the better part of a day. The tide was on the ebb, which meant heading somewhere in the direction of Tunisia. Effectively, *Mona Gorda* was almost standing still against the tide-pull, waiting to be swept in. A powerboat or *cigarette* would have simply burnt over in ten minutes, ignorant of the ocean's underwater tug. But at *Mona Gorda*'s speed and weight it was all about mathematics, vectors and Lúcio resolved that equation with equanimity.

Ceuta is Spanish territory. From there they could access Morocco without actually entering the country and so avoid the tell-tale, incriminating stamp.

Ceuta harbour in the late 70s was, and probably still is, something of a cesspool. It's in the nature of most ship-shelters, be they manmade or natural. A delightful rocky cove in Cornwall, Hurricane Hole in the Bahamas, or in this case the wide-jawed shallow maw with its lengthy seawall that is North Africa's first and last port of call.

It's only a matter of degree. Harbours suffer from poor circulation, since their primary function is to keep out any agitating motion of that very water which might sluice them clean. Tides do their modest part towards sanitation, but they tend not to get 'right under the rim'. Add to this a general tendency by their occupants for tipping and spillage of fish-guts, effluent, diesel oil, plastic, plus any and all of the human detritus you can imagine and some you won't want to. In all these ingredients Ceuta was especially rich. Something in the name hinted at it, sewer sprang to mind.

Apart from the slick, generous, caramel-coloured topping of jettisoned oil from tankers plying up and down the strait, there was the familiar multi-hued flotscum of used condoms, turds, food scraps, corrupted jellyfish, net corks, frazzles of twine, all of which bobbed in the gloopy soup like so many liberally scattered hundreds and thousands. Add to this the fermentative element of an African sun and the smell was pestiferously foul. This was one of those all too turbid loo-bowls urgently in need of flushing and one of the last places on planet water you would dream of taking a dip, unless that is you were absolutely compelled to.

Shyno nosed the *Mona Gorda* round the western extremity of the breakwater and throttled back as they entered the unruffled passage that formed the approach road of the main channel.

The parking-lot that was the port could have usefully employed some sort of signage such as *spaces available*, or *prats in pleasure craft this way*. As it was the eye swept from left to right through 180 degrees, taking in rusting merchantmen, commercial fishing trawlers, grubby mid-size

47

tankers, several half-submerged wrecks and there at the heart of it all an inviting expanse of almost unoccupied pier, several hundred yards long, all kitted out with stanchions for tying on to and neat white cubes which were housings for power points and running water.

Perfect. Shyno made a near immaculate docking, coming up alongside without so much as a bump behind a handsome ketch which was the only other vessel moored there. Lúcio held *Mona Gorda* off at the bow by dangling his legs over the side. Nev was at the stern, one hand on the warm pier.

Shyno cut the motor and sat in the wheelhouse and the boat just wallowed there in the motionless water. Each of them was quietly congratulating himself on a job decently done. Time for the ropes then and a couple of fender buoys, boys.

Shyno was in the process of stretching his neck muscles when on the second left swivel he clocked the incoming cross-strait ferry about a quarter mile off at the mouth of the channel. A big beast, impressive. The sort you imagine yourself handling after years of practise but know you never will.

Four knots is the prescribed speed for any vessel within harbour limits, No Wake they call it, but this one was doing considerably more, probably double. Some grizzled boy-racer no doubt, or maniac, or simply running late. No matter, it came thrusting in with a big bow-wave, heading straight for their pier, the skipper seemingly intent on driving his thousand ton bus right into the African interior like some latter day Kurtz.

Shyno had ample time to assess the situation, about twenty seconds easily. At a glance: Lúcio, legs dangling dockside, fiddling with a rope around the starboard bow cleat. Nev, still holding off but half-leant over the gunwhale swabbing at some smear or other with a cloth. And the ketch with its half dozen large teardrop shaped fenders strung at six feet intervals all down her side.

'Fuck! Fenders, fenders, fuck, quick!' was all Shyno managed as he lurched out of the cabin. He grabbed Nev by the scruff and hauled him back in, flipped a blue and white plastic sausage over the side and saw Lúcio do the same as he retracted his legs. Then they just braced themselves and watched and waited.

About a hundred yards out the ferry skipper flung both engines into reverse at full revolutions and spun the helm hard to starboard. The effect was similar to what a downhill racer achieves as he comes barrelling down into the spectators' enclosure at eighty miles an hour and at the last minute stands hard on his edges, throws up a sheet of snow spray and comes to a sliding stop.

In this instance the spray took the form of a yard high wall of churning water that came sweeping towards them like a set of swells. Each time *Mona Gorda* was thumped against the pier the fenders squished flat like flimsy balloons hissing and squeaking as they relinquished their air. And they could feel in their bones the crump of stone against concrete as they hung on and were simply battered there.

After, when calm reconfigured, they inspected the damage. Some to the forward decking, none to the flesh. Nev just kept glancing over the side at the disfigured fenders muttering,

'Fuck man, that might have been me.'

'Or me...' Lúcio concurred.

A fruity, not unfriendly Home Counties voice dissolved their reverie. Deck shoes, tanned hairless calves, pink knees, khaki shorts, horizontal striped *matelot* t-shirt, creased leather features and all the rest. The owner of the ketch.

'Sorry chaps, but you can't park here I'm afraid. Sail only.' He gestured to a motley collection of stink-pots tethered up further along the key. 'Should find a slot somewhere down there. Cheers.'

They cast off, chugged over and since the boats were moored stern-inward, dropped anchor from their bow, ensuring it was firmly hooked. Shyno edged backward, reversing gingerly into an available berth. This time before they did or thought about anything else, they tied safely and securely up. Then double-checked.

WALKS ON WATER

Alan pitched up in the harbour 24 hours later pretty much on time and at the appointed date, around noon on the 30th of September.

This in itself seemed a reasonable omen since neither side had spoken for over four weeks, Mustapha's farm being not only remote but mercilessly free of any modern convenience such as piped water, electricity, or telephone. The nearest call box was a four-hour trek by rutted track back down the mountain and given the somewhat dilapidated state of the camper and the general trend toward banditry among the lower slopes, Mustapha had advised against it. Besides he could spare neither of his two sons to act as cohort until the pressing was completed.

The van would have been noted during its ascent to the eyrie and there was a limit to the efficacy of the various bribes and threats he had already handed out to key headsmen and officials to ensure their future safe passage. His budget had run to two further journeys: one for Alan back to Ceuta, the other for YaYa and the mules down to the beach. Beyond that, he told them, no guarantees.

The news of the revised security arrangements had a doubly disconcerting impact on Dave.

'Ah, the dinghy thing, ya, an ah Mustapha...'

Alan had developed the skills of a diviner as regards Dave's Morse code.

'Listen mate you'll get a day on the water once you're

down at the beach. More than you'll need. And Mustapha's only fucking around. He likes you.'

Alan could not have chosen his words more incautiously. YaYa was serenely and mutely married to an inoffensive devotee from Essex called Lucy, with whom he had duly and dully conceived twin blonde girls. He was besotted with them. At fourteen months when these babes ventured forth their first emphatic utterances, he discovered a common language. Of das, mas, aaahs, naahs, and of course yayas which induced in him an ecstasy that he tried to convey to the Guru in his quarterly one-to-ones.

Meantime Mustapha had taken to giving Dave a morning tour of his allotment. Runner beans, courgettes, knobbly carrots, podding peas, cucumber, marrow, all dewed and ripening in the autumn sun. It took a kind of mock heroic indifference, almost stoic on YaYa's part, not to acknowledge the vegetable splendour on display. Mustapha, miffed, mischievous and somewhat dispirited, then proceeded to contrive frequent encounters with his hirsute, carbuncular, plump and stumpy but ever eager niece Alya-Alyahoun, of whom he would declaim most magnanimously,

'Is my gift, Dave.'

Dave was in no doubt he was being challenged to show his hand. To Act The Man. In Mustapha's realm this meant be either one or the other, or both, but definitely not none. YaYa managed to make it perfectly plain to Alan.

'Nah, can't stay alone here, ya?'

'I'll sort it mate, ok?'

Alan had a lengthy pow-wow over a few flasks with Mustapha which went on into the night. YaYa sat clenched and determined as he gazed deep into the camp-fire coals which blazed and flared, *light of logs meeting to be lit*, then settled to a mound of ashen embers.

'Right mate, no more bother. Trust me.'

'Ya, what did he say?'

'Nothing.'

'Nothing?'

'No mate.'

'Ya, what did you tell him?'

'Only that you've got a dose of syph and you're crawling with crabs. Thought that should do it, and it did. Now relax.'

*

Alan made his unhurried way around the periphery of the port, skirting the sea-wall. The impression he had gained from his few meetings with Lúcio and Shyno – Nev he already knew – was that they were somewhat naïve. Track-record, previous, decent credentials, all suggested that they were quite capable, but they were amateurs, in the sense that they seemed to think this was some kind of adventure or boy's own story; whereas Alan was a career lag and had been at the sharp end, both giving and receiving, more times than he could count. Which was why YaYa would be doing the ferrying and not he.

It was a calculated risk to take up residence at Mustapha's *finca* but he had got away with it, as he had thought he would; but from here on in he would definitely keep the whole business at arm's length. Just give the guys the beach co-ordinates, then wait it out until YaYa made it to their rendezvous, if he did. Call it cynical, he simply thought of it as wise given the circumstances and the players. Call it practical.

To that same end he was garbed *à la Maroccaine*: an

ochre-coloured knee-length cotton tunic, loose black linen trousers, worn leather slippers, battered turban, accessorised with various dyed scarves, beaded necklaces, silver wrist bangles and sunglasses. Slung like bandoliers across his shoulders, a goatskin water bottle and a muddy green hessian bag completed his motley.

In what you could still see of his face behind a month's worth of swart growth only the blue eyes when he removed his shades hinted at any anomaly. From afar it was a pretty – though pretty is not the word – reasonable simulacrum of a natural indigent as opposed to some stoner gone native. That is, of course, until he opened his mouth.

Nev, who was in the stern, clocked him a hundred yards before he reached the pier and chortled. He recognised the somewhat ape-like walk. Alan made a great play of not acknowledging him as he ambled by the *Mona Gorda*'s berth and Nev for the fun of it went along, studiously ignoring this dockside hawker peddling his tat to the ignorant and unwary.

Alan shambled on further down the jetty to where a shabby little hippy sloop was tethered up. He pretended to engage the occupants with odd trinkets from his shoulder bag, grunting the while and employing the odd words of French and Arabic he had picked up from Mustapha, curses mostly, then shrugged, turned back on his way and stopped at the stern where Nev was waiting; then as if he was about to repeat his pantomime, looked around and muttered,

'Hullo mate, alright if I come aboard?'

Lúcio was in the shower taking advantage of unlimited water, Shyno in the galley fixing lunch. Nev beamed and did his version of *salamalekum* with one of his wings. 'Course you can. Christ, where did you get that gear, got any smoke?

I'll call the guys.' And almost as an afterthought. 'Where's Dave, man?'

'Up at the farm, Nev, slight change of plan.'

Any reservations Alan had about this crew were tempered by the fact that they had actually got to Ceuta, crossing the better part of 600 miles, but what really impressed him was the *Mona Gorda*. Vehicles of all kinds were his speciality and there was something special about her quarter.

Once Lúcio had persuaded him to remove some of his more outlandish guises – no one in the port was paying the slightest attention to them he explained, but they might do if he carried on like that – the four of them sat ranged around the stern benches drinking tea, all eyes inescapably returning to the large riveted rectangular panel at their feet.

Shyno had removed all but a dozen of the fastenings, leaving one at each corner, two at each end and a couple on either side. Taking them all out and screwing them back in was a time-consuming procedure, as there were probably a hundred all together. As it was they now had relatively instant access and easy withdrawal. Shyno had been down there a few times already checking out the hold.

'So that's it then? How much room have you got? The bales are bulky you know, about three foot square by one thick, and there's ten of them. 30 pounds each.'

'Ample,' said Shyno and proceeded to explain. 'It's just an empty space really, nothing down there apart from a few old life-jackets and some jerry cans. From where Nev's sitting it runs the full width of the boat up to the rear of the wheel house, a good 15 feet easy, and because the hull is curved, it's made of concrete you know, it has these metal ribs, just like you see on building sites sticking up out of the blocks, except here it's a sort of lattice-work, if you get my drift. Anyway apart from the bump that houses the prop-shaft, you've got these ridges on either side. I reckon we could pack five bales up on each one and I bet, even if you had this panel open, you wouldn't see them unless you got down on your knees and stuck your head inside.'

'Mmm, goodun,' murmured Alan. 'Might take a little look later, when it gets dark.'

ES CARGO

Rich Lee was feeling quite utterly wretched and having a rough ol' time of it, literally, as he rolled from clammy synthetic bunk to *aluminum* panelled washroom-cum-shower, in the below deck waterline cabin of the crossover ferry from Southampton to Bilbao, via Biscay Bay. It was entirely his own choice and one that he was now repenting but not at his leisure.

Lúcio had offered him the option of the route previously outlined, or any variation on it, but Rich had set his heels, typically Taurean, and without wishing to cast as it were any aspersions, or seem politically incorrect, he was Republican after all, confessed that he just didn't think he fitted the profile.

In his over-powdered imagination he had conjured up a succession of knowing leers from beefy officials as he explained how he was delivering this car, 'not mine mind you,' to his boss, 'Oh your Boss, I see, and what is it exactly you do for him, you do *do* for him don't you?' And all this in a variety of accents designed to enhance the insinuation that he was, not to put a fine word upon it, queer. Guilty merely by association if nothing else.

On top of which he was convinced he would need to cut his hair to offset the worst of this hallucinatory gauntlet and he was just not prepared to do it. He really did possess a splendid tonsure, one of those glossy thick west coast wheaten affairs which he cultivated in a contemporary layered style and which he was forever flicking back off his forehead with a couple of combing fingers or a twitch of his neck which only made those lustrous locks shimmy then settle where they nestled just above his shoulders. Nothing could have been more unconsciously camp.

Perhaps his instincts as regards the fear of being labelled proved him right. He insisted on the shortest route to Spain, and for fourteen hours in a moderate force four, as he heaved his already vacant insides out, reckoned he had drawn the shortest straw. Rich's gift for recruiting transporters stopped short of actually becoming a mule himself. He knew, coward that he was, that he would inevitably spill his guts.

Dockside in Bilbao at the customs booth a mild-mannered young officer took a cursory glance at his papers and waved him through. During the four day uneventful drive down south the only disappointment were the snails. *Los Caracoles* were small, chewy, and to Escargot's taste, over-spiced nuggets of tomato-based gristle that compared unfavourably to the plump garlicky morsels he was accustomed to.

The Spanish estate agent in Malaga assured him that the villa, which Señor Lúcio had booked, was all in order.

'The maid has laid fresh linen. There will be a welcome basket of fruit and a bottle of Cava and milk in the fridge; bread and other foodstuffs can be purchased at the nearby village store. Here is a map how to get there. The pool has been skimmed of leaves but Señor Lúcio has dispensed with that service and said you would take care of it. Sí? Here are the keys to the front door and the garage. If you have any needs, please call me.'

All this, in a perfectly accented, accurate but somewhat formal English sent Rich upon his way.

Villa Nova was anything but new, built some fifteen years earlier in the usual Spanish style. It was an undistinguished three-bed bungalow set back off the road in half an acre of rampant foliage and a mixture of palms and overburdened fruits trees, citrus mostly.

The pool was neat, clean and inviting especially in the still fierce daytime temperatures. There was a distant view of the Med though you couldn't see it thanks to the trees. But the two main characteristics which Lúcio had specified it had in spades: seclusion and a large empty garage.

Rich housed the Jag, unpacked, opened the Cava and settled down on one of the poolside loungers to while away the afternoon. He reckoned he would have the place to himself for the better part of a week. Things were looking up. Plenty of time for *tapas* and *fino* and exploring the delights of Puerto Banus. The one location in which Rich imagined the colourful Jag would not look out of place. Or he either.

GOING GOING

Shyno unloosed the few remaining rivets on the stern deck hatch, removed the four metal strips that comprised the frame, prised out the heavy marine plywood cover, and torch in hand lowered himself into the fusty gloom. He crawled forward a few feet and felt Alan's bulk plump down behind him.

'Phew.'

Shyno played the beam around the small cavern, pointing out salient features; stone spine protecting the prop-shaft, corrugated steel ribs visible through the pale grey concrete.

'It's still drying out apparently, even though she's ten years old. Just goes on getting harder with age. Not much you can do to it, unless you ram her on a rock or catch a torpedo. No joking; any normal prang and most likely she would only suffer a splinter crack.'

Shyno, rapping with his knuckles, produced a sonorous hollow note as if from a stone gong.

'This stuff is near two inches thick. It's what gives her her weight.

Alan was assessing available storage and devising camouflage. Tarpaulins for a starter, strew a few more life-jackets about, maybe some fenders; keep the jerry cans, throw in some rope, generally cram the remaining volume with all the usual boat rummage and clutter and then some.

'Great mate, no sweat fitting the bales all in, let's get some air.'

Topside Shyno reset the hatch while Lúcio spread out the chart which featured in detail that section of the Med coast covering Ceuta south towards Tetuán.

'The beach is five miles north of the port. Completely deserted along the shore. Just a few local shacks back on the hills. It's got no name, so it isn't marked on your chart. Mustapha's going to build a...cairn, that's it, a pile of stones as a landmark. Natch it'll be night for the pick-up, so I reckon you should do a day run tomorrow. Take a couple of fixes, plot it all up, time there and back, look mate I'm not trying to teach you to suck, you know about this stuff, right Lúcio?'

'Actually I do,' he replied.

'Well, should take about six hours there and back. Set off again around nine and we'll do the business near midnight. They'll have a torch to flash you, nothing fancy, just three quick ones at intervals. Can't afford too much in case someone spooks. Mustapha won't start until he sees your running lights. It's deep water so get in close, about four hundred yards, but no more as there's breakers. You'll hear them. When you do that's near enough.'

And that was it. Alan sloped off around ten that night and the three of them sat smoking and sipping brandy, each more or less lost in their own private reverie, rather like raw recruits on the eve of battle.

CANDY COLOURED CLOWNS

'...if it be life to pitch
Into the frogspawn of a blind man's ditch,
A blind man battering blind men.'

Shyno mused on Yeats. Nev had Roy on the tape machine, the Voice crooning and keening, *'Only in dreams'*. Lúcio was poised in the fore cabin re-Vita-lising Virginia Woolf as she,

'Went turning to water
And inescapably
Had to undo her wings.'

Hart Crane, drowned off the stern of the Orizaba, way back from Mexico. Shelley off Ischia. *'Phlebas the Phoenician, a fortnight dead'*. Stevie *'not waving but drowning'*. Whalers from Nantucket, Ishmael, all hail, well met, fellow swimmers, white oars beating in monotone, *'till human voices wake us and we drown.'*

It was this kind of interior sea-shanty, a funereal dirge, that grogged Shyno to wakeful sleep as *Mona Gorda* rocked on the echoes of a mounting Mistral.

November 1st saw the three of them awake by dawn. Breakfast was the usual fare. A couple of hours of moody procrastination and terse exchanges gave a sombre tone to their imminent departure. Without actually admitting it to themselves or each other they knew that the prologues were over. Time to get down to the business of the dummy run, and then the night escapade that they all sensed might alter them for ever.

Nev loosed the stern ties and cast off. Lúcio was busy with the anchor rope up on the bow. Shyno eased *Mona Gorda* forward as he took up the slack. They had about sixty feet of rope out. Lúcio was hauling and coiling and as *Mona Gorda* came up on the hook, Shyno put her to neutral, called Nev to take the wheel, and went forward to help with the chain.

'It's pretty well bedded' said Lúcio, the sinews in his torso, much like a Donatello bronze, taut with the strain. 'I can't seem to shift it.' Shyno leant his weight to the burden, but after a minute or two of impotent heaving came to the same conclusion. He lashed the rope round the bow cleat and went back to the wheelhouse and took the helm.

'Going to try and drag it free.'

He spent the next ten minutes manoeuvring the boat forward and back and only succeeded in making slow circles like some pondering elephant on a short tether. Lúcio looked aft, hands spread in a what-do-we-do-now gesture. Nev was preparing a roll-up. This was not a problem to which he could impart anything useful so he kept out of it. Unbuckling his braces was a fiddly business and Shyno seemed impatient.

The skipper was just coming to terms with the fact that he was going to have to dive the anchor up when he remembered they possessed neither mask nor flippers. Snorkelling had never featured high on their agenda. Sure they could simply reverse back into their berth and go in search of equipment, even a diver maybe, but he was brassed off at this latest indignity. Besides they were attracting attention from the denizens of the stink-pot community and they were running late. It was already past ten. Sod it. Shyno stripped to his trunks, slipped off the bow and plunged into the ordure, which felt icy at around 65 degrees.

The anchor was only fifteen feet down, snarled in a mooring cable. Beneath the scummy surface the water was surprisingly clear. Eyes wide open he consoled himself with the idea that the salt might act as some form of palliative against the infections he was exposing his orbs to. It took three lung-withering excursions to the bottom before he got the bugger free and on his final frigid breaching roared out,

'Haul that bloody anchor in and fetch me some bleach and a dry towel!'

Shyno was as gentle as a cub, but when aroused, as brutal as any beast at its kill. Not the most auspicious start to the most serious leg of their venture. Later he would refer to it as the end of the idyll.

Out past the seawall they turned right then right again, set the log, plotted a track on the chart and bore south a few hundred yards off the pristine Moroccan coast. A wide-spaced glassy swell rolled in from the north and pushed them along at ten knots while *Mona Gorda* surfed the motion, accelerating down the blue-green valleys as the sea gave a propelling pat to her broad rump.

Shyno handed Nev the helm, had a brief confab with Lúcio, then climbed up to warm himself on the wheelhouse roof and periodically scanned the shoreline with a pair of binoculars. The tape machine was pumping out Sister Morphine and all-in-all he felt more or less well.

Two hours later he spied a heap of flat stones piled up in a cone midway down an empty beach and whooped and hollered as he scrambled down the wheelhouse ladder and grabbed the wheel. He pointed *Mona Gorda* in and the three of them stood staring at the cairn, a couple of hundred yards offshore, just outside the collapsing surf.

No doubt about it, this had to be the spot.

Lúcio took a pencil and marked the chart. Nev did a kind of pirouette on his crutches and Shyno silently apologised for being an uptight shit.

'*What then?' sang Plato's ghost. 'What then?*'

Well, turn around, head back, moor up, rest, eat, get ready for the night shift. Pumped and primed, they up-anchored without problem at around nine and retraced their wake in darkness along the African shoreline. In out, in out, as rowers on the stream, they plotted up then idled in the same spot where they thought that they had been and waited for the torch beam which never came.

Around 2am Shyno fired up the diesel, for the nth time, and moved the *Mona Gorda* out from the beach where the swell was pushing her on. Nev and Lúcio were both succumbing to a kind of Morphean gloom, as was he. A few lights still sparkled back up in the hills, but nothing that indicated any kind of rendezvous.

Shyno took her a good way out, about a mile offshore and cut the motor, intent on snatching a few hours sleep. He woke at dawn, noted the booming surf almost within earshot and turned the engine key. He was greeted with a few metallic clicks, then silent nothings; not even the merest hint of a turnover. The battery was flat. Too many turnings on and off without charging had drained and done for it. They were rudderless, immobile and at the discretion of the sea.

RESCUE REMEDY

To say the *Mona Gorda* was going nowhere was not strictly true, except in the sense of not under her own power; but motion there was and it was noticeable, as the combination of tide and swell exerted their inexorable pull shoreward. Shyno got the engine hatch open and had a poke about below, jiggling the battery terminals which were caked in a coppery blue gunge, tried the key again but to no avail. It was a dodo, dud, dead, a no go.

The temptation to hark back to Lúcio's dismissal of the 'trivial' was strong; but it was pointless casting about for a scapegoat, when he knew that he should have dealt with the matter of a spare battery himself. The words 'auxiliary power' and *Mona Gorda*'s lack of it only compounded Shyno's sense of negligence. What had they been thinking of? What they had not was transparently clear. The hapless trio sat huddled in the wheelhouse and Shyno felt the burden of expectation focused on him.

'Basically we're stuffed. No power means no radio, so a mayday's out. We could try to swim her off I suppose but I doubt that we could shift her. No one's going to drown, but at this rate of drift we'll be on the beach in an hour. Best bet is to get the anchor out before we're into the surf. Just pray it's not one of these steep-shelving types, you know, a hundred foot of water and the next minute bingo, it's up to your waist. Lúcio, have a look on the chart and check the depths. I'm going to drop the hook anyway, maybe the drag will slow us down. Listen if it comes to it, we'll have to jump ship and swim for it when we get in close, there's no way we'll be able to hold her off on the beach.'

Shyno glanced at Nev's braces.

'If we're going to end up in the water, mate, give yourself a bit of time to get them off first.'

Ironic that when they had just written off the coastguard as a viable option that self-same coastguard, unbidden, should promptly show up with the *whoop whoop whoop* of a powerful siren announcing their arrival.

'Splendid' said Lúcio. 'Just what we need, the Navy.'

And it was – or rather one half of the Moroccan coastal force as they were later informed. She was a long, sleek, shark-grey 120-foot cutter, making about 25 knots and bearing down on the *Mona Gorda* at a rapid rate, slicing through the wide spaced glassy swells with the grace of a porpoise and plenty of purpose. Fifty yards off, she throttled back and came to a halt, the siren still blaring, more than audible and duly intimidating.

What might have been a 10mm squat-barrelled gun was mounted in the bow and Shyno could make out a flurry of activity by a group of machine-gun toting Moroccan sailors toward the stern, preparing to launch a tender. This was a large rigid inflatable which they swung out on a davit where it did a sort of seesaw dance while they tried to lower it to the water. The cutter was beam on to the swell and rolling heavily. For a minute or two it seemed she might well spill not only the tender but the four occupants trying to keep their seats as their colleagues winched them down to the surface. Then they were under way and speeding over, all the while hailing and gesturing in that universal language which always translates to 'hands in the air'.

Lúcio and Shyno obliged, smiling and waving like friendly natives, while Nev did his best with one of his crutches, praying that they wouldn't mistake it for some sort of firearm.

As their RIB came alongside it was clear they were serious. Guns were un-shouldered and pointed in the trio's direction. One sailor grabbed a rope and leapt onto the bow where he promptly slipped on the wet deck and went arse over tit and gave himself a nasty thump as he struggled not to fetch up in the water.

Shyno could have sworn he saw a quick smirk from the other recruits but then they got efficient and gruff and went about their business: which was to tear the *Mona Gorda* apart from stem to stern and uncover the dope.

Lúcio felt the time was not yet right for any elucidation, plenty of scope for that later. In ten minutes they had penetrated every possible orifice and had drawn a blank. Not content, the sailors each got out a large screwdriver and jabbed into every sealed bulkhead and panel until the walls in the forward cabin resembled a colander. They seemed disappointed and now that the first frenzy was over you could tell they were puzzled, as they took in Nev's disability and then the guiltless and affable mien of their captives. This was when Lúcio came into his own and with the faultless and fluent French of a native speaker began weaving his spell.

'Nous sommes des poètes, on peut dire maudits, mais le Bon Dieu nous a fourni des sauveurs sous la forme de vous-mêmes, vrais navigateurs.'

Nev looked at Shyno who, all the while smiling, murmured,

'He just told them we are a bunch of dippy poets who don't know the first thing about boats and thank Christ you've come along to rescue us in the nick of time just like the proper sailor fellows you are. Or some such flannel. Look, they're buying it.'

And so, apparently, they were. The transformation from raiders to rescuers was already under way. Lúcio turned toward his chums and in unfamiliar demotic said,

'Just cool it, guys, and let me handle this.'

The cutter took *Mona Gorda* under tow and made steady progress toward Tetouan few miles south. There was a fair to-do and kerfuffle when they got there. The Captain quite simply commandeered the entire harbour. First he had all the commercial fishing boats cast off and reposition in a tight cluster in the middle of the port. Having thus freed up the whole length of the sea wall pier, he subjected the displaced boats and their crews to a masterful demonstration of how to manoeuvre a large vessel in a confined space and moored up like some visiting but unexpected Pasha. They were suitably awed. Authority in action.

Mona Gorda he close-hauled like a remora to his belly, slinging deflective fenders between them and letting her nuzzle at his flank as the guest of honour. A novel form of protective custody. To be frank, nothing could have been more deliriously absurd, apart from the events about to unfurl.

THE CAPTAIN'S TABLE

Lúcio had this uncanny knack of reading his readers. By which it is meant he could immediately intuit at a first encounter whatever a person might desire from him and by the same token what use he might make of them in return. It was a magical gift, almost metaphysical, the ability to see 'the bones behind the bones' as he put it.

Call him what you like: necromancer, conman, catalytic psychopath, mind bender, genius, he could sway anyone he wanted to his will, such was the force of it. A deep dark Orpheus always up against the wall and never looking back. A piper who had lead many distinguished rats on a merry caper, often without them being aware of it. All this packaged in a compact bronze boyish parcel of wit and charm that bore a striking resemblance to Rimbaud, without the lice but with all the venom and an equal talent. Echu, Elegua. You either loved or hated him, but usually both, and overlooked him at your peril.

Shyno and Nev sat out in the stern trying to absorb this latest twist in the affair. The crew of the cutter were busy about their chores on the deck which loomed above them but every now and then one would lean over smiling, thumbs up, and mouth the word *poète*.

Within half an hour a rope ladder was dropped over the host's side and two young sailors in broken English asked if they might come aboard. Of course you may. Shyno went through the wheelhouse to the cabin where Lúcio appeared to be organising documents and had a quiet word. By all means. Their visitors did a bit of a dumb show but the thrust of it was obvious, they were there to effect repairs and extend an invitation. The Captain wished to speak with Lúcio, at his convenience.

Lúcio donned the slightly crumpled cream linen suit which he had packed much to Shyno's annoyance, gathered up the documents and a copy of his bilingual book of French and Portugese poems. Armed with this, escorted by one of the crew, he made an elegant and agile ascent of the ladder and disappeared. The sailor who was left behind then set about filling with white mastic the myriad perforations his chums had not long previously made.

While waiting for these restorations to go off he busied himself cleaning up the battery terminals and called aloft for a mate to send down a set of cables which he attached, placing *Mona Gorda*'s power source on a slow charge. In time he rubbed the in-fills down and with an artist's brush touched up the repairs with near-matching paint.

Nev was still sat abaft. There was a twice-daily ritual that he performed before sleep and upon waking, which involved his callipers; namely the taking them off and the putting back on. The braces were weighty, unwieldy and uncomfortable. Each one consisted of two 2 inch wide metal struts, hinged at the knee with a locking mechanism, continuing up to the inner thigh, widening to accommodate the only slighter thicker girth. A pair of broad leather straps fastened by Velcro, one near his crotch, the other at his knee joint, completed the armature. An iron bar welded at the base of these struts formed what was in essence a stirrup for his boot.

Shyno had watched him once or twice quite unselfconsciously unburden his legs of this apparatus. It was a humbling sight and not for the squeamish. Perhaps it was the heat or fatigue, but Nev had unbuckled out in the open and the two discarded props lay side by side on the deck at his feet like a pair of abandoned weapons.

A group of recruits had gathered on the cutter's gunwale; they were ostensibly attending to some routine maintenance but it was curiosity that had got the better of them. Nev knew it and was basking, like the Leo that he was, in the attention. One sailor was making a show of testing the fixity of rivets in the cutter's hull with a heavy stainless steel spanner when he overreached himself and the expensive tool slipped from his grasp, pinged off the rail and plopped into the water. Much consternation and a bit of a huddle. Someone was going to have to get in and fetch it back.

Nev looked up, gave an airy wave and promptly flopped over the stern like a performing seal. Shyno had taken for granted that Nev could swim, something to do with his polio and hydro-physiotherapy, but this was out of the ordinary. Nev's body mix gave him what in aquatic terms was the equivalent of the wings of a manta ray. Huge shoulders, powerful lungs with nothing of any weight trailing behind. With just a couple of sweeps of his flipper-like hands he was 20 feet down to the seabed; then adjusting his flaps, glided back up to the surface with the spanner in his teeth. He was hardly breaking breath.

These acquabatics provoked an ululating howl of approval from the sailors on the cutter but Nev was not finished yet. He could just about reach with his fingertips to the lip of *Mona Gorda*'s gunwhale. He clung for a minute then with a gymnast's upper-body power, in true slow motion, hauled himself up level with the deck, swivelled and lowered his bum into a sitting position. And there he posed, dripping and glistening in the afternoon sun.

The applause from the Moroccans was sustained and more than respectful. They were stunned, as was Shyno. Lúcio took this opportunity to reappear and called out to them both,

'Get your glad rags on, lads, we've been invited to dinner.'

ALL SOULS

The Fellows Buttery of that idiosyncratic, occasionally over-rated yet still venerable institution is an intimate oval space with a domed ceiling beneath which, it is rumoured, every mot, bon or mauvais, may be overheard, the acoustic rendering every word spoken audible to all should they choose to listen. A boon to the brilliant and witty but somewhat constraining to any mere mortal who by mishap or mischief finds himself supping there.

Then there was the tedious business of the cutlery, seemingly intent on testing your etiquette and ingenuity: three pronged forks with which to chase the bullet-like garden peas, blunt knives for the inevitably tough chunks of meat and what to with the deliberately placed pit in the cherry compote: spit it out insouciantly on to a flat pudding spoon and risk it running off into your neighbour's lap, or palm it surreptitiously to the side of your plate?

All petty amusements no doubt. And among these discomfort foods 'brain seizure' featured high on the menu. As you tried to digest some subtle disquisition from an ancient Professor of Roman Law, meanwhile fending off some under-table fumbling from a late dementia Fellow who for 40 years has been writing his un-memoirs.

Scholars, as Yeats memorably described them, coughing in ink and polishing the carpet with their shoes. Then the call for port where some minion ushers you to the uncommon common-room for further tippling and high-brow banter amid much fingering of costly cigars. Lordy.

Lúcio and Shyno were occasional guests of a certain A.H, at 21 the youngest Fellow ever elected to the hallowed walls. All Souls has no undergraduates, only fellows, and there is no point even applying for a Prize-Fellowship unless you have an exemplary First. If you survived the draconian fellowship exam, you faced the Interview. This consisted of a public inquisition by any or all of the resident fellows, up to fifty at a time, who would fire off questions on whatever subject they chose for you to answer.

It wasn't a matter so much of what you knew, though that counted, but of how dazzlingly you dealt with what you did not. A species of up-market press conference to a quorum of hostile well-informed journos that you were eager to placate.

AH had sailed through it all and was comfortably bedded in the inner-sanctum bosom of Academe. Once in, it's a seven-year tenure, renewable, paid and maintained, to do what you like or, if you like, do nothing at all. Many were there to write minority interest unreadable books, but it was not obligatory. One Fellow, a quantum physicist had published nothing but obscure papers for over a decade, furthering his 'research'.

All that was truly required was to demonstrate sufficient wit, intelligence and original thought not to bore your fellow travellers should you emerge from your padded suite into the common parts, to sit at table or take port in the fug-filled overheated snug of their sitting room.

A members only club for semi-certifiable brainiacs.

After lunch AH led them back to his apartments. He was expecting three other guests: a junior research Fellow at Merton called Mark and his boyfriend Tim, plus the *pièce de résistance*, Henry Panter, an important and self-important critic of the Opera who wrote for The Times.

These get-togethers were straightforward in format and followed a regular pattern. Shyno and Tim were present to provide the aesthetic, the decoration, while the other four limbered up with a bit of mental duelling to prove who had the sharpest rapier. Lúcio could parry with the best of them, but he treated it as sport, not some spiteful game where the object was to inflict wounds and draw metaphorical blood. Our Critic took it much more seriously; he was there to win.

Tim looked as if he would rather be elsewhere, shagging probably, or downing a couple of ales in the pub. Shyno had been through this several times before and was easy with his role. Muse to the Maestro, maker of a few fine sonnets, pretty, nothing more.

Besides, AH had a plentiful supply of decent booze and could be extravagantly catty, which never failed to amuse. A rather beautiful doe-brown kohl-ringed pair of eyes beamed out from behind round-rimmed spectacles beneath delicate dark brows. A tumble of black hair to his shoulders attested to his part-Indian origin. The only weakness he would admit to physically was his big-girl bum, which he swathed in long tunics, at one and the same time trying to hide it and invite the attentions of a decent man.

Although he had not yet had time to read everything he would declaim '*J'ai lu tous les livres*' and he made a pretty convincing show of it. He owned a verbal and imaginative *sprezzatura* you could only describe as virtuoso. He was a mediocre and prolific poet but a Master in prose. See his *Journey to Ladakh*.

Mark was a first-class listener with a five-star mind and didn't speak much or often. When he did it usually gave you plenty to think about in the interval before his next utterance. Tim was a bluff bright chunky Northerner studying Geology at Durham. Of the six he was the only one drinking beer and took an immediate scunner to the critic. There was nothing entirely unpleasant about the man but Tim, who was bucolic as regards his own sexual predilections, sensed in the silver-quiffed bouffant the unmistakeable whiff of the closet queer.

Every time Panter glanced at Tim, which was frequently, his sharp pink tongue made an involuntary sweep around the even pinker lips of his plump little moue of a mouth. Tim found this both disgusting and pathetic. Fuck's sake, own up, man. But he had promised Mark no bother and best behaviour.

Lúcio and Harvey were batting it about with Henry, winding up the tempo, both looking for the blow that would set him off. Panter leaned toward Tim, moistening as he did and enquired,

'And what sort of music do you enjoy, young man?'

This was already patronising and presumed, rightly as it happened, that Tim had neither the taste nor temperament for opera. Load of balls-ache and bad actors and a few good tunes.

Tim as he was expected to rose to the bait.

'R and B, Soul mostly.'

'Ah, I see, anyone I might know?'

'I doubt it.'

'Try me.'

'Don Covay.'

'Mmm, no, and who might he be?'

'A soul singer,' and then as if he couldn't help but blurt it out, 'He's got the most amazing voice you've ever heard.'

'Really…'

Tim was in deep and Panter, sensing his hook was well set, decided it was time to reel in this *ingénu* and put him out of his misery. Lúcio liked Tim, as he did most people who were honest and unassuming, so he intervened.

'I think Tim is alluding to the Duende, as Lorca defines it: the difference between mere technical brilliance and true spirit. What aficionados of Flamenco and Fado debate endlessly over a few cups of Fino.'

This should have been sufficient for Panter to release and put back, but he persisted. You could almost see his mouthing brain wrap its tongue around Ferrier – '*la voix mêlée de couleur grise*,' or Caruso. Then he simply turned his back on Tim, ignored Lúcio as some minor irritation, and addressing A.H launched into some superior anecdote.

'I was in Tramontano recently and had the privilege of a private performance of a new work-in-progress at the Villa Castellano, owned by La Contessa Annalina Magnani di Frotelli, in her delightfully intimate theatre. Even managed to rouse Maria from her bed to run through some of the arias. Terrific sets. Thinking of roughing out a few paragraphs for the Thunderer. A small diary piece, you know.'

'I am glad you enjoyed it' murmured Lúcio, 'Anna will be so pleased you approve. I shall be sure to let her know.'

Panter reacted as if he had been winded by some below-the-belt blow.

'You know her?' he woofed.

'She and I are old friends, as are our families. She asked if I would give a hand with the libretto and advise on the set designs, that sort of thing.'

Lúcio then quietly proceeded to give Panter a lesson in humility which lasted about half an hour during which time no other voice was heard. It seemed to encompass most of the -ologies and -isms with a few juicy titbits thrown in for light relief. Ten minutes in, Panter got down from his armchair and went and sat on the carpet at Lúcio's feet. By the time he had finished his impromptu lecture the not-so important Critic was hurriedly scribbling on a scrap of paper. He was taking notes.

Shyno reckoned dinner at the Captain's table might prove something of a doddle.

PIPED ABOARD

And so they were whistled and cheered aboard, in an improvised version of what would normally be reserved for visiting brass.

A bosun's chair was rigged for Nev, in which cradle he sat like King Kitten as they winched him up. Shyno wore a pair of fading pinstripe lilac flares and a white cotton pirate blouson with blowsy sleeves, Nehru collar and rolled cuffs. Lúcio stuck with his linen suit. Nev sported his regulation boots, the other two wore flip-flops.

Don't these Moroccan servicemen, Shyno mused, have something better or more important to attend to? Apparently not. All along the scrubbed iron walkway the crew stood half-easy, smiling and nodding favourably as the odd triumvirate passed by.

When Shyno ducked beneath the portal that gave to the main saloon and came face to face with cutter's Captain, he got some inkling of what this parade was all about. Books. Hundreds of them. Lining, where there might have been maps, charts, or barometers, the serried teak shelves on all four walls, each one with its own polished restraining brass strip, behind which like soldiers the volumes were ranked. No more or less than a seafarer's library of which the Captain, 'call me Ali, please,' was custodian and connoisseur. North Africa's very own Captain Nemo.

The Skipper was a memorably good-looking figure and as it transpired a committed bibliophile. Not exactly what you anticipate from a senior officer of the Moroccan fleet, but then why not? Dark of course, serious, close-cropped hair, neatly trimmed beard, height and weight proportionate, surprisingly delicate long tapered short-nailed fingers. But it was the eyes that compelled. A deep sapphire blue pair of jewels that gleamed out of crow's-footed sockets like semaphores. '*Warum gabst-du uns die tiefen blicke?*' Pace Goethe, the kind of close-up long-distance gaze that befits a sailor or a movie star.

Captain Mansour had other surprises in store. He was fluent in several languages, devoted to poetry, and now possessed, pride of place, a copy of Lúcio's '*Le vrai le vain*' (Paris: Actuels, 1971).

Another of those few who know.

Supper was a jolly affair, Mansour apologetic for the over-enthusiastic attack on the *Mona Gorda*, but as you will appreciate a duty of care to international law, a regrettable mistake, easily made, given the circumstance, let us not dwell upon it, please, you are my guests, shall we proceed and have something to eat, forgive me, turning to Neville, I gather you are quite a swimmer, what is your name again, ah, *splendide*, good chap, well done with the spanner, *on y va*, after you sir, I insist.

Followed a good old feast: simple fare, choice of chicken chasseur well spiced, sweet potato mash and steamed fresh vegetables, or honeyed *mille-feuille* pigeon pie with fruit and cheese for afters, all washed down with several bottles of Château Musar. Present were Captain Ali, two senior officers, and the happy trio.

Lúcio topped the whole thing off with a reading from his poems which, though Nev understood not a word, judging from the Captain's profound appreciation, soft eyed and hand on heart, must have been something exceptional. It all went over extremely well.

Later, back aboard the *Mona Gorda* still basking in the afterglow of the whole affair, Lúcio broke the sobering news,

'Chaps, we are now officially in Moroccan territory and I am afraid that they have stamped our passports.'

As they absorbed this latest information Shyno refrained from a sulky rejoinder. Hardly matters, does it, if you've nothing to declare.

RICH'S LITTLE GIRL

Rich was feeling restless. After two days of solitude he had run out of interesting things to say to himself and needed an audience.

The local village had proved less than responsive to his limited Spanish and the urge for a more sophisticated ambience pushed him toward Puerto Banus. Only caution held him back. Lúcio had been quite specific, keep a low profile, knowing that that would be tricky wherever Rich showed up.

Banus was not the *Mona Gorda*'s intended port of call for their return journey, far from it. The landfall they had in mind was a sleepy marina they had visited on their way down south, further back up the coast near Nerja.

Banus was no longer the cake-walk it had once been. It had become a catwalk for the watchers and the watched. Four years after its splashy launch, it had already gained a reputation as a favoured gateway for Morocco's finest. Lúcio just didn't want Rich drawing any unnecessary attention to himself or to the Jag.

So Rich worked at the itch of boredom with regular laps of the pool and channel-hopped the cretinous TV output. Frequent tugs of his tent-pole whiled away a few hours but the truth of the matter was his real discomfort resided in his nose. It was over a week since his last toot.

The debate about the addictive properties of coke is ongoing. Ethical issues about dealing in it will have to be addressed later. But in those days, unless you were a free-baser, committed to smoking the unrefined coca paste, its grip over its users was mostly mental. Crack had not been invented yet, although like internet porn it was a pustule waiting to erupt. Back then it was a media-class-only drug, far too expensive to destroy your septum with unless you were a rock star or millionaire.

Over in Colombia they called it *perrica*, as in parrot, because it made partakers loquacious, compelled to chatter. It had the power to convert an introverted mute into a fluent orator, although what he uttered was likely to be largely drivel.

In short the only thing Richard was suffering withdrawal from was the sound of his own voice. He decided it was time for a buff-up and a night out. This entailed one of those puzzling contradictions in his world view which he had yet to resolve to his total satisfaction. He held it as self-evident that the Old Country was superior on almost every front to his native America. History, culture, aristocracy, culinary invention, architecture: the list is familiar but he could not comprehend how Europe in so many instances had simply failed outright to get to grips with something so fundamental as plumbing.

Villa Nova and its unpredictable pipes he took to be a case in point and, once more submitting himself to the capricious waterworks of the shower, he shook his head in dismay and wondered whether this might qualify as one of what the estate agent had described as 'his needs'.

It was not the preliminary rusty drizzle which he had quickly learnt to avoid but the way in which the colour of the water would continue changing throughout the quarter of an hour that Rich felt constituted an absolute minimum, for a decent douche.

So he found himself ducking in and out of the variable spray as it moved through a spectrum of brown, green and yellow, with intervals of clarity in between. This discouraging palette was mimicked by an equivalent range of temperatures, no matter where he fixed the tap or thermostat; from icy to scalding to lukewarm and back, without rhyme or rhythm, so there was no way of judging when to advance or retreat.

Something about the soap as well, which was the only kind supplied at the villa or available in the village store. Strangely foamless and studded with granules or possibly grit, it did certainly give a thorough type of exfoliation which bordered on sandpaper and left his skin tingling, medium rare.

He had even considered washing in the pool, but that had been laced with some cocktail of chlorine and chemicals at a municipal level, which Rich was convinced he could see evaporating off the surface in a shimmering vapour. He swore his hair was already several shades lighter and had restricted himself to breast stroke whenever the heat or tedium compelled him to enter the water.

At least it was clean, as were his teeth, which, as with most *yankers,* were near perfect and took pride of place in his face. Rich had devised his own elaboration on the thrice daily two-minute brushings, one that he considered unique since he had never heard anyone else describe it and which he kept to himself as a kind of competitive edge. He chanced on the method one day after eating some corn on the cob.

First, tug loose half a dozen strands of hair from their roots; twist into a twine, then wind around both forefingers and using a bow-saw motion move it back and forth between the affected teeth.

A few years later, when flossing was officially introduced to the public, he took some consolation from having been an early pioneer, and privately kicked himself for not having the nous of an entrepreneur.

Thus far not too bad on the ablutionary obstacle course. Just a minor skirmish with the single bladed *Bica!* and the inevitable nick which he patched up with a dot of double-ply loo roll. A quick blast of *Bruto* which left his sparse pits humming, and then there was his hair.

Villa Nova's towels were a poly-cotton blend biased toward the manmade that left Rich's barnet with a pronounced frizz. Unacceptable. There was nothing else for it. Head back under the shower, squeeze out the excess, then set up the ironing board. Adjusting the iron to *lana* (wool) not *seda* (silk), a few judicious sweeps produced a creditable result, less the slight blister to his left earlobe.

Again, ahead of his day, this time in the matter of tongs.

On into the final straight: denim strides, faded, boot cut; big collar paisley print shirt; Frye kickers; thick braided silver and turquoise buckled belt. Add two-tone aviator shades and he was ready for the road.

Rich tooled the big cat down the switchback tarmac, Randy Newman on the stereo. *Gone Dead Train*, a favourite, with Ry Cooder bottle-necking in fine form. Rich liked the lyric, laughing at the conductor who said his coal would never last. Especially that bit about 'the fire in the boiler up and quit before I came', as this was something that had never chagrined him. He always went fully fuelled.

Richly thought of himself as a bit of a Performer, not mad or anything, no in that division he was strictly little league, but he liked 'to put it about'. In those days you could still pimp your wheels at grease pace along the dockside drag, it was almost obligatory; to primp and brag, establish your mag-cred, like on South Beach in Miami, checking out the bars, the impossibly svelte and available girls, though it's all probably footfall equations and pedestrianised now.

Mindful of Lúcio, Rich slotted up in the public car park and set out on foot.

Puerto Banus was just another nouveau arrived like countless before. A small fleet of supra-yachts fronting a line-up of fleecing boutiques and eye-wateringly priced part-starred restaurants. Only in that era it was Saffas and Yanks not Ragheads and Ruskis who made up the owners.

Rich settled for a well patronised *tapas* bar at a table for two with a good view over the marina and perused the menu. None of your quadrilingual printed plastic tat, just a small chalked board listing the daily specials in the lingua franca. Rich enlisted the help of a waiter for a quick run-through.

'*Caracoles*'. No, thanks.

'*Tripas, estilo Madrileño*'- tripe in tomato sauce. Mnah.

'*Angulas*'- tiny eels, elvers. Erm.

'*Chipirones en su tinta, muy bueno*'- baby cuttlefish in their ink. Maybe.

'*Ceviche*'- You mean like sushi, no, ok.

'*Patas de gallo fritas con salsa verde al ajo*'- fried chicken feet with green garlic sauce. Nope.

'*Culos de pavo a la parrilla rellenos con trufa y hierbas frescas*'- turkey 'tails' grilled and stuffed with truffles and fresh herbs. Arseholes? Parsons' noses, señor.

'*Plato de mariscos*'- seafood, but for two.

'*Paella a la Valenciana*' - ditto, and a forty-minute wait.

Rich took a deep breath, 'Ah, just gimme a steak, medium, and fries.'

'*A tomar*?' condescended the waiter.

'*Cerveza, por favor.*'

The trials of abroad...foreigners.

The talent on display was tantalising as Rich leant back replete and deferred the bill with a succession of jolting espressos, surveying the potential. It wasn't long before one of these cuties made her approach.

'*Holá bebe*, are you alone? Want some company?'

It was one of those perfectly redundant but to Rich perfectly acceptable opening gambits to which the only possible reply was 'Sure.' Her name was Gloria, from Medellín no less, and clearly a pro.

Rich was unfazed, he sometimes preferred it this way. No ambiguity and the 'benefits' included certain *droits de seigneur*. In a neat reversal of the popular cliché she said 'Luv your accent hun, what part the States you from?' Rich bought her a glass of Cava and started loosening his tongue.

She was a patient and attentive listener and she needed to be. After an hour or so Rich had barely got going and Gloria's almond eyes were starting to glaze over. Resting a delightfully manicured hand on his thigh she murmured,

'Wanna come back to my place, I need to powder my nose?'

Rich required no further encouragement, he paid their bill and she took his arm.

'*Vámonos, chico*'

Gloria was dressed in a style best described as 'latina slut', which by no means implied any defect of hygiene. On the contrary, every detail about her was contrived to bring out the worst in a man, which, of course, was precisely what she hoped for. The 4-inch heels, briefest of skirts, bare midriff, tank-top over braless little-girl breasts with, as Rich noted, prominent cone-shaped tips, did nothing to detract from her considerable beauty. Glossy tinted mullet, eager eyes, lightly downed upper lip, admirable bone structure. She might have been on the street but she was no street-walker, she had undisputed class.

Her apartment kept up the profile. A modern minimalist work with plenty of sharp points and soft rounded features and an industrial quantity of glass, most of which was devoted to creating the impression that Puerto Banus was her own front garden and the Med a private infinity pool. This sort of set-up took major monkeys, more than you could earn from a few well-heeled punters, there had to be a sponsor. Rich switched one part of his brain to transport mode and settled on the black velvet sofa.

'Be right there, baby.'

Rich watched her back as she moved away. One of those neat high-riding almost boyish bums, slender athletic legs, turned ankles. Just how he liked them. Something about these girly girls brought out the Daddy in him. Gloria returned moments later with a ziploc bag of powder, which she placed on the pink granite topped coffee table, then knelt beside him.

Except it wasn't really powder: that ready-chopped fructose or amphetamine-cut white grained sand that passes for coke in your everyday wrap. It was a good half-ounce of *Escama De Nácar*, Mother of Pearl, or in the tooter's lexicon, the Holy Grail. This is hardly the moment for a lecture on chemical procedures, degrees of purity, or manufacture. Suffice to say this was the stuff of connoisseurs, the equivalent of Château Petrus or d'Yquem: nectar.

Such a knower was Richly Bizarre.

He unclasped a small bone-handled stiletto flick knife and with the blade tweaked out of the ziploc a mussel sized lump of the iridescent product. No need to chop. Just prise off a couple of flakes with the point and then, thanks sweetie, gently mill and grind with a polished stone, rose quartz in this instance, until you have something the consistency of snow dust. There you go. Now snoof it all up with a bill roll and let the numbing chill penetrate the membrane into the blood's swirl as you ride on the current. Around midnight. Pure cocaine.

After a brief exchange of pesetas Gloria curled up against him, murmured '*Papi*', and set about her ardour. By the time Rich was stoked and beyond recall, lips around her teat, fingers fumbling at her hem, Gloria whispered in his scalded earhole the immortal words,

'I have a party in my panties Richy, just for you.'

Rich was already too far gone on the guest-list to heaven to grasp her meaning and besides he was experiencing a slight hardness of hearing as a result of the nimble little tongue darting in his ear. Gloria expertly guided the prowling digits away from her surprise and toward that delightful derriere.

'*Me gusta por atrás, papi...*'

And Rich was eager to oblige.

There are certain enigmas, as in the case of Gloria's, which are sometimes better left unsolved. She guessed that this *gringole* might be less than delighted to have her mystery made clear. So she plied him with powder and took advantage of him in the way that best pleased her and sometime toward dawn dispatched him with a phone number and a small rock, wide-eyed , wired, wrung-out, and none the wiser.

DONKEY BUSINESS

YaYa, Mustapha, his two sons Razah and Rezah, the deflated dinghy, one outboard motor, ten bales and two donkeys, were cloistered in the medium sized baking dish of a corrugated tin-roofed barn, midway between the abortive launch site and the Port of Tetouan; about half a mile inland, in amongst some cypress trees on a patch of parched, unworked farmland that belonged to one of Mustapha's many cousins and which now represented their fall-back position.

It had all seemed to be going to plan when, around ten the night before, the clopping caravan had begun the last leg of their pilgrimage down to the foreshore. One donkey was burdened with the dope, the other with the blown-up dirigible and the 25-horsepower Seagull engine. Mustapha was the point man followed by YaYa. Raz and Rez were leading the beasts bringing up the rear. There was just sufficient moonlight to make out the trail. A rocky well-tramped single file path flanked by indigenous scrub on either side.

All was peaceable until the donkey with the dinghy gave a sharp jerk of its muzzle, yanked the bridle rope free and moved off the track at a brisk trot toward a dense thicket of acacia trees where it set about munching on the vicious thorns. Rezah went in pursuit, which only encouraged the brute beast to penetrate deeper and get really stuck in. All it took were a couple of well placed kicks to its balls and Rezah dragged it out backwards by the tail with much cursing and braying, the two sounds being not dissimilar.

The fierce whispered shushes from Mustapha were followed by silence and then the unmistakeable hiss of escaping air. Puncture repair kit, anyone? Mustapha rallied them, only a few hundred yards from the beach and the cairn.

'We go on, check for damage later.'

YaYa was already experiencing a new sensation to replace his fear and it tasted of relief. As it was he need not have worried. The sight along the foreshore as he stood by the cairn provided every answer he needed as to whether it was still a goer. Sure, if you were a kamikaze or a world class surfer. The big fat booming swells were rolling in from a hundred yards out in successive sets, the barrels exploding with plumes of spray as they dumped their ordnance and hissed up the shore.

'Never get out in this,' YaYa shouted, to make himself heard above the roar.

'We go back, come again tomorrow,' bellowed Mustapha.

As they turned to retreat they thought that they could just make out through the swirling mist of spray what might have been a boat's running lights rising and falling in the distant dark, approaching or receding, it was impossible to tell. Pointless using the torch. If it was the *Mona Gorda* they had nothing to communicate except keep the hell out of here; and for that they had not thought to devise any kind of code.

Moderns have it so much easier with the cellular.

They trooped back up to the barn, unpacked and snatched a few hours sleep. When Dave awoke, Mustapha was already gone. Razah said they were to stay inside, sit tight, he would return soon. Dave looked over at the donkeys which had been quite freely making use of the limited facilities and inwardly thanked his guru that his guts were empty. Besides he was so dehydrated from a month of squits he would probably have bottled his own piss and drunk it rather than squander so lavishly on the concrete floor.

Mustapha hitched a lift on his cousin's tractor to the outskirts of the town and made his way to a bar on the fringes of the port. Even without the buzz that was on everybody's tongue, he quickly grasped the situation, especially as he had a clear view over the small harbour to where the *Mona Gorda* nestled alongside the navy vessel. He let the most voluble of the regulars fill in the detail, which only told him what had happened but not more importantly what was going on. For that he required some inside information. How to acquire it was the only question on his mind as he downed the first of several whisky chasers.

At the entrance to the dock proper was a makeshift cabin with a hand-managed wooden barrier manned by a pliable customs officer. Foreign passports and local documents were examined there, though natives with business in the port could pass freely with no more than a few words and a touch of baksheesh. One option, but risky.

An off-duty sailor from the cutter on shore leave, maybe? Another possibility. As was often the case, Mustapha mused, when in doubt, do nothing, just wait and see. Besides they had no dope aboard and as he dwelt on the barn full of bales back up the road, felt that if anyone was not sitting pretty it was he and his crew and a couple of crapping mules.

Alan was parked up in a campsite among an identikit collection of beat up VWs, psychedelically daubed Winnebagos, silvery Airstreams and the odd sprinkling of Beamers and Super Glides.

The scene had the look and air of one of those impromptu mini-festivals now known as a rave, though given the total lack of amenities apart from an acre of blasted pasture, there was not a great deal to rave about. Nothing daunted, the motley commune were quite oblivious to any defect in the environs as blissful oblivion was the one quality they all had in common. THC heaven. Bongs and bongos, pan-pipes and hash pipes: the whole hippy *caravanserai* that the authorities tolerated and regularly raided to encourage tourism '*et pour décourager les autres.*'

No harm in a few token tokers, it was the serious traffickers they liked to make examples of. The Alans of this world.

At first light, he slipped away from the remains of a few smutty, smouldering campfires, motored to the rendezvous two miles north of the cairn and took up a position where he could scan the expanse of beach. No sign of Dave and it didn't look promising; the unbroken line of breaking surf was closing off any approach to the shore.

He hung about for an hour or so then like some uneasy revenant made his way back toward the campsite. His first instinct was to split before the shit hit, maybe hook up with Rich over the border, high u-haul it out of there, pronto, quick, put some distance between them as it were. But then he figured that he was, barring some grass-up, clean; so maybe just linger. He didn't much fancy either option. In the end he decided to stay put and wait it out for a while.

Mustapha reprised his route back to the barn on foot bearing gifts. Dates, fresh figs, water, whiskey, bread, dried meat, smoked fish and a bicycle repair kit. YaYa gave an involuntary scratch to his crotch, which Mustapha dismissed with a cheery gesture.

'No much fun, ya? I go find Alan. Maybe get you doctor in Tetouan, fix carrot. Shave you curls, ya. You son bitches stay inside, many dogs sniffing about.'

Mustapha located Alan within the hour and they had a frank, *mano a mano* discussion about the issue, what was at stake and how there would be the devil to pay if Alan cut loose now.

The import was as follows. No move matey until I give the order. Forget the border. You won't reach Ceuta if I say the word. Dave is ok, a bit itchy, but no bother. Boat buggers, they look safe. Stick with your tourist tune. I'm sitting on the bundle and plan to get paid. Not fucking trucking that shit back up the mountain. I am going to deliver. And so are you. Just play up and play the game, if you're worth your part. So what if the drop-scenes drop on all of Allah's stages?

Words or words like these Mustapha freely employed, all the while illiberally cursing. After a bout of ugly haggling Alan conceded with a few surly grunts.

Mustapha was neither blowhard nor bottle-merchant. He managed to persuade Alan that what appeared a major reversal was no more than a minor glitch that required a slight change of plan. What that alteration might involve Alan knew better than to ask or Mustapha to volunteer. It was a work in progress, an 'improv' that needed a fair bit of working on with little time for rehearsal.

PASSING THE PORT

Shyno was forward in the cabin, Lúcio by the wheelhouse, Neville astern. Each had retreated to a private meditation on last night's business with Captain Ali who had since issued a further invitation, this time to breakfast, which Lúcio declined on both their parts, making excuses, but would himself attend with pleasure.

Shyno knew better than to meddle, this was no mere social visit. Lúcio was working some juju, he could tell without asking. Unlike most conjurers Lúcio was happy to disclose his methods once he had pulled off a trick. His view was, atypically, that it hardly diminishes a performance to have it explained afterwards; on the contrary it makes it more magical.

'I'll fill you in later guys. Captain Ali means business and we are not off his hook yet, of that much I am sure.'

***

'Bonjour, Monsieur le Poète, I hope you slept well?'

'Yes, thank you Captain, though my companions are somewhat worse for wear, too much of your good wine I'm afraid; the fruits of the Bekaa Valley have ensnared the unwary.'

'Help yourself to pastry, there is coffee in the *cafetière*; make yourself comfortable.'

'You are more than kind.'

Lúcio had the sensation of one who enters the Headmaster's study, not guilty, because not yet found out; but about to undergo the ritual derogation of a suspect who appears to have got away with whatever mischief he was contemplating for the simple reason that the deed was stillborn. Since thought-crime was not so easily punished, he might reasonably expect to get off with a theoretical warning and a hypothetical pardon.

Ali was pacing his stateroom, one arm at the small of his back, his free hand stroking the peppery beard.

'Monsieur, it has been a privilege beyond coincidence, this brief encounter. Quite unforeseeable and unexpected. I am, as you must realise, an admirer. But to be brought face to face in these unusual circumstances with the creator of such – dare I say immortal – poetry leaves me gratified, yet perplexed. Do please enlighten me. What is it exactly that you are doing here?'

'Ah, *bien sûr*; let us just call it a *folie du grandeur,* nothing more nor less, I assure you.'

'Ah yes, a great adventure. It may well be. But perhaps you could clarify a few matters so that we may both proceed on our way, un-shadowed by any doubt as to what we have been party to? Forgive me if I speak formally. In my official role.'

This somewhat mannered exchange was partly the result of Captain Ali's desire to display his linguistic skills, particularly in English which was his third language; but also he felt that any awkwardness brought about by having to cross-examine Lúcio might be discounted as the stilted enthusiasm of an eager amateur.

Captain Mansour was in all matters strictly professional, as befits an officer, and notwithstanding his genuine delight and surprise at this rare encounter with a literary master, he was not so far out his league as to overlook any anomalies in Lúcio's story. Allowances might be made, but to be at peace with his sense of duty and conscience, he required further persuasion.

'Forgive my impertinence, but it is clear to me that you are none of you experienced sailors. Your friend you have told me has some working knowledge of boats but not to put too fine a point on it, goes unprepared. It is true of course that we get many pleasure boaters and pleasure seekers patrolling our shores, some even less proficient than yourselves. No offence intended. Yet we are bound by our law and the nature of our, how shall I say, unofficial exports, to be especially vigilant. And now I shall be indelicate, which pains me. Why were you out by night upon on the water when any voyager bound for Tetouan would have simply made passage by daylight, *en pleine vue*, and not given the impression he had something to hide?'

'I see your dilemma. As it happens we did take a daytime cruise down this remarkable coast of yours, the day of our night sortie. A reconnoitre, so to speak. So we could familiarise ourselves with the the lie of the land. But I'm running ahead. Nor do I dispute your imputation. I admit it wasn't clever and might appear sinister, even underhand. I shall try to put your mind at rest. Please excuse anything that may strike you as vulgar or indiscreet or overly intimate.'

Captain Mansour stopped pacing, settled to a mahogany carver, retrieved from his humidor a stout *Cohiba* and offered the box to Lúcio. A few moments of silence ensued as they both fingered the fine rolled tobacco leaf, snipped tips, struck matches and with a couple of deep draws, each set glowing the stogies on which for the next thirty minutes they would chew and puff.

'Do continue.'

'Let me come to the point. Nothing worse than a wool-gatherer.'

'D'accord.'

'Shyno, our skipper, my companion and friend: for some years now I have been his lover; formerly his tutor and mentor at University. Are you a married man, Captain?'

Ali coughed over an involuntary inhalation of cigar smoke, by which Lúcio construed a 'yes-but'. The exigencies of the itinerant seaman, many ports of call, poetic sensibility, loneliness.

'So am I, or was rather. And happily I imagined."

Mansour murmured, '*Soyez bref, mon frère.*'

'Of course. Our relations, though intimate, resemble those of two brothers. As the younger, he often feels 'put upon'. My very existence he treats as a challenge. For some time now he has been in revolt against my seniority. It makes him obstreperous. Or then he slips, as he puts it, into the 'passive porcelain'. A childish vulgarism, by which he means he feels sat upon. He is moody. One minute ornery, the next ornamental. Let me give you the facts.'

' My *copain* lost heart in our joint project a year or so past. The few poems he had written in response to mine – fine ones mind you, I have made translations to the Portugese – well, they simply dried up. The moment he ceased to believe himself a poet, our whole enterprise collapsed. Suddenly it seemed no more than some queer parody of the Socratic paradigm.'

'I looked for a way to restore his *amour propre*. He has always been at heart a creature of the water. His upbringing among islands I imagine. But it is more than that. He is by temperament a natural seaman. You know the sort of character. So I acquired our boat. Gave him a chance to take the lead, since as you have rightly observed, this is an element in which I am quite out of my depth. A first command, as Conrad would have it.'

'He took it seriously, much more so than I did. And he was right. A maiden voyage with a novice crew is not something to be undertaken lightly. Neville, well, more a case of charitable friendship. The options open to him were few and limited. It was meant to be a challenge to us all. A kind of outward-bound holiday.'

'*Charmant*. But to put it in the vernacular, what were you doing out of bed after lights out?'

'We made our first night crossing from Ibiza to Alicante. It was only our second day out at sea. We were buoyed up by our initial success and became overconfident. My friend was left in charge. In truth, I had already become bored with all this bossy skippering business. Precepts, repeated admonitions, fastidious concerns. Ordering me about. I put it down to fear and the need to assert himself. Well, I was wrong. We had a nasty scare with a cruise liner in a bank of fog off Ibiza. We were almost run over. Not long after we had a very close shave with a Spanish trawler nearby Benidorm. On both of these occasions we might have been sunk.'

'Yet still you run risks, Monsieur Lúcio?'

'I accept your censure. I have been for some time half out of mind with care. Careless of my self and others. A sort of dereliction. Of duty I suppose. And now we are fetched up here. Ignominiously rescued by your intervention. It is as simple as that. There is an old saw. If you fall off your horse you get back on again. Regain your confidence or lose your nerve completely. I fear this latest escapade may have knocked him somewhat. And for that I have only myself to blame.'

'Let me see if I have this right,' Mansour took up the running. 'A fortunately married man, with prospects, a feted Poet, a prize-winner, throws it all over for a *folie à deux*. A grand passion. Then as that passion fades, acquires a boat. Appoints his cooling paramour as the hired owner and thwarts every attempt on his part to instil order. Either on a whim, or a perverse refusal to slacken the reins. Names him Skipper and then blithely obstructs his every direction. Are you mad? Or merely The Fool. Pardon my habit of speech, *khayroo elkalami ma kalla wa dalla.* Barking, as my crew say. I call it plain speaking. Am I too severe?'

'Admirably frank and to the point. We are all somewhat shaken out by these recent events. Innocents abroad and all that. We may well have crossed that line Crane warns against. The bottom of the sea is undoubtedly cruel.'

'So how do you intend to get yourselves back on course?'

'Make our way home, I suppose, cautiously. And begin again. Michael Finnegan's Wake if you will forgive the pun. Just take it on the chin.'

Captain Mansour appeared to concede. There was a subtle easing in his posture as he exhaled a plume of smoke toward the cabin ceiling and whatever disquiet he may have harboured seemed to drift away on the vapour.

'I have to say Monsieur that you and your friends make for the most improbable cast of international smugglers ever to have crossed my wake. Foolhardy would not be the word for it. I doubt if I could sum up your prospects without resorting to insult. Should such a preposterous crew actually succeed in this type of endeavour, well – *hats off to them.* The very idea strains credibility. I feel myself somewhat credulous to have even entertained it. Say no more and we'll let the matter rest. I am grateful for your candour. I only regret that this chat of ours has forced you to disclose details which you might have preferred to remain private. The temptation to be evasive must have been fierce. I appreciate your honesty.'

Lúcio made a slight bow of the head and drew on the stub of his cigar.

'*Inshallah*! You will require a life craft and a spare battery if you are to avoid further unacceptable risk. Your friend may be a novice but he has grasped the basics. You would do well to listen to his advice. As for myself and my crew, we have our own business to attend to after this diversion. Or should I say *divertissment*. We sail for Casablanca tomorrow at noon. I shall ensure your boat is made seaworthy and arrange with the relevant authorities for your safe passage. It has been an unusual privilege. I wish you *bon voyage*. Here are your passports.'

Thus with a kind of admonitory grace, Captain Ali bestowed both his blessing and dismissal. And Lúcio deferred to this patronage, calculating that perhaps he might have just got the better of and the best from him, given the circumstance.

'One or two further matters, Monsieur. I strongly advise you restrict any future excursions to the daylight hours. Boats are not toys and the sea is no playground, however much the evidence may suggest otherwise. If you insist on 're-mounting the horse' as you put it, choose your pasture wisely. We have received a forecast for unusual weather in the northern sector heading this way. Now, if you would be so kind as to sign my copy of your book, I should be most grateful.'

Lúcio withdrew his Meisterstück from his breast pocket and rose to the Captain's desk. This instrument was a rare sight in that time, most writers finding the squat wide-nibbed pen too unwieldy and too expensive. Lúcio found it indispensable. He had small delicate hands and the weight of the plume allowed him to employ it as a painter does a brush, sweeping the gold tip across the page with the deftness of a calligrapher. In his florid style he inked a couple of improvised couplets onto the frontispiece of his book and signed off with a flourish.

MONKEY PUZZLES

Lúcio clambered one-handed back down the Cutter's ladder, clutching in the other a straw pannier which contained the excess from breakfast. At the bottom rung, level with the *Mona Gorda*'s gunwhale, he swivelled, extending his right arm and lobbed the basket towards Shyno, who pouched it.

Lúcio hung there briefly, like some mid-wire trapeze artist acknowledging applause, before springing off into the air. His *jete* was almost balletic, while the landing owed more to a vaulting gymnast planting a dismount. Heels together, knees apart, arms akimbo, he centred himself. Then as if to bamboozle his adjudicators, he started bobbing up and down, pogo-like, all the while mimicking a capuchin monkey, scooping at his armpits and favouring his audience with a banana peeling mime, hooting and squeaking 'mico, mico, hoo hoo hoo'.

This brief skit segued into a parody of a parrot – *loro ludens* – as he slowly shifted from foot to foot, raising first one leg then the other, extending his neck in counter revolutions, then added to this pantomime an ear-splitting vocal 'harara, harara...'

Neither of the two lads batted an eyelid; they had seen this comic turn before, though Shyno did cast a wary and weary glance upward to the gods, in case the audience hanging over the cutter's rail might mistake this caper for some kind of mockery. Quite the contrary. The modest knot of recruits looked down beaming in astonishment at these childish antics.

Lúcio stood up and with a sudden change of tone, launched into one of his lurching Afro-Brazilian trance dances. What with the shuffle and the jig and bass incantations, Shyno thought for an instant that Lúcio was about to enter into Maya mode and have himself mounted.

He was chanting praise songs to his tutelary deity, *Elegua*: Lord of the Market Place, Guardian of all Cross-Roads, and Keeper of the Keys to the Highway. *Echu, Legba*. A tricky little black-hearted Rumpelstiltskin who, should you not invite him, will stamp his foot and spoil your party.

After a couple of choruses of this mambo jambo, Shyno looked aloft once more but the audience had vanished; called to their duties perhaps, though it occurred to him later that this was a ritual those African souls might not have cared to witness, for there was nothing in this latter summoning-up that was the slightest bit humorous. Lúcio's eyes were blazing with the glazed intensity of one who gazes out over some interior landscape and the rhythm he was swaying to belonged to a darker order.

Abruptly he was back, as if awake from a coma.

'No need to stand on ceremony chaps, get stuck in. Cakes courtesy of Captain Ali's kitchen. Delicacies! Absolutely delicious.'

Shyno set the kettle to boil and sat down beside Nev at the saloon table facing Lúcio.

'What was all that about? For a moment there I thought you had cracked your teapot. What on earth got into you?'

'Three large espressos and a couple of *puros*, just for openers. A great way to kick-start your day but I wouldn't recommend it on a regular basis. And all that monkeying around, just letting off steam. Captain Ali gave me quite a quizzing. For the past hour I have been eating humble pie instead of excellent buns, would you pass me one? Besides, if you knew what I think I know now, you might be a mite frisky also.'

Lúcio bit into a pastry and chewed appreciatively. Nev followed suit as did Shyno. In the galley the kettle started its low whistle but nobody moved.

'Captain Ali is on to us, of that I have not the slightest doubt.'

Shyno could no longer ignore the kettle and jumped up to turn off the gas. He put together two brews, poured a glass of fresh lemonade and returned to the table. He was about to urge Lúcio to get on with the business when his friend produced their passports from his jacket pocket and fanned them out like a three card trick.

'Pick one, any one, go on.'

Nev hesitated, so Shyno leant forward and after dithering a moment chose Lúcio's.

'Examine it. Take your time. Imagine you are the immigration officer who no doubt at some point in the near future will be doing exactly the same.'

Shyno kicked himself. Lúcio was a frequent world traveller. Nev had only been abroad half a dozen times.

'You can always pick another if you prefer, it makes no difference whatsoever. Look, if it makes it easier, just pretend you are skimming my papers. I have told you that we are coast hugging and have just made our way down from Nerja. Never heard of Ceuta, ha ha. Go on, do it.'

Shyno was getting annoyed. Bloody trickster. Okay. He flicked through the pages and drew a blank.

'Now, consider yourself a suspicious, crabby bureaucrat with a diminutive prick and irritable piles. Scrutinise.'

Shyno played up and fingered and thumbed each page as if it were a holy script ready to divulge its anathemata.' Nothing. Shyno had had enough.

'Look I'm not in the mood for arsing about. Did he stamp us or didn't he? It only matters if there's dope on board and there isn't, and there's a fat chance of that anyhow, now it's all cocked up.'

'Would I lie to you? Or Captain Ali to me? Just look closely and you'll see.'

Nev was nervy. He hated any kind of aggro, especially between these two, whom he looked upon as above baseness. He palmed his own passport and swung off to neutral territory at the back of the boat. Shyno snatched his blue hardbacked booklet and made for the cabin. Lúcio smiled and ducked into the shower.

HAPPY SNAPS

It must have made a curious picture: Nev sitting bolt upright on one of *Mona Gorda*'s white painted stern pews, arms stretched out before him, scrutinising the pages of his passport as though it were the Book of Common Prayer. He was rather long-sighted – hence the odd posture – but it brought all the details of the document into sharper focus.

And so it appeared to Mustapha, squatting on his heels in the shade of a tree, which was one of a modest grove planted on a steep terraced slope some two hundred yards above the harbour. A peaceful vantage where only the fitful noonday breeze disturbed the silence with the irregular patter of falling olives. He passed the battered brass pocket telescope to YaYa and pointed toward the navy Cutter.

'What you make of that?'

YaYa fiddled with the aperture and after some consideration made a sound which might have been Om or Um. It *was* curious, but not as strange as the scene they had witnessed shortly before, when Lúcio had first appeared, reversing down the rope ladder to indulge in some sort of inebriated dumb show before the three would-be smugglers dipped out of view into the wheelhouse.

'Piss-up?' queried Mustapha, 'Is not too early, maybe.'

YaYa kept the scope trained on Nev, who had begun a kind of zooming movement with his arms, bringing the little book forward and back in front of his face.

'Let me see that!' Mustapha gruffed as he relieved Dave of

the view.

Next into vision came Shyno, apparently in a state of advanced intoxication, waving what looked like a small pamphlet above his head, in the manner of some Seventh Day Adventist who has actually been invited in through the doorway on which he has been knocking and doing a rather quaint imitation of what in other cultures might pass for a rain dance.

These two were not long at their boogaloo before Lúcio popped out onto the stern, dawdling at the wheelhouse door, while the others made jokey bows and mock salamaleikums, followed up by a deal of juvenile high-fiving and pats on the back.

Even from this distance, one thing was obvious and required no soundtrack: these were no prisoners and unlike any suspects that Mustapha could summon to mind. The only thing he could think of to explain their behaviour was drink.

Whether it was his own thirst or some unconscious prompting, Mustapha felt the first stirring of a positive impulse, something which had been signally lacking over the past twelve hours. Under the sway of this newfound enthusiasm he announced,

'We fetch Alan, ya? Go for a drink-up in town.'

YaYa was confused but docile. They stood, stretched, flexed their knees, retrieved the two crumbling bikes with their almost circular wheels and mounted; they wobbled back down the trail, crimped past the harbour walls and at a steady mule-pace unsteadily pedalled the two miles north in the direction of the campsite.

STARTER FOR TEN

Nev beat Shyno to the buzzer by a second but they had both solved the puzzle by the time Lúcio emerged from the shower. One glance at the sheepish happy faces told him all.

'Up to speed then, shipmates? Knew it wouldn't take long. Funny old business. Seems as if Captain Ali has a little explaining to do himself, though we certainly won't be asking. What do you make of it? A pretty rum manoeuvre for a man in his position, don't you think?'

The three of them had reconvened in the wheelhouse where they were comparing passports, though this time in a more congenial atmosphere.

'He must have done it on purpose,' murmured Nev.

'I would tend to agree,' added Lúcio.

'Crafty old devil, what's he playing at?' said Shyno.

'I'm not sure,' Lúcio went on: 'I am still working it out.'

Shyno extemporised. 'Well, if he suspects us, as you say he does, it's a trap. But he must have known we would spot his sleight of hand. Or does he think us cocky enough to call his bluff? Or...'

'Could he be giving us a chance?'

'Pretty weird either way.'

'Yes, a tricky one,' admitted Lúcio, 'what our cousin Rich would term a judgement call.'

The object of all this conjecture was the Tetuán border stamp in each of the three passports. What Captain 'Camouflage' Ali had contrived was a 'marriage' between this latest seal and an earlier and more innocuous one. In Lúcio's case, a three year old imprint from the airport at Lisbon. For Nev, it was Durban, and for Shyno, Nassau. These were not the random haphazard daubs of a careless official. Some thought had gone into creating just the right kind of blurred imprimatur; so that the letters of Tetuán were either hidden or indecipherable and the numbers that should have read 3 11 78 appeared as 8 12 73, or to similar effect. Most officials would have selected a blank page to make their mark. For some reason the Captain had not.

The net result was that unless you were in receipt of a sudden Pauline awakening, the Moroccan stamps were to all intents and purposes invisible. Officially there, but ostensibly not. Why this should have so exercised the trio was as much practical as psychological. If they had nothing to hide, like three hundred pounds of Moroccan hash, then a recent border stamp from that country was neither here nor there. But if they *were* carrying such a load then they would hardly wish to advertise their recent visit.

Their whole itinerary had been designed to remain in Spanish territory. Despite their unplanned detour into Tetouan, Captain Ali's behaviour meant they still had a chance of pulling off the subterfuge.

'The way I see it we have a 24-hour window. If Mansour doubts our motives, there is not much he can do about it while we are tethered up here, going nowhere. And he can't actually *prove* anything. YaYa did us a considerable favour by not showing up. Meanwhile there is a schedule to stick to. He leaves for Casablanca at midday tomorrow. His sister ship *Aurora* won't reach these waters until noon the next day. He roundly dismissed us as hypothetical smugglers on the basis of our sheer incompetence. Whatever his private reservations, as far as the local authorities are concerned, we are sightseers now.' Lúcio paused and took a sip of lemonade.

'I doubt he is a gambler; it wouldn't do for an Officer, though there must be occasions when he takes a calculated risk. Perhaps this is one of them. I won't say he has let his sympathies get the better of him. After all, his hands are clean as far as his superiors are concerned. Something in his nature. It must have to do with *boat business* and all that claptrap you banged on about Shyno, while I was spouting *fol de rol de roly o* and putting you down. Beg pardon. Besides, I know he enjoyed our company. Must have made a change from ploughing the same old furrow.'

'I have a feeling he secretly admires us. Eccentric Poets, would-be desperadoes. Something that he might have been. He doesn't believe we have the remotest chance of actually committing any offence, other than suicide. And if that is our choice, well on our own heads be it. You know, he even declared that in the extremely unlikely event that a bunch of cack-handed amateurs such as ourselves managed to bring off this kind of caper, he would *doff his cap*! Extraordinary thing to say, if you think about it.'

Shyno harrumphed and said,

'He may not be a gambler but he's certainly hedged his bets. And if you're right about all this, it looks as though he has even taken a punt on our hundred to one outsider. I think he must be touched. Too much imagination and too many books. Did you ever see so many crammed into such a small space? Bodleian-on-sea. I reckon it was your poetry that swayed him. He was pretty cool about it on the surface but you just pitching up in his cabin must have seemed downright spooky. Perhaps he had some kind of brainstorm.

You didn't do anything to him did you? You know, *Juju* stuff. I wouldn't put it past you.'

Shyno gave Lúcio a reproving look which he ignored.

'All I asked for was free passage and we have it. Nothing more. *Things are as they are. Unborn, undone.* The rest is up to us.'

'Fancy a trip into town?' Nev ventured. 'Now we've got tourist visas we might as well use them. I'll go stir-crazy if we don't get off this boat for a bit and I could do with stretching my leg-irons. To say nothing of a drink, I'm parched. Hair of the dog. I could murder a pint.'

'There might even be a chandlery,' Shyno added. 'That's a ship shop to you, Lúcio; get a spare battery, a few flares, ask about a dinghy. Never know what we might find. Maybe even YaYa. He must be skulking about somewhere round here. He can't have been caught or we wouldn't be having this conversation. Anyway I've got a lousy hangover as well. Not sure that Musar wasn't past its best. Or maybe I'm a lightweight. Either way, I'm up for a shoofty. Shall we make a move?'

TREBLES ALL ROUND

It should have come as no surprise, but somehow it did. And an agreeable one at that. The Old Quarter of Tetouan – there wasn't a new one – lived up to its reputation. Progress had not yet cast even a cursory glance over this unpropitious stretch of lowland coast, let alone the town. If the trio had anticipated some tourist mecca, they were swiftly undeceived. Imaginary vistas of gleaming condominia, restored riads and lushly sprinkled golf greens were no more than that. A nightmare mirage in some developer's rheumy eye, two decades down the road.

What greeted them as they paid off the taxi was a dreamy narcoleptic backwater. A white maze of cobbled alleys peopled by a few scabrous mongrels and the occasional black-shawled figure peering out from behind peeling shuttered windows. The Medina was closed, pending refurbishment. What should have been a bustling hive of hucksters and artisans had been reduced to an abandoned fortress of silent battlements and eyeless minarets. The whole place seemed unnaturally empty. As if everyone had just clocked off, gone home and shut themselves indoors. As if all life were taking place behind a series of barred gates, within enclosed courtyards, *in camera*.

Still, theirs was no cultural tour. And Nev had a range of no more than a mile before chafing set in. They were searching for a bar.

'Not exactly a laugh a minute' said Nev, as he loped

alongside a pensive Lúcio and a petulant Shyno. Each one of Nev's swings saw him cover a couple of yards, so the other two were pressed to keep up.

'Bit lifeless, I admit.'

'Bloodless morgue, if you ask me'.

As they rounded a corner into a small courtyard they were confronted by a flickering neon sign tacked onto a flaking façade above a pair of blue painted saloon doors. *Auberge du Port*. On the wall beside the entrance hung the tattered remnants of a bill poster advertising a matinee performance of a Spaghetti Western, several years out of date. Clint, of course. From the hidden interior there issued forth, above the tuneless whining of a plangent zither, the sound of laughter and the unmistakeable war-cry of a dumb familiar:

'Ya... ya ya.'

'Well, I hate to say it,' said Dr Know, as he stepped toward the tavern 'so I won't.'

Shyno was about to shoulder his way through the entrance when his eye caught the title of the cinema poster, or what was left of it. Smiling, he pushed through the swing doors and stepped inside. It took several moments before his vision adjusted to the smoke filled murk. On the left two stacks of empty soda crates with a warped plywood top made up the bar. A half-dozen rickety tables with plastic cloths congregated in the centre. To the right a couple of alcoves afforded a degree of privacy. The lighting was perfunctory. A few bald low watt coloured bulbs and the stubs of some guttering candles. And in one of these dimly lit nooks sat laughing and drinking The Good, The Bad and The Very Ugly.

Alan had his back to the room. YaYa was half-hidden by the alcove wall. The unfamiliar face of what appeared to be a living gargoyle broke into a vile grin of welcome and exclaimed,

'Boat buggers! Why you take so long?'

There were no other patrons and no sign of a barman. Alan swivelled in his chair and YaYa poked his gormless fizzog around the partition. Shyno sensed Lúcio come up at his side just moments before Nev announced his arrival with a purposeful clunk. The two sides just stood there as if sizing one another up. Then Nev broke the stand-off. He raised one crutch, pointed it at YaYa and with only a hint of irritable menace said,

'Make mine a treble, mate; where the fuck did you get to?'

The how, the where and the why not of the whole non-event were reprised at length over the next few hours. Once all the outstanding introductions had been made, each of the participants in this earnest farce gave his and his players' account of the previous action. All were keen to have decent reviews. So prompts, fluffed lines, obscured sightlines, mislaid props, missed cues were all discreetly overlooked. In short the whole performance turned out to have been a minor triumph in the face of near total disaster. It had been simply too rough to launch. As for the crew's encounter with the Navy, the prologues were over and it was time to choose.

All that was required now was a swift rewrite, a touch of inspiration from the director, and under the reviving influence of a few stiff measures they would be ready to face the curtain for the second act. Before that could happen, however, there was the small matter of the interval and with Mustapha's encouragement the cast, with the exception of Lúcio, proceeded to get enthusiastically drunk.

It wasn't that Lúcio held back, quite the opposite. He downed two shots to their one, smoked three *puros* to their two, but all without any noticeable effect. Shyno had seen him carve his way through a small molehill of *perrica* on numerous occasions, then fall asleep like a baby; whilst others around him were chewing quaaludes like candy, desperate to crash. In this respect he was like Maya when she went into her trance. Except in Lúcio's case there was no obvious sign of any transition. His voice remained the same. He didn't speak Patois, sprinkle himself with perfume or develop a sudden interest in flowers and shrubs. Nothing spasmodic in the slightest. In fact, all the usual antics of the spirit-possessed, such as foreign dancing, mime, prophecy, speaking in tongues, only transpired when he was coolly sober or had drunk too much coffee. This had proved a singular advantage in business transactions with various Latinos, who laboured under the illusion that deals should only be concluded after heavy imbibing. A superstition loosely based around *vino* and *veritas* and the popular fallacy that it is difficult to lie when you are completely fish-faced.

Each member of the gang had his own quirk of character which under the influence of a steady flow of liquor became ever more pronounced. Mustapha cursed wildly and ogled Shyno. Shyno got vainer and waxed philosophical. Alan practised anger management. Nev giggled a lot. YaYa was mute or monosyllabic.

After the first bottle of Black Label had slipped down their gullets, Mustapha got up, went behind the bar and fetched out another. The mystery of the absent bartender was soon cleared up. No such character existed. *Auberge du Port* had no license to sell liquor, was not open to the public and was simply Mustapha's own private watering-hole. On his frequent forays down from the mountains he would swing by, open up, and entertain whichever cousins or clients happened to be on hand and in need of drink.

It was his peculiar conceit to have decked out the den as a shrine to his hero Sergio Leone. Hence the mock-western entrance, the adobe walls plastered with iconic posters, the haunting Morricone soundtracks transcribed to local instruments and played on a recurring loop through a pair of antique speakers. No doubt Mustapha cast himself as the villain in these various epics, since even his lurid vanity could not stretch to the silent avenger. YaYa on the other hand was a dead ringer for the lonesome cowboy. Looks and speech patterns, perfect. Just don't expect him to do anything violent.

Most of this was lost on Lúcio who had a tolerable indifference to popular culture. A state of affairs brought about by the inexplicable adulation afforded to various strummers and balladeers in his native Brazil. And the widespread neglect, except by the *cognoscenti*, of his own soaring lyrical ballads. The mere mention of Jobim or Gil would provoke a withering diatribe on the pre-evolutionary tastes of the general citizenry. *Entertainment is not Culture*. Critics he deemed insects. *Alas, like cockroaches they will always be with us*. As for the *soi-disant literati*, he reserved for them a circle all to themselves in his Dantesque and equally extensive inferno. Sounds that could move many to sentimental tears simply pained Lúcio's ears, literally, and gave him a headache.

What no one could dispute was that the ambience of the drinking den was entirely conducive to hatching plots, closing deals and the pursuit of lucre. It was midway through the second flask of JW that Lúcio proposed a toast to Captain Mansour and made what on first hearing seemed an absurd proposal.

'Dave should come on board with us and bring the dinghy.'

No one laughed. Lúcio obviously thought it was obvious. But it had a sobering effect on the rest of the gang. Mustapha scratched at one of his random patches and was silent. Nev reached for a roll-up. Alan looked almost amused. YaYa had the air of an intended victim. Shyno wondered whether to adopt the role of Official Opposition. Lúcio ignored all this and proceeded with his colloquy.

'It's quite logical, if you think about it. We are just following the Captain's orders. It's what he would expect.'

Lúcio had lost them. A line from one of his darker lyrics unspooled in his head.

'I guided no one. I only knew
(it happens that I know)...'

Sometimes it seems not common to explain.

'The cutter will be gone by noon tomorrow. The local officials are under instruction to ensure our safe departure. They'll be happy to comply if we bring a dinghy on board. I have a chit from the Captain. My only worry is the weather.'

'Actually it does seem to have dropped off a bit, the breeze that is.' Shyno forbore to add the half formed thought, *the lull before the storm*.

But it was true. As they meandered through the labyrinth of the Old Quarter they were sweating keenly. A pale grey quilt of low unbroken cloud spread out as far as the horizon and smothered the peaks of the High Rif to the west. The air was clammy and difficult to breathe. The sky was what they call *lowering*. Glowering was more like it.

'Dave knows the coast. He can guide us to the cairn and launch from the *Mona Gorda*.'

Alan thought it wise not to draw attention to this minor flaw in Lúcio's logic. YaYa's experience of handling the din-

119

ghy had so far been entirely terrestrial.

'As long as you fellows don't mind getting wet, we should manage. Alan, you and Dave can hold the dinghy so it doesn't get flipped. Mustapha, you and your boys form a line and pass along the bales. You'll only be in the water up to your waists. Chests at worst. There are ten, yes, so three trips should do it. Once everything is stowed we drop Dave off further up the coast a couple of miles. Alan makes the rendezvous and we make for Spain. It's just a matter of all hands to the decks. Isn't that the expression?'

Lúcio leaned back in his chair and sipped from a shot glass. There was an air of QED about his delivery. As if he had been demonstrating to a crèche of two-year-olds the simplicities of building blocks. For a recent convert to the discipline of boating he had acquired an authority that begged no questions.

Well, maybe one or two. But Dave, who was the querulent most directly implicated in this latest rearrangement, was beyond any protest his brain could muster, other than the usual – this time fateful – pair of syllables.

Mustapha called time on his depleted stocks and in the two minutes it took to shut up shop, ushered the gang out into the unlit courtyard. It was almost dusk. They walked as best they could toward the main square where the Moroccan commandeered an old Peugeot estate off a distant relative with the promise of a few *reals* and a future invitation to his bar. The six mile return journey to the port in the packed wagon passed without incident as Mustapha rarely left second gear and most of his passengers were sleeping long before they got there, forty minutes later. He dropped off the boaters short of the harbour wall at a spot out of sight of the customs booth. It was here he proposed that they meet around nine on the following night. Boozy farewells bid, he and the two lags rumbled off into the purpling gloom, they to the campsite, he back to the barn and his long suffering sons.

The Boat Buggers as they now referred to themselves managed to negotiate their way back to the cutter without further mishap. Her low slung stern quarters lay a little above level with the dockside and a short railed gangway was their point of boarding. A few riding lights helped to prevent anything more than the odd barked shin or grazed knuckle. So much unprotected metal to outflank and there was still the small matter of the bosun's chair to contend with. Shyno was as dubious as Nev was apprehensive.

'Sure you know how to work this thing?' he said.

Shyno slurred something to the effect of 'noshsoshur' and started examining the contraption. Two possible wrong options presented themselves. Nev unceremoniously dumped from fifteen feet onto *Mona Gorda*'s deck in a heap of bent iron and broken limbs; or hoisted skyward like some novelty ensign. Lúcio had already scampered down the ladder and was looking up. Shyno half-hoped to hear something to the effect of *why don't you pay attention* and then with the usual acuity have the method pointed out to him. No such luck. Not even with Lúcio's new found sea savvy. Shyno was inclined to pass the buck to Nev who after all had been in it twice already. Shouldn't he know? Nev spared him. One swing took him to top of the rope ladder where he peered over into the void.

'You first, mate. Take these with you. Or I can chuck them down and you catch. Up to you.' Nev offered him his crutches.

So, a bladdered, one handed swaying descent? Or have yourself speared by a blunt missile? No contest.

'I'll take them,' said Shyno.

It was probably the right choice. Once safely down the other two watched Nev perform his second defiance of the laws of physics. First buoyancy, now gravity. He was facing the Cutter's gunwhale, hands gripping the rail like the pommel on a vaulting horse or a parallel bar, elbows bent, supporting his legs. Then, there is probably a technical term for it, he pivoted forward, extending and straightening his arms until his boot tips were raised above the rail, his body folded in a tight v, a sort of halfway handstand. He released one hand and casually swivelled through 180 degrees and placed it back on the bar, all the while sustaining the touch toes position.

At which point he let go.

As his legs swung down towards the cutter's side they straightened out, moving in an arc until his boots connected to her armour with a dull clang. In the same instant as he fell he grasped onto the second rung of the rope ladder and hung there suspended. The rest was mundane monkey. Using only his hands he lowered himself down tier by tier and when he reached *Mona Gorda*'s gunwhale let go with one fist and posed in a passable imitation of Lúcio's earlier gesture. A near perfect ten on anyone's scoresheet. Nev looked toward an astonished Shyno saying, 'Pass me my sticks, matey' and winked at Lúcio.

'Christ Nev, where did you learn to do that?'

Shyno was arranging the saloon seat cushions on the wheelhouse floor where Neville bunked down. He was unbuckling.

'Special school. I was a bit of a gym freak before the polio hit me. I just kept it up. There was one teacher, Schmutts, he encouraged me, talked about competitions, 'para' something or other. What he meant was sport for cripples. The idea was to keep our spirits up, stop the self-pity. Funny, it worked for a while. Didn't help my Pa much or my Ma though. I guess they felt guilty. Not bothering with the vaccine or anything. It never occurred to them, living out in the bush. Nearest Doctor half a day's drive. Besides I was a healthy kid. They had this farm up country in the Natal. It kicked in pretty late. I was thirteen when it happened. The old man went down fast on the drink. He was old fashioned. Couldn't accept it. His only son a *cripp* - he never used the word, but it got to him. Took it out on the Old Lady. So she shipped us off back to England. Dad more or less washed his hands. She's holed up in a bungalow outside Worthing, doing justice to the gin and juice. I get down there now and then but when she sees me she cries. Can't handle it.'

There was a ripping sound as Nev tore back the strip of Velcro binding his knee. He eased off the calliper and began rubbing his leg. A black-bristled pipe cleaner no thicker than your wrist.

'It's ok mate. I get by with a little help from my fiends. Smoke a bit of dope and I feel fine for a while. Fuck, hope YaYa gets his shit together. I am here dying for a spliff. Jeezus.' Nev made a wry grimace and set about his other brace.

'Yeah, the old routines. You never forget 'em. Like riding a bike. Now, that would be a laugh. You know, when Rich got me into all this he did me a favour. He figured it was the other way round. Dude's a right shyster. Paying shit while I took all the risk, but it gave me some self-respect. Rather be a mule than sit around in some bung-hole bedsit on the dole, rolling with a few other losers, *dancing with Mister D* and dipping in the skag. Look at me. Toast of the fucking Moroccan Navy.'

With that Nev made to get under his sheet and hit the sack when Lúcio appeared from the forward cabin. He was clothed all in white, in what looked like a pair of cotton pyjamas, barefoot, with a linen bonnet on his head that resembled a chef's crushed hat or something handed out on a hospital ward. A kind of Tam o' Shanter, but with ceremonial overtones. Over his left wrist were three different strings of coloured beads, *collares*; and in his right hand a small squat cone shaped figurine discoloured by chocolaty streaks of dried blood with two brazil nut sized cowrie shells inset on one side midway up the face, forming a pair of eyes. *Elegua.* From the pocket of his tunic protruded the neck of a quarter flask of cane liquor that he kept in reserve; it was not for general consumption. He was drawing on a short sweet scented cigar. He set the statue down on the saloon floor, took a couple of deep draws and exhaled a jet of bluish smoke onto the conical figure. This he did two or three times then unscrewed the flask, took a large swig, rinsed it round his mouth, before spitting it all out in a fine misted spray that drenched the stone head. Nev looked as though he expected the eyes to light up.

'*O meu Pai*' Lúcio began chanting, as he reeled off a series of praise names followed by several verses of unintelligible prayer. He always addressed *Echu* first before going about any business. It wasn't just courtesy. It was the way to avoid mischief and ensure good behaviour. And favour of course. *Elegua* ignored might just as easily trip you up putting on your slippers as slam an open door in your face.

'I'd like you to wear this if you don't object.' Lúcio removed a necklace from his wrist and offered to place it over Nev's head.

'Sure, no problem. What's it for, some kind of protection?'

'Yes, you could say so. It belongs to *Obatala*. Think of him as a father figure.' The necklace was a string of pure white coral beads with a single red one breaking the sequence. Lúcio slipped it around Nev's neck where it lay gleaming against the jet black hair and burnish of his chest.

'So what's the story?'

'If you really want to know I'll tell you. It might upset you, I hope not. But it's true. Shall I go on?'

Nev nodded. He seemed to be in the mood for a bedtime tale, even a dark one.

'*Obatala, Oshanla, Oba.*' He goes by many names. He is the first and foremost among the *Orisha*. He is the creator god, the shaper of clay, the maker of men and all bodily forms. He moulds our matter; he crafts the models, the proto-types. And *Olorun,* who is Spirit, breathes life into those lifeless limbs.

'One day they say, *Obatala* got drunk while at work on some clay. He had a weakness for palm-wine. And what he created while out of his senses was not quite perfect. From that time forth he never touched a drop of liquor again. And those creatures that he had misshapen became his favoured and favourite children. Of all his creation the most sacred to him. These white beads are a symbol of his purity. This red one, a reminder that no one is entirely free from error or from blame.'

Nev fingered the beads of the necklace as though lost in memory, sighed, smiled sadly and looked up.

'Sort of a parable I guess.'

'Yes. I overheard you talking about your parents. I hope you don't mind. It seemed somehow appropriate.'

'Appreciate it. Thanks, Lúcio. Really, I mean it.'

Lúcio placed the second necklace over Shyno's head. Each

dark blue bead alternated with a white one.

'*Yemanja.* Goddess of the Sea and the Sea herself. Blue for water. White for the salt foaming crests of her waves.'

Lúcio placed the third necklace over his own head. Black bead followed by red, one after the other in a seamless ring.

'*Elegua*, my Father. Red fires burning out of blackest night, lighting the way.'

Lúcio lit a small candle and placed it, along with the glowing stub of his cigar, onto a saucer, into which he poured a few drops of *aguardiente,* which flared up briefly. He murmured a few words of *Yoruba* and set down this offering beside the effigy as a kind of impromptu altar.

'Sleep well, Neville. Any dreams, you can tell me tomorrow.'

Shyno rose and made for the cabin as Lúcio followed. They lay there in silence in the motionless dark and after a spell of urgent whispering, for the first time on the voyage slept as more than brothers in arms.

TIO ENRIQUE: 'EL COJO'

Rich Lee was having, as they say in the English game, 'a bit of a nightmare'. Yet it had all kicked off so splendidly well. He dreamt he was back home in CA, La Honda; snowed up, in both senses, in a snug log cabin in the foothills above San Francisco among the sequoias, spring coming on, the majestic trees resinous with sap, and a ripe little teenage peach of a beach bunny (flower-child, hippy type, always losing things, rings on her fingers and toes, one in her nose) curled up against him under a llama skin rug on the undulating water-bed, the air thick with patchouli and the fumes from a joint of primo *sinsemilla*.

She was a coast blonde, natural, pert, pink and downy in all the right places. A free spirited, uninhibited screamer whom Rich had scoped then scooped up from Malibu beach with the promise of plentiful toot and a mini-break in the mountains.

Right at that moment in his dream he couldn't remember her name. She owned very few clothes and travelled light, dispensing with the little she wore as soon as they hit the cabin. Her notion of bliss was a brisk al fresco frolic with Rich in the powdery snow followed by an invigorating dip in the jade green melt-water of a rushing spring, then back to the bouncing stage of her thrice daily performances.

As is often the case with dream sequences there was an abrupt and disquieting elision. Rich struggled to hold on to the snowy vista but it morphed into a low ceilinged room of clinical white tiled walls and fluorescent lighting. In the background he could detect a persistent mechanical drone. In the former scene this might have been the sound of a lumberjack at work, but here in this sterile zone it was more like the whine of an oversized mosquito. A voice, a female one, was tut-tutting in his ear in what appeared to be Latin. *Pediculus, pedicula.*

Rich realised he was reclining on some sort of apparatus that could have been a dentist's chair, except he was butt naked and his legs were in stirrups. He willed away this disagreeable image and succeeded, but not before he became aware of a pair of crimson nailed hands emerging from starched sleeves, one wielding a set of stainless steel clippers, the other a cut-throat razor.

A jump cut took him back to the cabin and the waterbed. He was now in that languorous halfway house between waking and sleep. He stretched out his limbs and his foot made contact with a satin smooth calf. Mmm...bunny. He indulged himself a while, stroking the warm alabaster. When he finally allowed himself to wake, he pulled back the blanket as if searching for the girl and found he was alone.

As for the hairless leg he had been caressing, it was his own. Along with the billiard ball pate and a follicle free mound. There wasn't a hair on his body. He was completely shaved. True, it was only a dream this time, but back then it was real. Rich could remember her name now. It was Alice. She was a Cancer. And her parting gift: a colony of crabs. He recalled a confession to Shyno.

'Man, I saw these black specks in my pubes. *And then they moved.*'

Now Rich was waking again. The sense of discomfort was too real to be a dream. Bolt upright in his bed, he ripped back Villa Nova's synthetic sheet, scratching furiously at what felt like several livid boils in his neatly trimmed thatch. No doubt about it, something was biting.

Rich embraced the haphazard shower, the abrasive soap. He swam dozens of lengths in the toxic pool. He almost called the estate agent. He cursed, then prayed, after a fashion. He doused his crotch with copious doses of after shave and when he could no longer abide the stinging, anointed it with olive oil. He scoured the phone book for a pharmacy and found *peluquería:* hairdresser. But the pustules persisted, stubborn and mysterious. So he did what he knew he should have done in the first instance and telephoned Gloria.

The voice on the other end of the line was not exactly unfriendly, somewhat curt and guarded it seemed, but neither was it familiar.

'*Diga! Quién es?*'

The words came out in a terse rasp which might have belonged to a clapped-out drill sergeant, a miner in the late stages of pulmonary disease, or a lifelong smoker. All three as it transpired later. Rich did his best to present his bona fides in a mix of pidgin Spanish plus a bit of yank, alluded to his friendship with Gloria, and returned the courtesy.

'*Soy Enrique, El Cojo*'.

El Cocko? Rich stifled a snort as the image of an aged punter with a Lothario delusion rose unbidden to his already scrambled brain. The two fat lines he had snoofed to clear his thinking had had the opposite effect. Perhaps he had hallucinated the whole episode or was he still dreaming. Or was someone dreaming him? What a nightmare.

'I am her Uncle. I shall pass you over.'

'*Holá bebé*, did you miss me?'

Rich flicked through a rolodex of responses ranging from

indignant to sarcastic but the best he could come up with was a compliant 'Uh, sure. Listen, we need to talk. I have this, erm, problem.' Gloria giggled. 'You mean like an itch you want to scratch?' This was all too much for his boiling synapses, to say nothing of his crotch. 'Listen, I'll be there in half an hour. Ok?' And hung up.

The youth who greeted him at the apartment door was no more than late teens and offered no greeting. He made a gesture with his upturned palms and Rich figured this was an invitation to a frisking so he raised his arms. The welcoming party looked down and tapped one of Rich's boots with a sneakered foot as if to say *spread 'em*. This was followed by a thorough inventory of his person including a neutral pass over his groin, rounded up by a satisfied grunt and the instruction, '*Pase!*'

Rich obeyed and as he walked down the mirrored hallway behind his escort, clocked the pearl handled Glock thrust down the back of his stone-washed jeans. Nothing fazed, he allowed himself a grim smile. This was old-hat to Richly. During his various encounters with purveyors of powder he had established one thing at least. These *pistoleros* sported guns like most men wear watches; the more vulgar and ostentatious, the lower their rank in the pecking order. He doubted it was even loaded.

A second *goomba* was loitering by the panoramic glass windows that overlooked the marina. The blinds were drawn even though it was a sunless overcast day. The air conditioning was on. It felt chilly. The sense of having walked into a rich man's private mortuary was compounded by the figure stretched out on the chrome and leather recliner adjacent to the sofa: scene of a considerably more lifelike demonstration of the flesh not ten hours earlier. An elongated male form in unremitting shades of grey lay prone on the lounger. Any embalmer would have been proud of this work.

An iron black military buzz-cut bristled on his skull. There was a waxy complexion to the concave, lightly rouged cheeks. The shadow of a recently shaved beard spread like a stain over the thin upper lip and ruminant jaw. The worst of the effect was disguised by a clear surgical mask attached with a tube to a small oxygen cylinder and by a liberal application of talcum powder. Floris? *Corpus floreat.* The eyes were closed in repose. His arms lay folded in a mimicry of St Peter's cross, across a double-breasted silver sharkskin suit, beneath which a v-necked black cashmere sweater revealed a sprouting of wiry tendrils that climbed towards his chin over an outstanding Adam's apple that bobbled with each laboured and barely perceptible intake of breath. Enrique was snoozing. Rich Lee found himself momentarily appalled. This ancient assembly of bones in its ill-fitting sack, this montage of collapsed planes and oblique angles that resembled a late cubist sketch in heavy charcoal. He had a vision of himself as an under-assistant in a branch of haberdashery, protesting, in spite of himself, *oh, suits you perfectly, Sir.* Were it not for the jaunty aspect of a pair of crossed ankles sporting white Gucci loafers, one of which boasted a Cuban heel, this ghoul was a perfect dead-ringer for a corpse.

Rich sniffed and the apparition awoke and sat up. As if on cue, the two bodyguards made to assist but the old man waved them away with an impatient flap of his wrist. He unclipped his mask, rocked forward on the recliner, reaching for the cane propped against the armrest. It was a yard-long baton of polished hardwood with an egg shaped ivory handle into which was set a deep green emerald the size of an eyeball. Enrique's own eyeballs were of a similar colour but the whites were more like yellow. Rich had a sudden intuition about a lyric which had been puzzling him: *the great grey man...who squats behind the man who works the soft machine*. This had to be the sponsor. *El Patrón*.

The old man swung his legs off the recliner and levered himself to his feet. He was taller than Rich had assumed and a good three inches taller than Rich who was almost six-one. Lanky, whippet-thin, he made his way across the room toward his guest walking with a severe limp. Each step involved a precarious balancing act since the defective right leg seemed to have a mechanism all of its own. As soon as it lost contact with the ground it swung out in a circle, then hung there in front of his body, jerking uncontrollably several inches off the floor, until by an effort of will he brought it back down onto the built-up heel. The spasm over, he drew his good leg alongside. Rich would have spared him the journey but a grisly fascination kept him rooted to his spot. An outstretched fleshless hand preceded the introduction.

'Soy El Cojo.'

Rich took it in his own, half-expecting a claw-like grip, but it was surprisingly gentle, almost fragile. He had the uncomfortable feeling that if he squeezed too hard the fingers might snap. He had braced himself for this first utterance from the old boy's mouth, anticipating a carious tumble of yellowing tombstones. What greeted him instead was a dazzling display of upmarket dentistry even better than his own. He was about to introduce himself when a feminine voice whispered in his ear,

'*Cojo,* it means lame. It's a nickname.' And then louder, 'Tío, this is Rich, my American friend.'

Absorbed in the macabre spectacle of Enrique's siesta, he hadn't noticed Gloria come into the room. This was fortuitous, for the person now standing at his side was unrecognisable from the evening before. Gone was the tinted mane, the do-me heels, the pelmet skirt. In its place, short auburn hair pulled back severely from her face and gathered in a brief ponytail which was pinned up in the Spanish style with an antique comb. No makeup, not even lipstick and her eyelashes, though luxuriant, seemed somehow shorter. A plain black bolero jacket, white linen shirt, dark trousers and sensible pumps gave her the air of a convent schoolgirl dressed for an *exeat*. A pair of quick demure kisses to both of his cheeks completed the performance. Her demeanour was that of a passing acquaintance, nothing more. Rich barely managed to conceal his astonishment from the uncle's gaze.

'*Carino*, be so kind as to bring us some refreshment,' Enrique said, in perfect if somewhat formal English. Gloria smiled agreeably and as she turned, Rich seized his moment. 'Uh, let me give you a hand.' This elicited a slight frown from her uncle but he waved them on. The two youths who had been silently observing the *gringo* shrugged and Enrique motioned them to pull up some chairs.

Rich was in the kitchen, his back to the door, surveying the expanse of stainless steel units and white marble worktops while Gloria busied herself arranging the drinks tray. He was struggling to find the precise diplomatic gambit to broach his predicament when she turned to face him as if reading his thoughts.

'What's up, *papi*?'

'Well, it's this, you know, I've got, down there, I mean, healthwise, these things, bumps, bites kind of, are you, no, sure, of course not, but, you never know, it could be nothing, maybe, or something...'

Rich just couldn't get it out so Gloria did. She knelt on

one knee, unzipped him, and combed her fingers through his patch. After a brief recce she turned her gaze upward, pouted, smiled sympathetically and burst out laughing.

'*Pucha*! Is just some mosquito *molesta*, don't worry *papi*.'

The intense flood of relief and the unexpected rush of affection he felt for her produced in Rich a predictable result.

'Mmm, not now *bebe*...' she murmured. 'Business first.'

MEMO FROM TURNER

Enrique's poison of choice was Crystal. Not bubbly, not *meth*, but an addictive and deceptively powerful aniseed flavoured firewater distilled in Colombia. At 17% proof it is no stronger than a fortified wine, though in sufficient doses it will produce a hallucinatory high not unlike *mescal*. And a legendary hangover known as a *guayabo* for which there is no other remedy than to keep on drinking.

Rich possessed none of Lúcio's spirit powers and decided his best bet was to pace himself. His only experience of this particular tipple was not one he was keen to repeat. He had an uncomfortable memory of himself perched on the second floor window ledge of a dilapidated colonial house in Cartagena; arms outstretched in the attitude of a glider, chanting a ditty he had memorised somewhere, midway through his second flask of the licoricey liquor.

'*Pista...pista. Vengo en avioneta. Voy a aterrizar.*' Which roughly translates to: 'Runway...runway. Small plane about to land.' As a preventative measure, he made several early forays into the fatty *chicharones*, pork-belly scratchings of a superior kind, which were heaped up on a plate in the middle of the table and with which he hoped to line his gut.

The potion itself, clear, colourless and viscous, is hedged around with rituals, the two most important of which are simple to follow. Take it neat and down in one shot. There was a simple rule of etiquette as far as Rich could determine. No refills until every glass was empty. And the host, in this case Enrique, dictated the tempo.

There passed an hour of commonplace pleasantries: the weather, unseasonable. The fluctuating state of the property market, on the up. The influx of foreigners, Germans mostly. Despoliation of the Spanish *costas*, unfortunate but unavoidable. The exorbitant cost of first-class air travel, highway robbery. Desirability of motor-yachts, debatable. Advantages of berthing at Puerto Banus, many. Gloria's further education and the prospects for a career in modelling, promising.

Enrique raised his glass with a fifth '*salud*', one for each round, and addressed Rich directly.

'And what kind of business are you in, American friend?'

Rich had a stock response to this line of enquiry, which was both insinuating and non-committal, or so he thought.

'Transport.'

And had he been required and felt the moment was propitious he would have elaborated in a neutral fashion,

'Import/Export.'

Capped off with a conclusive,

'Distribution.'

It wasn't necessary. Enrique fixed him with a knowing look, downed his medicine and wheezed,

'We speak later. First we drink.'

It was at this juncture that the two bodyguards appeared to relax. Upon some unseen signal from their boss they produced their pistols, ejected the loaded clips, fingered out the bullets one by one, swept them into two small piles like poker chips and put down their guns on the table.

In the spirit of the occasion an already tipsy Rich rummaged in his jeans, looking for his flick-knife. To spare him further effort or indignity the youth who had frisked him produced it from his jacket and placed it on the granite top.

Enrique dug two skeletal fingers into the breast pocket of his suit and retrieved a small paper packet which he proceeded to unwrap. Rich could sense his nostrils flaring and suppressed a sniffle. Leaning forward he watched as Enrique unveiled not powder, but three small pea-shaped opaque lumps of greenish mineral.

'*Soy esmeraldero*. These are the tools of *my* business.'

If Rich was disappointed he managed to disguise it and made a murmur of approval. Enrique gave a phlegmy sort of chuckle.

'*Pura mierda*!'

Dipping into an inside pocket he produced a second wrap, which revealed a solitary blue-green rectangular stone about the size of a 10d stamp.

'From Muzo, my home. Exceptionally rare...'

Rich had a working knowledge of the topic, picked up over several years. A useful social lubricant in the company he kept. He was familiar with the four Cs: cut, carat, colour, clarity. He had reckoned with occlusions. He also knew that above a certain level there are no gradations regarding the quality of emeralds. Such stones are purely, as he ventured,

'Theoretical?'

Enrique cackled,

'Excellent! Precisely!'

And added in a gnomic undertone,

'No one can be certain they exist for sure...'

He turned to Gloria.

'*Amor*, condoms *por favor*. And scissors.'

She came back a moment later with a pack of flavoured prophylactics which Enrique opened. He tore the foil from one and placed the emerald in the teat. After a couple of deft twists and tyings-off, he snipped the excess latex and, as if it were a lozenge, placed the jewel in his mouth and swallowed. Clearing his throat he said, 'Safe-keeping. I have a flight to catch this evening. Schipol...' and poured another round of Crystal.

This set the pattern for the remainder of the day. For all the insouciance of the old boy's actions he might as well have been popping candy. Rich counted fifteen stones of varying sizes that disappeared into his gullet.

Around tea-time, five hours after his arrival, Rich was entering that airspace in his head which according to all the instruments at his disposal told him he was flying and about to crash. *Pista...pista.* Completely pissed.

Gloria had occupied the lounger and was snoring gently. The two youths sat rigid but asleep, flanking Enrique like bookends on the sofa. The old buzzard was talking business and was inexplicably still sober.

'I should like to meet this *socio* of yours, *Señor* Lúcio. When he returns from his cruise.'

Rich had a fuzzy recall of some immodest boasting about a yacht and a Latin American colleague with impeccable credentials.

'Yeah, shure, when he gets ashore,' was all that that he could manage. Speaking was becoming difficult – too many esses – but he was determined not to do a YaYa. Talking of whom, at that precise moment, in some adjacent whiskey parlour thirty miles across the water, under the influence of another Latin Master, he was also experiencing a not too dissimilar dislocation of his senses.

'A taxi, perhaps, unless you prefer to walk. I do not recommend you drive.' *El Cojo* was escorting Rich towards his exit. 'Give my nephew a call in the next few days. Let us have a meal together. And talk some business. *Encantado.*'

Rich Lee somehow landed on his feet, got his small plane down to ground, the runway lights of the marina twinkling in the early evening penumbra. The tick-ticking of a thousand yacht stays pricked his ears. The sodium flare of night lights along the finger piers seemed faintly narcotic. A dry distant rumble of thunder mumbled something but he lost count waiting for the enlightening lightning to appear. The car park. The pink cat. He ran his fingers over her curves. Beauty. He sat behind the controls and flicked a switch. Feeling randy. A new man. No empty cellar. *Gotta teach it to learn.* He fell asleep across the wheel with the radio on.

IMITATION OF DAWN

A stiff persistent offshore breeze that had sprung up during the night swept down from the High Rif across the low lying foreshore and out across the coastal waters, ruffling the crests of the swells and creating a foamy chop which ran counter to their motion. The effect of this change in the wind direction was gradually to offset the prevailing tendency of the waves and, over the course of the day, to iron out the surface. A series of intermittent squally showers acted like countless tiny hammers until, by late afternoon when the breeze suddenly and without warning died out completely, the water was beaten flat.

In the stillness that followed, it lay like a gently heaving mirror, silver in colour, with the vitreous sheen of liquid metal. This smooth undulating belly was mimicked by the shallow dome of a sky whose iron grey canopy of low unbroken cloud stretched to the horizon, where it merged seamlessly, making it impossible to tell where one element ended and the other began. It was as if everything was enclosed in a vast shrinking bubble from which the breath was slowly but inexorably being sucked out.

The sun remained obscured and only by subtle gradations in the leaden tone of the sky indicated its invisible passage beyond the cloud. Dawn might have been dusk, noon dawn, and the half-light of evening a rapid descent into black. As though the unseen hand that had been steadily lowering it, abruptly clamped the lid on that unlit cauldron and its liquid contents. Such was the weather for their final day in Teotuán.

When Shyno awoke and stared through the starboard porthole it appeared as if a filter had been placed over the lens of the glass, reducing the world to a dull monochrome, bled of all colour. The port side window gave onto the cutter's flank whose iron painted plates and immediate proximity served only to emphasise the oppressive intimacy of the cabin. The steel hull acted as one wall and the peephole of the seaward window gave to the low ceilinged berth the feel of a cell, into which he half expected the face of a gaoler to peer. He pressed his nose up against the glass and saw instead the blunt stern of a fishing trawler with its tangle of gear proceeding down the passage of the harbour channel towards the great stone boulders piled up either side of the gateway to the port. The fleet had up-anchored at dawn, taking with them their temporary moorings. And the vessel which presented to him its receding back was the last in a line of a loosely strung out procession of boats, diminishing in size to a point where the most distant of them was no more than a dot midway to the horizon. The basin of the harbour was now free from encumbrance, apart from a few small skiffs moored against the opposing wall. *Mona Gorda* and the Cutter were the only incumbents of note: like strange bedfellows from some revelry who wake up to find all the other guests have departed.

***

Alan and Dave surfaced to a military tattoo of knocking on the camper door and an intricately inked moustachioed face which belonged to their neighbour, peering in through the rear window. A solitary, exiled member from a chapter of Hell's Angels who called himself Mountain. Alan opened up to be greeted by a glowing fist no less swarthy or decorated than his own, proffering by way of breakfast a half smoked spliff and a tin mug of coffee. Apart from the VW and the angel's dusty chopper ticking over nearby, the campsite was deserted.

'Time to make a move, man. Word is out we are due for a visit.'

Alan scanned the acre of abandoned pasture. In the false light of dawn he could pick out the remnants of a few damped down fires and the scent of cedar and burnt litter drifting over on a chill autumn breeze that was gathering strength. Overnight the caravanserai had quietly upped sticks and gone on its way. Alan took a swig of lukewarm coffee and a drag on the number.

'Take it easy mate, catch you later.'

They followed the tail light of the Harley to the metalled road where it broke left toward Ceuta. Turning right, the camper made its way to the barn. Mustapha was waiting with the doors open. He had put the word out himself. He didn't want witnesses to the night's proceedings. The VW rolled inside. The barn doors were sealed. They all hunkered down among the donkeys and dope. Father and sons, two honoured guests and a patched up inflatable, waiting it out.

*

Rich did not really awake for he had not truly been asleep. He was skimming along the surface of unconsciousness, drifting in and out of images, fragments of music, half-remembered lyrics. To paraphrase an anachronism, to go back to the future: *If I medicine you man, you'll know you've been dosed.* He fumbled for the key in the ignition. *I've got silence, on my radio.* The battery was flat. *What I need, Turner, is a photo. You gave him a whole one?* Rich was head down under the cat flap playing with the terminals. *I like that, turn it up.* A voice belonging to the owner of the Merc in the next door slot piped up in a beguiling Queen's Land chant, 'Quit on yer, did she sport? Want me to give ya a jump?' *Rosie dear, dontcha think its queer?* It was three o'clock in the morning. *Still singing my song for you.* G-l-o-r-i-a. Yes, please. *You don't know where I'm going.* Yes I do. Rich took a look around *to see which way the wind blow.* Purred up to Villa Nova. *Nice mo-ah!* Parked the Jag in the carport. Gave a blast of *Flit* to the bedroom and hit the runway, hard .

CUTTER OFF

It was just forty eight hours since *Mona Gorda* had first lain alongside the navy vessel. The prospect of her imminent departure was the source of a mounting controlled urgency on the part of her crew, which filtered down through the open cabin hatch where the poets lay dozing in the semi-darkness. Brief barked commands, echoes of running feet on the gangways, the odd whistle and snatch of foreign sounding song. Frequent clangings and slammings of heavy doors and equipment. The occasional half-stifled oath.

For the past two nights they had fallen asleep then surfaced to the steady pulse of the ship's generator. This morning was different. What finally aroused them from torpor was the cutter firing up her engines. Adolescents on omnibuses know the unexpected effect of a thrumming diesel. Men who think they know better will be stirred in their seats by the rev of a growling V8. Several thousand horse powers coursing through your bones in time to the beating of your heart is another matter. La *Gorda*, all twelve tons of her, was vibrating like a tuning-fork. Shyno stuck his head up through the propped hatch and watched as a black plume of oily smoke floated out over the port from the ship's stack.

'Looks like she's getting under way. What time is it?'

'Time we got off, I should say,' muttered Lúcio, who was usually at his best come mid morning, but seemed somewhat distracted by the sudden intrusion of this minor sea quake and its continuing aftershocks. 'What a racket! I hope they are not planning on keeping this up.'

They were not. It was only ten o'clock. No sooner had the diesels started drumming than they abruptly ceased. It was an alarm call from the Captain, followed by a trio of emissaries sent down below. The first one was the recruit who had the mishap with his spanner. He came aboard in search of Neville who was propped up in his corner. This youth was still not out of his teens, barefoot, with a fuzz of bum-fluff tufting his chin. He bobbed and weaved in a nervous shuffle, so Nev stuck out a hand in greeting and received in return a kiss on each cheek which had them both blushing, upon which the grateful lad salaamed and scurried back up the ladder. Next on, the painter-restorer, lugging a 24-volt back-up battery, used but charged, which he insisted on placing next to the main one and explaining how in an emergency it might be deployed. Lastly, a junior officer, all on his dignity but clearly delighted with his commission, bearing a signed monograph from Captain Ali, unpublished of course, on *Le Bateau Ivre*, and a weather report. *Small craft warning, extreme low pressure*, with a terse handwritten note appended. *Be advised. Anticipate severe conditions. A. Mansour.*

'Don't much like the sound of that,' said Shyno.

Lúcio was non-committal. They both knew this was a done deal. *Aurora* would be patrolling these waters within twenty four hours and might well prove less hospitable than Captain Ali. Postponement was simply not an option open to any of them, least of all to Mustapha and his crew, who were sitting on what must have felt like an explosive device with an unpredictable detonator. Time was running out and in perverse fashion, not quickly enough. Working backwards to an ideal schedule they would reach the Spanish coast by daylight the following day. A six-hour journey from the point at which they would drop off YaYa. Say one in the morning. Thirty minutes up the coast from the cairn. Two hours for the transfer. So leave port at ten. Half-nine should see Dave and the dinghy on board. Fine, if the weather held off. There was no telling and no alternative, other than to abandon the whole daft scheme and that occurred to no one as a working proposition.

The trouble with a bare boat like *Mona Gorda* was that there was so little to do. In other circumstances this might have seemed a bonus, in the way of low maintenance gardens, or a dinner date with a prospective mate who does not drink and is on a diet. But the buzz around the cutter and the contrast with his own idleness struck Shyno as symptomatic of something he was aware of in himself. A passivity, a yielding to the inevitable, which went against every sense of being in command, the contrary of Skipper, a pawn in someone else's game. He had an intuition of some future state of impotence against the general run of fate; of not having control over anything, not even himself, and this induced a kind of lethargy. Hose down the stern deck? Why bother? It would rain soon. Polish the spokes of the helm with a wad of Brasso? They will tarnish again before long. Nevertheless he did it and five minutes passed. Fire up the Perkins and check the battery charge? Done. Fuel gauge? A quarter full, more maybe, enough for a hundred miles. Plenty, surely? Fuel dock, closed. Water-tank? Brimming. Lúcio on strict three minute showers. Stern hatch at standby, twelve rivets to remove. *I have forgotten/ And remember*. Nothing. An insidious sense of irrelevance and his own shortcomings washed through his already diluted egoism. Poetry? Perhaps it does more than survive. Here, in this un-tampered-with patch of Moroccan coastland it had made something happen, though precisely what still remained to be answered. *Not, I'll not*! It was the old Carry On Comfort.

Shyno hauled himself out of this morbidry and did his best to busy himself with whatever he could, steeling his weakened will against the tedious day's journey into night.

Shortly before noon the drumming began again, this time in earnest. They cast off, made a short tour to the far side of the harbour and tied up against a floating pontoon out of the cutter's way. She had no thought for them, her crew busy at their stations.

Captain Ali had moored his vessel bow-inward along the sea wall. It would have been simpler to reverse out of the confined port to the open sea but that did not sit well with navy tradition. It was a tight circle. A brutal employment of stern thrusters produced a roiling turmoil of foam at her rear as she swung away from the pier. She still had a bowline attached. From this fixed point her hull arced slowly through 120 degrees of the compass, like the second hand on a clock ticking backwards. A quick counter blast from the starboard propellor and she settled in neutral, the helmsman gauging their trajectory. At an unheard command a recruit cast off.

Shyno had a clear view through the wheelhouse window of her uncompromising rump about forty yards ahead as she began reversing at low revs towards them. At twenty paces the plates of her stern blocked out *Mona Gorda*'s widescreen. Stop all. A change of gear, signalled by more boiling foam, and she moved slowly forward, hard to port at first, then straightening her bow until she was head on to the harbour entrance, under way at last. Once clear of the channel her stern dug down, the prow angled up. A great belch of black smoke erupted from her funnel followed by the thunder of her turbines and in under half a minute she was doing twenty knots, her wake opening wide like a silver zip in the fabric of the sea as she sped away towards Ceuta.

Shyno took *Mona Gorda* back across the empty basin to a point on the mole where a set of stone steps led down from the promontory and tied up against the wall. They were at the extremity of the port. The fishing fleet would settle in behind them in a line on their return. By the time they were ready to bring Dave and the dinghy aboard the crews would be long gone to the bars or their beds after a day's toil. For the time being they had the harbour to themselves.

The silence following the cutter's exit was broken only by the occasional cry of the few gulls too lazy to have followed the fleet out to the fishing grounds, or wise enough to wait and have their scraps brought home to them. They dozed and preened on various prominences or made the odd desultory swoop around the port before returning to their stations. The oppressive stillness in the air and the overbearing closeness of the cloud cover had the trio talking in undertones, though there was no one within hailing distance. The port seemed sepulchral, the cutter a phantom. All her solid metal, her living crew, that mixture of menace and welcome under the sway of a bookish Master, gone like a spell lifted. Malign or benign? As with Lúcio, at times it was not easy to tell.

'Going to look for a telephone, chaps. Give Jade a call. I may be a little while.'

OMD

Lúcio had been gone a couple of hours when the first of the fleet returned from its labours, earlier than on previous days. Shyno put it down to the weather and possibly a disappointing catch. The rest of the flotilla followed in dribs and drabs, mooring up in their customary slots. Several of the crews acknowledged *Mona Gorda* in a cordial fashion, but there was a sombre, disconsolate air about them. No doubt they would lose a day's fishing, maybe more if conditions turned really foul.

These were small trawlers, lightweight, not built to operate in extreme seas, several of them patched and splintery in places, their wooden hulls leaky, their pumps unreliable. Shyno had imagined a last supper of fresh hake or red mullet, but on the evidence of the meagre haul being offloaded, he prepared not to haggle. Nev was dozing in the cabin, still sleeping it off.

Lúcio reappeared around teatime, walking along the dockside with a characteristic brisk stride, toes turned slightly outward like a ballet dancer on the balls of his feet, a legacy of the beautiful game and his position as striker.

Instead of heading for the *Mona Gorda*, he climbed up onto the heaped boulders of the outer sea wall and made his way over with a series of considered leaps to where Shyno was crouched contemplating the crabs. Lúcio hunkered down at his side and they both stared out across the glassy millpond as if scanning a radar screen. Not a blip nor a blot on the horizon. The fishing fleet was all in.

'Flat calm, eh? Let's hope it stays that way. Sorry to be so long. Sheer murder getting through. Jade wasn't there. Anyway, I tried a bit later and managed a brief chat. She was ambivalent, green going amber, a few prevarications. When I put her on the spot, she wouldn't be moved. All she would say was she saw us back in Oxford. Just be prepared for some difficulty. Well, I could have told her that. Still, it's better to have it confirmed. Come on, let's get back to the boat and eat something. I had a word with the chap at the barrier, gave him some *reals*. He won't trouble us with any mischief, might even be asleep. He said try not to wake him.'

Shyno smiled and though he was full of foreboding managed a playful rejoinder which was lost on Lúcio. Something to do with *Little Joe never once gave it away*, but like many of his obliquities it slid by unrecognised. They reconvened aboard, brought Neville up to speed, reassured themselves, forced down some muddy tasting mullet and a bland pat of couscous, took a sip of the precious fortifying cane liquor, and each in his own way endured the run-in to the finale.

At eight forty five, the two poets left Nev out on the stern deck rolling a snout and strolled as casually as they could along the mole, past the customs barrier where a lubricated Mohan was already snoring, bottle in his lap and squatted on their haunches, backs against the exterior of the harbour wall.

Three quarters of an hour had gone by without any sign of the farmers when they heard the first faint clopping of mule heels breaking the silence. Shyno was so pent up with the absurdity of it all he could have hooted as the beasts hove into sight. Mustapha was astride the first one, urging it on with vicious kicks to the withers which it completely ignored, muzzle thrust deep in a ragged nosebag. The Moroccan had hold of its ears instead of the reins and was alternately tugging and yanking at them, cursing, as though it were one his wives, reluctant to submit to some backward desire. YaYa was following behind in a white cotton ensemble, meekly resigned, the complete Nazarene, encouraging all forward momentum from his flyblown mount in his imitable fashion.

Alan, they explained, had put down a marker, refused to bring the camper anywhere near the port. It was not part of the agreement. Mustapha for once was reluctant to involve a cousin, so it was donkeys at dusk. The two mule-miles had cost them a couple of hours and a pair of saucer sized blisters on YaYa buttocks from riding bareback. Neither was in the mood to be humoured and YaYa had about him the melancholy air of an unwilling martyr to a cause he had once espoused and was now eager to recant but couldn't. Mustapha dismounted, managing to suppress his indignation, and greeted the two poets with his snag-toothed grin and a gesture of magnanimity towards the animals.

'Bastards bear anything, so long as you feed them.'

YaYa humped the Seagull engine. Shyno hefted the collapsed dinghy like a yoke over his shoulders. Lúcio took the five gallon gas tank and the foot pump. Mustapha gathered up the reins of the transport and turned back on his way.

'Midnight we meet. This time we make it. *Inshallah*.'

The trio carried their baggage toward the makeshift Customs booth where Mohan was sleeping. They ducked under the wooden barrier and proceeded without let back to the *Mona Gorda*. It could not have been simpler. They shipped the gear then set about inflating the dinghy. It was a patched up, somewhat pathetic little craft, maybe twelve foot by five, with a wooden stern plate where you bolted on the engine.

One of those junior outboards with a steering arm and a hand crank, like a motor mower. When it was fully blown up, Shyno poured a bucket of seawater over its tubes looking for bubbles of escaping air. He couldn't find any. She was more or less sea worthy. He tried to imagine the dinghy in a shore break, but the image disconcerted him. He gave Dave what was meant as a reassuring nod of approval, but which might have been taken as a *rather you mate*. They bolted on the outboard, connected up the fuel tank and inserted the wooden plank that served as the helmsman's seat. She sat there like a tubby, eager little goer, taking up most of *Mona Gorda*'s stern deck, her taught underside pressed against the hatch where she would deposit her spoils a few hours hence, then carry YaYa back to the shore further up the coast, there to be abandoned.

Shyno had a flashback – he'd taken the odd trip in his time – to his interview at Merton, three years previously. With John 'Davey' Jones, Senior Tutor and later Professor of Poetry at Oxford although he only wrote prose.

JJ was an aficionado of Conrad and against the general run of opinion (those big-canvas protagonists who favoured *Nostromo*) argued that the *Nigger of The Narcissus* (120 pages) was the author's masterpiece. After the usual opening gambits, *hail fellow, well met,* he lunged straight in.

'Do you see any sexual symbolism in Conrad's depiction of ships?'

Shyno was momentarily thrown. He had prepared, but not for this. *What, boats as fucks? Creaking, groaning, needing to be seen to, sails like brassieres, corseted in rigging, impaled by the mainmast, big bellied, leaky?*

'Well, feminine, of course, but in the way of the *Anima*. Ship as *soul* say?'

He could see nothing erotic about YaYa's dinghy, though the patched up rubber tubes did resemble a pair of wide open blistered lips.

Five nautical miles on a calm sea, with only a hint of swell and not a breath of air, is about one hour at five knots. And a quarter of a mile off shore there was no significant current to take into consideration. So they slipped away just before eleven, leaving behind the fishing trawlers, the lights of the port, the constellation of the town bedded down and sparkling under the bulk of the Rif mountains.

As they chugged through the jaws of the harbour mouth, a green light signalled on their port side and a red one blipped at their right. Winking and blinking, like Dr Johnson: beckoning them on.

Once outside the wall, Shyno bore north, noting the subdued, gently heaving belly of the interior ocean. An early autumn sea mist crept out from the shore enveloping *Mona Gorda* up to her gunwales. Her crew stood waist deep in the cottony stuff, only their upper torsos visible. At intervals it would part and peel off, unfurling from their bodies as if they were corpses shedding raggedy shrouds, before it closed back in and swathed them once more. They rode without running lights and the vapour, like a blanket, muffled the hammering of the diesel.

Five miles by the log, Shyno throttled back into neutral and listened out for the swell. It was scarcely audible. No one was speaking, but all eyes were fixed on some distant point in the mist when a torch flashed on and off three times. Shyno switched on *Mona Gorda*'s riding lights to the same pattern and cut the engine. It was time to launch.

YaYa and Shyno raised the dinghy to the stern and slid her over, outboard first, with a short painter tied to the nose to prevent her from drifting. Dave clambered over the gun-whale and lowered himself in, sitting down gently so as not to lose balance or aggravate his blisters. He cranked up the Seagull and it fired first time. Pointing the bow coastward, he put-putted off in the direction of the shore break. In a matter of moments he was lost in the mist. Not long after the torch came back on, flashed for a few seconds then went out. There was a brief pause before it resumed, repeating the beacon, guiding Dave in. Without it he might as well have been heading for Zion for all that he could tell.

It was almost half an hour before the dinghy reappeared. Shyno had the riding light on and had taken up a position on the wheelhouse roof, the point of greatest elevation. YaYa emerged out of the white smog grinning and wet as he bumped the rubber nose of the dinghy against *Mona Gorda*'s side.

'Ok?'

'Ya ya.'

Dave had only four bales aboard and the dinghy was overloaded. It was going to take three trips. Shyno leaned out over the gunwhale and grabbed the first of the packs, hauled it aboard and set it down on the deck. It was a bulky mother, mummy-wrapped in silver duct tape, glistening like an over-size ingot. A lot of dope. He lugged in the next three and without any further chat YaYa backed off the inflatable from La Gorda's flank and with what looked like a new self-possession turned shoreward for his second run.

Shyno ducked down into the hold and with Lúcio assisting stowed the bales just as he had imagined they would, there on the raised ridge, up along the concrete sides of the hull where they sat snug and wedged as though it had been designed for precisely that. And so it went. Fetch and ferry, haul in and stow.

In just over an hour they had nines bales stashed down below and one left sitting on the deck which Nev was attending to with a Stanley knife. He cut through the layers of wrapping and sliced off a small corner from the uppermost slab before plastering over the wound with some spare duct tape. He sniffed at the lump and nodded his approval. Shyno humped the remainder below, resurfaced and slid the deck hatch back into place. It took a couple of minutes to screw in three rivets at each corner. This was enough to hold the metal framework in situ. He thought he would have the opportunity and leisure, somewhere en route, to screw in the many remaining dozens back where they belonged. Anyone can be wrong.

Dave climbed aboard, soaked and shivering but pleased with himself. The dinghy they tied off on a short painter at the stern. Lúcio was bent over in the wheelhouse perusing charts. Nev was busy constructing a spliff. Shyno commandeered the helm, fired up the diesel and guided *Mona Gorda* out and away from the Moroccan coast heading Northnorthwest at a steady five knots. It was glassily calm. The mist continued to lift the further out that they went. *Mona Gorda* trundled forward, beam-on to the uneasy swell, rolling imperceptibly. It was one thirty am.

Nev produced a big fat carrot of a number, lit up, took several deep tokes and passed the glowing brazier over towards Lúcio who was deep in mathematics.

'No thanks,' he murmured but took it anyway and inhaled. He passed it on to Dave who swallowed a couple of lungsful and coughed his approval. Shyno took a drag or three and snorted the smoke out through his nose.

So this was what they had come all this way for.

Olive green and brown, freshly pressed, first shake, primo THC crystal resin, fragrant and powerful. Within moments they were all exceedingly high. It was top quality stuff as they had been led to expect. The smoke, well, it induced a type of relaxed euphoria, an alert torpor. Things went on normally. The boat got steered. A course was plotted. But there was no urgency about anything as they cruised unconcerned toward the rendezvous where Dave would depart. They forgot about the weather, the forecast, Mansour's warning, the Moroccan navy, time and chance. They were at ease with themselves and the present moment, as if it could only last.

Shyno had a look at his watch. It was one fifty. Time for YaYa to be on his way and they on theirs, although Dave seemed to be in no hurry. He was chatting, if you can chat in grunts, with Nev out on the stern deck. A sparkle in Shyno's fuddled mind told him something was out of sync. It made no sense. Dave could have simply taken one more trip back to the beach and hightailed it with Alan, there and then. Unless Alan hadn't been there for some reason. And if The Mechanic had gone straight to the rendezvous further up the coast, a point which *Mona Gorda* was just about to pass, why didn't YaYa simply say *adios* and head on in for the meet and retreat, a twenty minute ride, no more? Yet he was lingering.

'What time are you hooking up with Alan, mate?'

YaYa gazed up and there was a faintly haunted look on his face.

'Ah, dawn, ya?'

So that was how it came down. Whatever the scruple of their arrangements, Dave was facing at least four hours out on the water, on his own, in the dark, in a small dinghy, unless he took the chance of beaching alone without a light to guide him in. It seemed as if his chum Alan had reverted to his original position. Arms length to it all. Not willing to risk a night light but willing to risk his companion. It only took a moment to assess the options. Shyno put *Mona Gorda* into neutral and slipped down the companionway stairs to the front cabin. Lúcio was hunched over on one of the berths, jotting down what looked like verses in his notebook.

'I don't think he wants to go,' Shyno announced.

Lúcio frowned and looked up from his muse.

'Well he simply has to. He should have gone already by my calculations. We are heading in the wrong direction. He will have to get off. I quite understand his reluctance. But if he's not up to the dinghy then he will have to stow aboard with us. We'll take him to Spain.'

Shyno could find no obvious flaw in this reasoning. Captain Ali had camouflaged their Moroccan border stamps. No guessing but Dave's would be plainly visible. What matter. They weren't planning to expose themselves to Spanish border control. Four blokes in a boat cruising the *calas* off the Costa del Sol? Plausible. Maybe. Perhaps they could wing it. Shyno didn't envy YaYa's prospects out on the water and despite an incriminating stamp, he wouldn't have used that as an excuse to be rid of him. Put him overboard? He had seen the fear lurking in the fellow's face. Suppose he got lost in the mist, or flipped in the shore break. No, it wasn't something you did. He possessed neither Alan's ruthlessness nor self protective streak. This had to be dealt with gently. The two poets made a joint approach. Eventually they got it out of him. Yes, Alan had refused to come to the cairn. No, not his job, never was. Not in the plan. Mustapha and his boys had handled the bales. Alan would be waiting but not until daylight.

'Dave, don't you see, we are past our turning point, we are

heading back towards Ceuta. We need to be off. Now. Come with us if you don't fancy the dinghy. We can work something out.'

Shyno was almost pleading.

'Ya, but my passport...'

'Yes, we know.'

'Na. I haven't got it with me. Ya?'

It hadn't occurred to them. Lúcio's next proposition revolved around stowing YaYa in the hold with the bales, as a precaution, and then once safely in Spanish territory declaring his papers lost. But it didn't wash. You could see Dave picturing himself bunked down with the dope in the hold, like a rat in a drain and the denial in his eyes showed just how much faith he put in them not getting caught. A bit like Alan. When it came down to it, it was the *Mona Gorda* gang putting their necks in the noose and Dave, deep in his fear, doubted them. It was the old *every man for himself*.

Nev was rolling up the last of the taste he had cut from the bale and looked over. He was the closest to Dave. All that lost time spent footling with the Guru in Malaga, *darshanning* under the midday sun. He fixed him with a fond, unforgiving gaze, lit up his number, sucked on it and said,

'Dave...' he exhaled. 'Either you are on the bus, mate, or you are *off*...'

YaYa made a hopeless defeated gesture with his hands, as if it was he who was abandoning them and with as much lethargy as he could summon, spent the better part of ten minutes getting his shit together. The little of which entailed simply standing up, transferring from the boat into the dinghy, untying and pushing off.

For another quarter of an hour he tailed the *Mona Gorda* like a stray pup and Shyno hadn't the heart to speed up or to alter course. So they wasted a little more time and added some more distance to their journey, until in an instinct of self preservation he put the throttle hard down, spun the wheel to starboard and headed out to sea towards Spain. It was only then that Dave stopped dogging them. Shyno looked back once and watched the dinghy turn about in their wake and disappear into the night. It was the last time they saw him for over a year.

Lúcio's revised course put them on a bearing pretty much northeast. At eight knots, a six hour haul to the coast. It was two in the morning and still calm. Lúcio and Nev were out on the stern deck chatting and casting the occasional glance backward at their empty wash.

***

The first wave of nausea gripped Shyno like a fist clenching deep in his gut and bent him double at the wheel before it passed. He straightened up, gasping, forehead frosted with sweat, eyes watery, his body trembling. He just had time to calculate the distance to the galley sink before the next seizure took hold of him and then he was head down in the steel basin retching and choking, deep wracking spasms that emptied him in moments and then kept on coming. Dry heaves, bitter dives into the further reaches of his bowels.

There was no point in trying to stand up. As soon as he did, another bilious convulsion had him bowing from the waist like some obsequious courtier still making obeisance long after the dignitaries have passed. *Mal de mer*. There is nothing quite like it to reduce its victim to the status of a puppet. And disabuse him of the notion he is master of his flesh or of anything else for that matter.

Shyno managed a mute sideways glance up the companionway steps where Lúcio stood looking mildly unconcerned. Nev must have been at the wheel, abandoned in the rush to the galley.

'Pretty strong stuff?'

Shyno wanted to explain that it was the hour or so spent wallowing about beam on to that innocuous swell while YaYa had ferried back and forth that had made him seasick. Not the smoke or the fishy smelling mullet, ok maybe the combination, but what came out was a strangled croak. So he waved Lúcio away and crawled into the cabin and curled up in a foetal hug on the starboard bunk. The two low-wattage companion lights glowed amber in their sockets and he closed his eyes against their dull glare before yielding to the fever and a queasy unconsciousness.

For the second time on the journey Nev found himself alone at the wheel. Lúcio had followed Shyno down below, ostensibly to check on his friend, but finding there was nothing to be done, decided to carrying on composing his villanelle.

Nev had a course to follow. All he had to do was keep his eyes fixed on the compass and his hands on the helm, since there was nothing else to see through the wheelhouse windows except the white expanse of the foredeck and the point of the prow, beyond which there was only impenetrable darkness. The dial of the instrument panel glowed fluorescent green and the constant slight oscillations of the needle were faintly hypnotic. Once or twice he felt himself dozing off. Each time he jerked back awake he was relieved to see that he was still more or less on track, barring some minor adjustments to the tiller.

They were making eight knots and the muffled drumming of the Perkins added a soporific undertone to the proceedings. He must have fallen asleep at the wheel a couple of times before the first big wave hit them. It came in from the starboard side, beam on, entirely unanticipated.

The last time Nev had been aware, the sea was still calm. But something had changed, changed utterly. The impact rolled *Mona Gorda* hard on her side and the motion had Nev pressed up against the wheelhouse bulkhead clinging to the helm, the skipper's stool teetering on two of its legs. It only lasted a few moments before the countermotion set in. *Mona Gorda* pitched down on her starboard side and began a steep plunge before she buried her nose in the trough and ceased forward motion, stern in the air, propeller out of the water, shrilling and churning in what sounded like despair. Then she managed to nose up again and began the uncertain climb to whatever was awaiting her.

Nev had a momentary vision of a plastic duck in some prankish child's boisterous bath before the onslaught began in earnest.

JUST A BIT OF BREEZE

The two poets surfaced simultaneously to the same thought that all hell must have broken loose. In fact it was not some blazing inferno but the cold liquid contents of the galley fridge spilling out over the cabin bunks. A sideways jolt had dislodged the two foot square white box from its housing in the kitchen and a violent pitch had flung the unit forward and up onto the mattress between their heads, narrowly missing braining them both, and there it sprawled, door open, its interior light still on, humming.

Shyno just had time to appraise this unexpected visitor before *Mona Gorda* lunged into another corkscrewing gyre. The motion forced them into a momentary embrace, sliding together across the vinyl cushions which were lubricated by sweat and a cocktail of milk and exotic fruit juice. It was all happening in slow real time as *Mona Gorda* reacted to the forces unleashed against her. As they clung there they had a clear view back up the companionway steps to the wheelhouse which allowed them a quick glimpse of Neville performing a third remarkable gymnastic routine except on this occasion not one of his choosing.

It was a cartwheel of sorts, with the metal spokes of his crutches and callipers and a pair of flailing arms describing an imperfect circle as he whirled though the air, briefly visible as he crossed through their line of vision. They saw neither the take off nor landing, only the arc of his flight, but the impact was immediate.

Mona Gorda began a shuddering giddy lunge down into an oncoming vortex and came up short like a diver repelled by the element he strives to enter. As her bow burrowed free and began the laborious climb back up the oncoming wave, Shyno released Lúcio, slid down off the sticky bunk and landed on his feet scrambling for the wheelhouse. Nev was crumpled up on the starboard side, dazed but conscious, bewildered by the force that had unseated him. Shyno grabbed the unmanned helm, glanced at the erratic compass flicking in its glass and waited for what the sea had to tell him.

The message he received was both violent and confused, as if a belligerent drunk were striking out blindly but with unexpected success, picking them off with a series of baffling blows which assailed them from every quarter. Under this onslaught, *Mona Gorda* reeled and staggered, drenched with the sea's spittle. Suddenly it was all too painfully clear. Shyno roared out to no one in particular,

'She is beam on, do you hear? She won't take much more of this before she rolls. *We must head up into it!*'

And so he began the necessary adjustments. Dragged the unwilling wheel by half turns through 90 degrees to starboard. Throttled ahead hard up an unseen, uneven slope. Reined her back, almost to neutral. Paused there at the summit. Tried to gauge the angle of the hull's plunge forward into the abyss. The twist of it diving down and in, rebuffed by the wind and the quixotic wave forms, until they were head on to the maelstrom. It was like a novice skier traversing blindfold across a snowfield of outsize moguls which were themselves in motion. When he glanced down at the instrument panel, *Mona Gorda* was on an entirely new course, due East, lumbering toward Egypt.

BLIND MAN'S DITCH

When he finally made up his mind to take his chance in the dinghy, the last sight YaYa had of *Mona Gorda* was her fat white rump disappearing into the night. She looked almost homely. Nev was sat out on the stern deck whistling on his spliff. Lúcio had his headphones on and was waving a farewell. Shyno was silhouetted in the glow of the wheelhouse. Were it not for the cargo of dope, YaYa would have travelled with them, passport or no. He no longer had much faith in his chum Alan. There was a callous streak about the bloke which went against his own gentler nature. That shabby business of not showing up at the cairn to give a hand with the bales; refusing to rendezvous before daylight; pandering to Mustapha's games.

YaYa had the impression that he was no more than some minor tool in the mechanic's armoury, of limited value, disposable. Sure, the boat trip had been his idea, but Alan had put him up to it, to be the spokes guy, the yes man. But the Man behind it all was AA, always pushing on, working the machine. The realisation that he was no more than an instrument in someone else's design made Dave feel unusually narked.

He throttled up the Seagull and the dinghy surged forward over the glassy swells. He was still two miles off, with a three-quarters-full tank of gas and he felt the time was now right to get some practice in. Better latent than never. An odd, uncharacteristic surge of peevishness and exultation coursed through his frame as he thought back over the six weeks holed up in Mustapha's mountain redoubt. Images of foetid meat, flies, unseemly acts, badinage, cruelty to animals, a distinct lack of anything you might call spiritual, all crowded in on his humility and bafflement. He drew a deep breath down into his diaphragm and held it there for as long as he could, then expelled it through his left nostril with all the slow force that he had learned in the bullring in Malaga. He imagined a bubble of white light enfolding him, pierced by the Guru's love, and with an exquisite act of futile surrender yielded to the present. Think no thought. Detach. Act without fear of consequence. Future plans are mere ideas if not realised now. Awake. Be. Become. Nothing. No one. One.

Primo stuff this pollen. Takes you down to the edge of the burning river and pushes you right on in. YaYa gunned the engine. Who needs light when you have a guide?

***

Dave was dawdling shortly before dawn in his motorised rubber-ring, two hundred yards outside the shore-break, ears tuned to the soft boom of collapsing surf, breathing rapidly from his unaccustomed burst of egotistical rebellion. For three hours he had been fooling around in his little boat, getting familiar with her, seeing how she handled. Mindful of the fuel he had putted about most of the time, but for the past half-hour he had been goosing the tiny outboard with a series of ever increasing twists of his wrist, extracting the maximum power from her twenty horses, skimming and bouncing over the black surface of the water. There was a buzz to be had in the low-level g-forces as he made sudden turns, abrupt decelerations, with the occasional exhilarating leap that took the small dinghy airborne as she skipped free of the meniscus.

On another day, in a world of perpetual possibility, he would have found himself astride his board, pumped and primed, hanging with some blonde dudes at Waimea Bay, waiting for the warning holler,

'Outside!'

Followed by the urgent, focused, hundred-yard paddle toward the mounting set of swells, eyes fixed on the first fifteen-foot wall, trying to gauge whether he would crest it and then imagining the bigger beast gathering behind, no thought of catching the wave, just the intent to beat the bugger, *not ever to be caught.*

But there were no buddies around that night, no secret sharers. YaYa's universe had resolved itself into an awkward singularity. Alone in his donut he had not the slightest inkling of the seas massing behind him. He was sufficiently far out from the shoreline, safe so he imagined, idling the time away before daylight. How was he to know that something other than dawn was about to break.

The four base elements that constituted his universe came into play one by one. He flicked at his silver Zippo lighter, cupping the flame to ignite another spliff. A dismissive gust of wind puffed it out and plastered the damp t-shirt to his back. A ten foot wall of water gathering pace as it encountered the shallows reared up behind him and, thundering in, picked up the dinghy in its mighty paw and swiped him landward.

There was no riding it.

YaYa gulped an instinctive breath, grabbed onto the side handles of the dinghy, stretched out his legs in a bracing gesture and entered the water chute. A brief eternity passed as the wave picked up its cargo and shuttled it earthward. For a few seconds he had the exhilaration of pure free fall before the wave collapsed and dumped him in a tangle of limbs and burning lungs onto the sandy bottom, where it bounced and abraded his body and then spat him back out on the beach. Time's Jonah. Ya-hweh! An unrelenting series of sucking swells threatened to drag him back out to sea, but the cumulative beating of the surge eventually deposited him above the high water mark, spent, still alive and spasmodically kicking.

Dawn light struggled to reveal his dismay.

Alan was two hundred yards up the coast, roving a pair of binoculars over the filthy sea, seeing nothing but the ponderous great swells sweeping inland, obliterating themselves against an obstinate shore. All the water was brown and windswept, confused, huge. At the periphery of his vision he could just make out what looked like a waterlogged heap of rags surrounded by a bunch of bedouins and a couple of low ranking provos. There was no sign of the dinghy or the dope. It had to be Dave. Drowned? Possibly not. The Mechanic made his habitual grim shrug of fatality, as if he had been summoned to a pile-up, multiple, on the M6, in driving rain. Muttering a few heartfelt blasphemies he tooled up the camper, took a last look back, then put his blunt head down, boot to the pedal and the rusting metal. Tutting he turned away toward Ceuta and the border.

'Cunning shunt. Shame about it. Baddun.'

YaYa spent the better part of an hour being alternately rinsed and spun by the surf, clawing his way up the beach in the half-light before dawn and only when he had convinced himself that he was beyond the reach of the breakers, allowed himself to collapse into unconsciousness. When he came to he was no longer alone. A group of local villagers stood around him a short way apart, surveying the wreckage. Among them, two young uniformed police recruits were debating his fortune. It didn't take them long to decide that Dave would be the making of theirs.

The laws of salvage, they argued between them equably, could be applied just as profitably to human cargo as to any *matériel*. So they arrested him, on no other charge than the impertinence of being there, undocumented, under suspicion of whatever mischief they chose to imagine.

As they dragged and hauled him handcuffed across the strand, something in Dave's soul was rudely unblocked. For months now he had been grappling with the Guru's abjuration *'silence your radio...turn off the voices in your head'*.

YaYa understood exactly what he meant. For the wireless in his brain resembled nothing so much as the demented twiddling of some hyper-active ham operator scanning the airwaves. What filled his head were the incessant, inconsequential bleeps of half-heard banalities, interspersed with white noise and electronic keenings, which he could not, try as he might, contrive to make quiet. So he had learnt to keep his mouth shut. Reduced his output to minimal syllables. Giving the outward appearance of inner tranquillity. But dams will break. Under duress.

A torrent, a litany of the most eloquent, foul-mouthed, Tourette-humbling scatological profanity spewed forth from his lips. YaYa had finally found his voice. Talk about talking in tongues. Most of the abuse was directed at Alan but there was plenty to go round. The initial salvo was a scattergun howl of indignation at the sheer unfairness of it all. The betrayal. He turned to one of his captors.

'Goatheed! Merkin mouth!'

The assortment of savage cuffs administered by the affronted provo did little to curtail his volubility. It appeared to encourage him. To the few, bewildered, largely sympathetic locals and the pair of uniformed thugs looking on, it came out something like this according to their unintelligible records.

'Cunners, ya? Oi, scusee, yew fat prack, dinnee fash, aw feck yuse yer raggy scabs, ahl spew mah guts all over ye, see me, wracked up hiya? lemme tell yaw, aah nay bother pluke features, did yer mather gang you on a goat horn? ...yon sea, ken tha wata, aye it's rank awfie, didna smell of fush till ure wummin went swummin, puss orf, ya gobshite!
'

Dave had Scots lineage and abruptly it showed.

On the short journey to the nearest lock-up, and from thence to a municipal holding pen, by way of various officious time servers, torturers, berobed dignitaries and placemen, nothing could persuade him to hold his tongue. A burly, sweating expert in extracting information was commandeered to wield his wisdom. But having administered the first few swingeing blows to the soles of Dave's bare feet he understood the futility of his enterprise. The prisoner was only too willing to cough. A veritable flock of canaries warbling above an offshore gas rig.

Interpreters were inveighed and departed baffled. All that could be construed from his rantings were various meaningless nicknames, horticultural references, innumerable appellations for the Divine and intricate innuendoes that bespoke unconscionable sexual practices. Cucumber, Pretty Fatty, Donkey, Mechanic, Tools, Fist, Goat, Flies, Diarrhoea, Seagulls.

If the Law is an Ass, or at best a kind of beast, then YaYa

became its burden. Since they could come up with no meaningful charge against him other than sprawling half-drowned on a foreign shore without proper identification, they had him up before a Judge in Tangier who gave him nine months for loitering with intent, time off for reasonable behaviour.

'It is no good, it will do you no good, lying on some third world beach, smoking detrimental dope, seeking consciousness expansion. Take him down.'

So Dave sang for his supper and for leniency. Of plots, conspiracies, literary hoodlums, betrayal, farming subsidies, in fact anything and everything that he could dredge up from his surprisingly fecund imagination. The power of speech, even that of delirium, became his weapon and means of survival. There was a method in his mania. As he recalled from his incessant troubling of the I-Ching: when at the court of King Wen, *feign madness.*

It worked. At the merest hint of a threat, be it from some overzealous official, predatory cellmate, impotent civil servant, Dave would simply engage forward gear and motormouth into the Thesaurus of profanity.

When one enterprising abuser saw fit, literally, to put a thick woollen sock in it, Dave managed by a virtuoso exertion of his limbs to mimic most of the abominations known to humankind, the whole sordid farrago given a running commentary by his muffled cries. Of course in the end they subdued him by means of various restraints. But their reprieve was temporary. At every release the colloquy began anew. It took the better part of a month, but a consensus formed. Leave the poor, touched idiot alone.

So they did. And Dave served his brief time, unmolested, suffering only the usual privations of the unjustly incarcerated, all the while scheming revenges on his chum Alan. And were it not for the assiduous, patient attention of a mid-ranking policeman, who staked his fortune on the ravings of a dragged-up, lunar-struck, hippy dip-stick, YaYa would have blasphemed his way to freedom with no one the wiser.

As it was it took nine months for the info to trickle back to the Thames Valley Police. And when they finally pieced it all together, they were ready to pounce on the ponces and the Pink Panther.

HARD NOSE

Halfway to the Spanish border Alan ducked up a dirt track and stalled the camper behind a stand of cypress trees. He did a thorough valet of the vehicle, every cavity and orifice, down to the sleeping bags and a cracked thermos flask. Just as well he did. Surprising the number of roaches, Rizla packets, nuggets of foil wrapped dope, improvised pipes and paraphernalia you could accumulate over a couple of months. He stacked the evidence, set it alight and after a brief consideration added YaYa's passport to the pyre. The bloke wouldn't be needing it for a while. He could always get a replacement in time. Alan didn't fancy having to explain his chum's absence if the authorities caught him in possession.

At Ceuta a uniformed pit crew waved him over to a lay-by designated for the purpose and tore apart the VW. It only took them twenty minutes to deconstruct the van, they even deflated the tyres. Then they turned their attention to the driver and gave him a thorough-over. They stopped short of any internal investigation, largely because Alan was well overdue a shower. For a moment though he thought that they might get their hoses out. It took him a long hour to gather his strewn belongings and pump up the tyres. It was the same hassle in France, the same aggro off the ferry at Dover. By then, after three days on the road, he was even more savoury. But clean. No one could or would touch him.

Dover was the familiar waste of stained concrete, rusting containers and weeping Nissan huts. The M20, under a dank autumn drizzle, the usual snarl of HGVS and bewildered foreign drivers hogging the idler lane. By the time Alan hit the A2 the camper was struggling. He thought about getting off and pootling up Shooters Hill but opted for Sun in The Sand instead. Mistake. Midway across Blackheath he had a blowout to his right rear tyre. As he hoiked the jack in to place, waving the irate tailback by, giving the odd finger, he took a moment to reflect. Dave was going down. Bound to sing eventually. Bamboo canes on your soles and toes soon get you chanting. Need to square Lucy, see the kiddies right. Poets? Just have to wait see if they made it. Maybe get word through, via the agent. Now if he could only get this cunted wheel nut loose he could be back home in Brixton before midnight.

As he turned left into Coldharbour Lane he saw two pandas, blue lights on, blocking the road. Four of Lambeth's finest were sussing a couple of surly spooks up against a fly postered wall. Alan thought he recognised the bigger one by his coconut. A shifter of mediocre shit from the Railton estate. Vinny or Vince depending on your acquaintance.

'Filth...' muttered The Mechanic. And it wasn't quite clear who he was referring to. 'This joint's about to blow. Fucking fuse is already lit.'

Al pranked his horn. One of the rozzers looked up, saw white, and waved him through.

The Mechanic parked up on the hard core outside the Victorian terrace and let himself in to the ground floor conversion of the pebbledash. The flat smelt musty with stale smoke and damp from two months of no heating. The kitchen walls had acquired a topcoat of mildew. He scooped up the pile of junk mail from the hall ignoring the brown envelopes, tossed the lot into the tiled fireplace, stuck on some

173

kindling, a few lumps of coal and lit it. Then he fired up the boiler.

The two through rooms that served as the living quarters were furnished *à la* garage. That is to say, they made no concession to any recognisable domestic interior. More like a greasemonkey workshop. A pair of bucket seats from an old Capri and a tatty vinyl bench out of a caravan made up the three piece suite. Lighting was perfunctory but functional. A series of caged high watt bulbs on lengths of cable that could be hung or hooked where desired. The décor was mostly black with hints of tobacco. Nick-knacks were predominantly plastic or turned steel and littered every surface. There was the odd poster. The Yardbirds. Nobby Stiles nobbling some poofter. No paintings, but a fair slickering of oil.

What should have been the dining room was given over to a disembowelled Triumph Bonneville. The bay window of the front parlour was dedicated to Al's stack. Two wardrobe sized speakers, a decent deck and a brutal looking amp. At each end of the sofa stood a yard high pile of vinyl which served as a side table.

The mechanic had a taste for skank reggae and when he was feeling truly mellow, skiffle. He racked up a Lonnie Don 45 on the spindle – *The Midnight Special* – and set it to repeat. He rolled a number from his private stash and lit up. Later, wallowing in the bath as he soaked away the road grime, he thumbed a few pages of the Old Wanker and fell asleep. No worries. He always kept the hot tap on a slow trickle to top up the water, letting the excess drain out through the bovver flow. The leccy and the gas were no problem either, as he had rerouted both to bypass the meters. Handy.

Al's gaff, home turf, no place quite like it.

MOUNTAIN DUES

By the time they had finished loading the last bale and pointed Dave's dinghy in the direction of the mother ship, Mustapha and his boys were near numb from the nuts down. It
was low tide but the beach shelved sharply. One minute they
were in up to their knees, the next it was chest deep. After an
hour and a half in the freezing brine they were well pickled.
No cucumbers that night, *cornichons* was more like it.

They whipped the mules back to the barn, stripped, lit a
smouldering fire of straw and rags and draped their soaked
cottons over the rumps of the beasts. Pretty soon they were
steaming. Mustapha handed out the remains of their provisions and then his instructions. They slept till dawn and
when they awoke the storm was in full fling. Raz and Rez
took the two bicycles and wobbled their way to the cousin's
farm. He lent them the Renault on a small rental and they
drove into town. No one was stirring as they pulled up outside the *Auberge du Port*. Raz unlocked the shutter over the
swing doors and they went inside. Behind the makeshift bar
was a trapdoor to the cellar. They put one half of the final
pay out from Alan behind a loose brick and picked up two
cases of adulterated whiskey. Then it was back out to the
courtyard, lock the shutter and return the taxi. They
marched off-road the mile to the barn, each hefting a case of
Johnny Water Black. Mustapha had the mules fed and loaded with straw bales by the time they got back. He strapped
the whiskey crates on top in plain view. The other half of the

pay out he wrapped in plastic and a rag soaked in mule micture. He stuffed the package deep into a nosebag and covered it with straw.

Mustapha had long rehearsed the numbers to himself. Fifty pounds a pound. Fifteen grand. Two years wages, ganging and slopping slops at the restaurant. The boat buggers could make ten times that, twenty if they parcelled it out. Enough for a farmer to retire on. If they made it.

It was a full day's hike back up the slopes of the Rif to their mountain eyrie. At noon they were waylaid by a local patrol. Mustapha had already paid for his passage home but the provo was insistent. Things had changed. Some fool tourist had washed up on the beach, without papers, making assertions. Disturbed, maybe crazy. Perturbing the peace be upon you. Mustapha fobbed him off with a crate of the watered down whiskey and a wad of *reals*.

Midafternoon the mule train came to an exposed promontory a thousand feet up. Mustapha called a halt. He took out his battered brass telescope and scanned the sea that separated Africa from Spain. At that distance it looked like a sheet of grey slate, the currents and waves no more than wrinkles on its surface. He made no attempt to spy the *Mona Gorda*, he didn't have the power.

Besides, from where he stood, one white speck out on the water looked much like any other. He folded the glass, gave a whack to the stern of the lead mule and they set off. The stiff breeze cooled the sweat on their backs as they began the final trudge up the mountain.

MEANWHILE BACK AT THE LAUNCH

Two of the three crew, the ones who could drive, were legless.

Nev, for obvious reasons. Although, for a while, they tried the less obvious expedient of lashing him to the wheel with his thick leather belt and a turn of rope. Employing his right crutch to thrust against any lurch to starboard, he managed twenty minutes of the hurly-burly before a particularly vicious set of waves flung him off balance completely and he buckled and sagged like a miniature Ahab strapped to the helm.

Shyno could stand upright for no more than a few moments before a new spasm jacknifed him and it was all he could manage just to straighten up again, try to assess their trajectory, before bowing to the next inevitable body blow.

At this point Lúcio, who had thus far displayed an otherworldly *sang-froid* in face of what he would have described as *a little loco difficulty*, pirouetted into the centre of the wheelhouse and with an infuriating mangle of the familiar cliché, declared,

'When the needs must, let the Devil drive.'

With which desideratum he pushed Shyno aside. Taking up a pugilistic stance before the juddering spokes of the helm he contemplated the steering mechanism. For what seemed a reckless spell he studied the involuntary jerks and gyrations of the unattended wheel, now and then lifting his head towards the darkness and planting his feet against the ever more violent motion of *Mona Gorda*'s hull. Finally, as if having absorbed all the necessary information that comes from a prolonged exercise and study of that craft, he took command of the boat.

Nev contrived himself a wedged position on the wheelhouse floor, callipers braced between the two benches, sitting upright, hands deployed as anchors.

Shyno had no choice but to mimic him, submitting to the now well established sea-sick rhythm, which brought his head down to his knees for the stomach press and empty release. He could feel his abdominals firming by the minute. From these slots, they had prime spots to watch as Lúcio got to grips with his latest ingenuity.

No need to exaggerate. There were odd lapses, experimental tropes, hubristic counter thrusts, lacunae. Gaps in other words, of attention. A worrying obliviousness to menace. An occasional lack of focus. Eagerness to showboat in the novelty of his mastery, but, no question, do you have, yes *I* do, I *do* have control.

You might well say that there is no great mystery about it. To take hold of a boat in extremity, with no prior knowledge of her workings, apart from a bout of desultory observation, and make her your mistress. Steer a fractious course through a force eight storm.

You could factor in a brief episode as a champion amateur flyweight boxer, attuned to incoming blows, dodging and giving as good or better in return. Or add to this a Latin dancer's possessed, fleet foot. He was a golden boot, after all. But this was not the beautiful game. By any reckoning it was what he would have termed: *Hunting in the dark. A dance upon no ground.*

How he mastered the conditions and their unquestionable peril was nevertheless mysterious. In short, without him, they would simply have foundered and sunk, more than full fathom five. As he was fond of reminding them, *The eyes are not seeds brother. Pearls are not eyes.*

It was both humbling and exalting to watch an amateur at work. Of course there was the odd quibble at the way he set about his business: that infuriating refusal to acknowledge precedents, established procedures, normalcy. A belligerent kind of self-possession which he pitted against the storm and as if he spoke in a common foreign language to the bemused elements, chanted to them, *subdue me, or be subdued.* Meanwhile he hummed and strummed the opening bars of Sibelius' 5th, as the boat cantilevered helter-skelter down the oblique faces of the hilly swells; then, as *Mona Gorda* wallowed in the lightless pit, he seemed to haul her upside with a stately cadence, his right arm urging her on like some conductor's twitching wand as he drove her to windward.

For the next three hours he manned the helm, and the longer the tussle went on the more like a dance it became. Although he could see nothing of the seascape around him, he seemed to have his own sonic apparatus tuned to the shifting masses of the waves. He knew intuitively when to yield and when to advance. He did it blind and by feel. It was unreal, yet altogether typical.

DAWN'S INVENTORY

Shyno guessed that he must have slept while the storm bludgeoned on.

Nev was still wedged in, wide-eyed and stoned, between the wheelhouse benches. Lúcio had one hand on the helm. With the other he was holding down a spread-out chart, assessing their position. He turned and looked down at the two of them prostrate on the floor. As if choosing his words without irony, he muttered the phrase of a poem of his which they both knew almost by heart:

'Their dawn is iron-black...'

And so it was. You would have thought that the first smudge of bleary light might have defused the imagined terrors of things that had gone thump in the night. Not so. What they were now seeing was like nothing they could have ever dreamed of. It had to be real to be conceived.

Shyno and Nev hauled themselves upright to get a proper view, straddling their bodies against the instrument panel. They were heading due east still and as the sun spread a gruel-grey light over their little world they began to make out the true dimensions of their folly. It was a seascape out of Brobdingnag. A panorama of swiftly moving cliffs and precipitous gorges. Shyno blanched. Nev whistled low. Lúcio hummed and muttered. Great slab-sided sullen waves advanced towards them.

Lúcio thrust the throttle down and the boat began its ponderous climb up the ragged face of an oncoming swell.

They stared out through the cabin windows, seeing only sky and the whipped spindrift of the crag above them, a long way above them. There was the interminable brief moment when it seemed she would simply slide back down the slope and then they were over the top.

Lúcio throttled off and they began the accelerating plunge down the other side. Ten, twenty, forty, sixty feet and still dropping into the wide-spaced valley floor, strangely smooth, but with sucking eddies, this time wondering whether she would pearl, keep on diving and founder. At the bottom of the trough they experienced a kind of lull, walled in by water. They could no longer hear the keening wind or the booming slosh of a wave top as it sluiced over their bow. Nor could they see any meaningful sky, just the rapidly advancing face of the next looming and somehow magnificent wave.

For the first time in a relatively short life, Shyno had reason to reflect on his own brief mortality. Not in that juvenile, abstract, down-the-road-a-ways way. But there, actual and imminent. Face it, you are going to die. It seemed somehow shameful to be quite so resigned and he glanced across at the other two, wondering if they felt the same presentiment.

TEMPEST TOSSED

All three of them were pressed up close to *Mona Gorda*'s streaming front windows as the 3D monster enveloped them. Lúcio appeared to have become possessed of an almost child-like glee. As if this were some extreme theme-park and he was the nerveless *enfant terrible*, airily daring and deriding a pair of reluctant parents he had dragooned for the ride.

It wasn't like a roller coaster, because they weren't attached to any rails and only the boat's stone weight kept them from being thrown into the sky. It was more akin to the motion of some kicking Brahman bull in a muddy rodeo, except no matter how wild the gyrations of the brute, they couldn't be unseated, even though they longed to be. So they clung on and rode the beast. Shyno had to resist the constant urge to shout a warning, indicate a turn, or cry out for more power but Lúcio anticipated the threat as if he had prior knowledge. There was no choice but to trust their new skipper. The seasickness had passed, only to be replaced by a different malaise. A lump like a brick in the centre of his gut around which he could feel his stomach contract and which he recognised for what it was. Fear.

As soon as it became clear that they were not in any immediate danger of sinking, Shyno allowed himself the first of several new dismaying thoughts. If *Mona Gorda* was making six knots, *if,* well the sea was running at least that, maybe more. So...

'We are not really going anywhere, are we?'

Lúcio gave him an unforgiving look, as if voicing the obvious were simply *de trop*.

'Well, at least when we go down, we appear to come up again.'

'Have you thought about the fuel?'

Lúcio had not. All three of them homed in on the gas gauge and saw that it was hovering a smidgeon below a quarter tank, or slightly less. Suddenly the eager drumming of the Perkins diesel seemed faintly profligate.

Shyno wasn't up to voicing any further conjectures. It was already eight in the morning, about the time they should have been making landfall. At the summit of each wave they had an unrestricted three-sixty view of the sullen chaos which surrounded them. A rough calculation put them standing still, if still was the word, midway between Spain and Morocco. Unable to head north toward land and just barely avoiding being funnelled back down through the Gibraltar straits and flushed out into the chilly, hilly wastes of the Atlantic. It was enough to make him want to regurgitate and reincarnate as a penguin.

Nev, as ever, found something to put it into perspective. Jabbing with his left crutch toward the port window he countered with a nervous chuckle,

'Check this fucker out.'

Beyond a certain number the odd inch or yard makes no great difference, it's just another digit. The crew were now deep in the realm of quantity. Each of them had had plenty of time to calculate what they were up against. So when *Mona Gorda* began the next strenuous assault on the wave face fronting her they could tell that it was steeper, deeper, longer, a good bit longer than her forty foot hull. But it was only a slope not a straight vertical. And if some commercial liner caught out in that same storm had radioed in a rogue wave sixty foot tall, would you have believed it if you hadn't been there, or wonder after all, if it was really *all that* or just *not small*?

Fishermen's tales. Hurracanoes.

What they saw on their port side a quarter mile off was a rust red oil tanker, a supersized one, beetling eastward as best as she could and making heavy work of it. She was long enough to straddle a half dozen of those chopped out hills, locked down and loaded. Yet she was struggling, they could tell. Each time she barged into one of the oncoming cliffs she put her bow down and piled into the wet mountain which fissured and then washed over her decks with an avalanche of foam. She must have had a cricket pitch's worth of freeboard on her but she was sounding and broaching like a harpooned whale.

The sight of her left them dumb. Big beast encounters bigger, thrashing it out. Meantime *Mona Gorda* corkscrewed on, bobbling like piece of pumice, ballasted with dope, nowhere bound.

Nev capped off this vision of his moment's loss of mirth with what had become the unreflective response of feckless youth in the face of every minor obstacle it ever stumbled upon.

'Bummer, man...'

To an already long list of morbid thoughts – *death by drowning, running on empty, police in different voices, going into the dark* – Shyno added the image of *Mona Gorda* being unceremoniously ploughed under by one of these wallowing beasts, oblivious to their presence, in possibly the busiest shipping lane on planet ocean.

'We have to change course.'

Just saying it cost Shyno most of his dwindling reserves of will. He had a sudden urge to wrench the wheel away from Lúcio.

'Zigzag! It's the only way, you fool.'

Now, to put your boat broadside on, in an oversized sea, is the depth of folly. First you rock, then you roll, then over, and out. Down the spout. Plug-holed. Definitely *not* the done thing. Even more risky than trying to turn your vessel about, if you can judge it just right, and run before the storm, surf the maelstrom and pray you don't get dunked, or sunk.

The first of the big swells they chose to traverse was neither the biggest nor the worst, but it was certainly the hairiest. Lúcio took on the approaching comber, a forty-footer, at about ten-thirty on the clock. Under the pressure *Mona Gorda*'s port gunwale pressed down hard into the water, her side deck awash, gushing with spume. There was a moment when it seemed like they wouldn't quite make the summit then she crested and teetered on the fulcrum. As she lumbered over and back down the rump of the receding swell, this time at four-thirty on the dial, it was her right side carving into the water. They were picking up speed. Instead of throttling back, Lúcio juiced her, top whack, so they were fairly hurtling into the suck. Just as she reached the base of the wave Lúcio spun the wheel hard to port and in surfing terms, pulled off a kind of slow motion bottom turn which left them running parallel between swells along the almost smooth valley floor, due North, battery to the left and to the right of them, at a brisk ten knots.

Shyno guessed the trough was maybe a hundred yards wide and they had no more than thirty seconds before the next onrushing wall. Inwardly he was counting down, eyes fixed on the follow up blow.

'Turn in! Now!'

Lúcio spun the helm to starboard. *Mona Gorda* laboured in response and began the next heart-stopping climb. It was another big one. It seemed that they had left it too late. The boat hit the wall at 45 degrees, too shallow an angle for that kind of ascent. Had it been a curler they would have simply wiped out. As it was they crabbed their way up the slope and took the summit almost sideways. Lúcio was correcting wildly and when they entered the *schuss* they were pointing straight down. Safe? More or less. It took a while to master the variations on this particular manoeuvre but they had plenty of time. There was a long day of this sport ahead and an almost indefinite number of precipices upon which to practise.

Shyno set his fragile mind on a single thought. *To be out of the swing of the sea.*

GEOMETRY ALWAYS SURVIVES

'Uh...Loose? Any idea where we are man, I mean, *roughly?*'

Nev had adopted the familiar, faintly wheedling form of address which he used when he had some pressing concern: like a letter he needed written for the DSS explaining why he hadn't signed on for three months; or backup for some minor dope deal he was planning. But usually it was money, as in,

'Got any *loose,* mate?'

On this occasion he wanted re-insurance.

Lúcio closed his eyes, took his right hand off the wheel and circled his forefinger above the creased chart before jabbing it down, speculatively, on a spot not far short of the coast of Malta. He opened his eyes to see where he had landed up and just managed to avoid being cats pawed by a vicious looking wave, before turning to a credulous Nev and saying,

'Only jesting. Actually, I was just working out the calculations myself.'

It was a complex formula. Triangulation times velocity. Nev tried to follow the meanderings of the equation but all he really wanted was the answer. The gist of it was as follows.

An estimated 38 miles from the point where they dropped off YaYa to the small port near Nerja on the Spanish coast.

A decent 2 hours progress with Nev at the wheel, averaging 8 knots, more or less on course = 16 miles. Take away leaves 22.

Storm hit at 4am.

Time now 10am.

4 hours heading in the wrong direction adds up to ZERO.

A couple of hours zigzagging, well, be generous. 2 miles.

Here Shyno's own slide rule kicked in. Each run parallel to the waves lasted about 30 seconds at 10 knots. That was almost 300 yards forward. But for every half minute spent advancing toward Spain they wasted twice that amount facing up into the sea, going nowhere slowly.

Which meant? Go figure.

Shyno reckoned they were only making about one actual mile per hour toward their destination at best. Which left roughly twenty more to go. At this rate it would be four or five in the morning on the next day before they reached Spain. By which time they would have long run out of fuel and possibly the will to live.

'I think we need to change course guys, you know, try to run *with* it. Pick up some speed. No?'

Lúcio looked at Shyno, then Nev.

'I'm afraid I have to agree.'

DA DO RUN RUN

Larry had been telling the truth when he flogged them *Laurene*. She was exceptionally stable and could hold plenty of water. Whether he had been referring simply to her freshwater capacity was another matter. He said that she had come through a force six gale on his trip down from Menton with only a slight easing of her seams, so perhaps he had discovered what her new crew were now finding out for themselves.

Bringing her about proved easier than imagined. At the end of one of their half minute, happy valley runs, they turned left instead of right and let the following sea take her from behind. Lúcio had never been near a surfboard in his life but he had seen the dynamics often enough on the Copacabana beaches to grasp the forces at work.

Mona Gorda's rump rose in the air and her high prow angled down. She began to gather speed. Her ten knots plus the six or so from the wave behind meant she bustled down the incline. It was a thirty foot wall of water but then there was the slope to take account of, so they had a good long drop-in before they made it to the bottom of the swell.

And that was when *Mona Gorda* put her nose in it, pearl dived and stopped dead in her tracks. Had it been a shorebreak they would have done a Dave. Technical wipe-out. But these were ocean giants, not rollers breaking on a beach, just huge haphazard combers dumping off their crests and rumbling on toward Africa and beyond. Still, *Mona Gorda* shipped several good bath tubs worth over her bow and even more of the same again at her rear. Lúcio throttled back and as the three of them turned to look around they saw the stern well almost full with two feet of frothing sea water, as if they had suddenly acquired their own on board Jacuzzi.

'Juice! Loose!'

It was Nev again. Saved the day. Lúcio put the stick down. La Gorda shuddered. She now had an extra five hundred pounds of wet ballast aboard and this was weight that she needed to shed fast. Crash diet or crash dive. There were two deck drains for just such a contingency but she had to be going forward for them to function. The next wave gave her some of the momentum she wanted and as she accelerated the water level in the stern began to drop. It took a couple of minutes to reach ankle depth but by that time they were already off again and surfing.

'Want to try some turns?' suggested Dr Know.

'Watch me' replied Lúcio. And proceeded to give a first rate impression of some Hawaiian pioneer, astride a waterlogged plank, ploughing up the waves.

ROSIE DEAR

Rich came to around noon that day with a hangover which he swore he would never endure again. And he kept that promise to himself over the years, although he broke many others.

At six months short of your 28th birthday you are not supposed to look down at your hands and watch them shaking uncontrollably, knowing that whatever you do or have done, there is nothing – not Quaaludes, codeine, exotic fix-me-ups, coke or Coca Cola – that is going to give you the stills. You have been derailed at Del Tremens junction. Rich accepted that what he needed was not a sedative, or a sugar fix, but an immediate sharpener.

Remedy: a glass of cold beer, a good glug of EVOO, a wedge of lime, followed by a *Crystal* chaser. Taxi into position. Await ground control. Ease off into the ether. Glide a while. Listen to some sounds. Choice is yours. A3 highly recommended. *Cumbia* if you have it. Eat plenty of fatty meat, pig's ears for preference. Re-boot with *Crystal*. Relax. Open up your palpitating, overworked heart and get with the plan. Revive if you can. Just don't dive.

Rich had only two of the ingredients to hand, so he swallowed down half a pint of cheap Spanish cooking oil straight from the bottle and sank a couple of icy Sols. Meantime he was trying to remember something he had forgotten or overlooked.

What sounded like several of Villa Nova's ratty shutters were clattering and banging in a staccato rhythm under the pressure of the wind. Rich looked at his watch, made a move toward the shower and thought better of it. The pool maybe. Got to *gush, flush the man.* Maybe not. He stumbled outside and scoped the thrashed foliage of the garden and the bruised sky. On an impulse he went back to the bedroom, dragged on a pair of bootcut Lees, t-shirt, his scuffed Frye kickers and went out foraging. He waded through a morass of unkempt vegetation, bypassed a thicket of gnarly rotting *árboles,* kicked his way through a tangle of melon vines, until he fetched up, six hundred feet above sea level a mile inland from the coast, contemplating what the estate agent had eulogised as *the view...*

Phew! This merited a line or two. A series of rocky, scrub covered, parched, descending scarps; odd drivelling rivulets choked with boulders; tinder dry slopes, cut through by a black snake of tar macadam winding down towards the block-busted tenements of Puerto Banus on his right. Numberless white cubes encircling a poisonous agglomeration of fibreglass and diesel with a few matchstick masts of actual wood. Over to the left, a couple of miles up the coast, the smutty hoard of Malaga.

But it was the sea that most discouraged him.

It just didn't look right. It was fucked up. The wrong colour. All over the place. Humungous. Black. But with an artex spray of caramel scum applied like icing to its surface. Ugly and scary.

'Pity any numbnuts caught out in that shit.' Rich muttered to himself and then remembered what he had forgotten in the brief lacuna between Enrique's opening *salud!* and this.

During the forty minute drag in the Jaguar sixty miles up the coast, Rich kept trying to reassure himself that at worst he was late for a pretty important date but that he would still show. *I'll be there.* Anyway the crew hadn't called to confirm. And who would contemplate a day trip on, of all days, a day like this?

As he pulled up to the entrance of the small private marina his best suspicions were confirmed. There were maybe three dozen berths of which only two were occupied. Both boats were modest day trippers, tarp wrapped for the winter. There was nobody about. Even the low rise half completed development that came with the docking appeared uninhabited. It was between seasons. It was perfect. Except for what was taking place just outside the protective harbour wall and which for the first time in his guilty rush Rich had the opportunity of experiencing at first hand.

The marina was no more than a diminutive natural cove, a typical Spanish *cala*, narrow but deep, maybe fifty yards wide at its mouth, across which from the left, two thirds of the way out, jutted a manmade sea wall of hewn boulders topped with prefabricated concrete plugs in the shape of jacks, dropped roughly into place. These interlocked in a random configuration, more or less level, creating a barrier about twenty feet high. The wall extended halfway across the throat of the cove leaving a fifty foot gap, then continued on to the other shore.

The water within the lagoon was barely ruffled by the wind, so tight and protected was the bay with its steep-sloped battlements on three sides. But it was heaving from the pressure of the sea at its post box of a mouth. The two cruisers were surging violently, twanging taut the slack of their mooring ropes. They looked like subjects under bondage threatening to break free from their restraints.

Rich stepped out of the Jag into the lash of a gusting thirty knot wind. He was soaked immediately. The whipped spindrift from the waves was sheeting back over the basin wall like driven rain. He was used to big seas. He was a child of Big Sur. He and a few fellow stoners would make the regular hike out from the San Fernando Valley and sprawl spaced out on the cliff top, looking down over the Pacific, tripping while the pipelines exploded.

Outrageous, dude

But this was something else. There was no pattern to it. No order or beauty. Just a harum scarum melee of malignant brute force.

He ducked for the cover of the car, excusing himself.

'No way they gonna be out in this kinda shit. No way!'

R Lee B poked the Pink Panther and flicked on the windscreen wipers to refocus his movie. He settled back into the fawn leather. It was 2pm. Spanish lunch hour. He was hungry. Hell, give those turkey tails a try, why not? A half dozen *escargots*. Time for a quick Nova siesta. Check out Gloria. Later. Back at Banuski? Sounding good to me.

G-L-O-R-I-A

Here comes the Knight, hehe...yeah, maybe, but I doubt it.

'Give my *nephew* a call...'

Hijo de puta Enrique! Metido. Cabrón.

Gloria extended a slender limb and drew the double bladed Babybliss disposable razor back down the length of a naturally smooth calf all the way to a creamy, caramel coloured inner thigh, sighed, and swished it in the bubbling water of her bath.

Shaving was a daily ritual, as for most men, but in her case almost unnecessary. Still, it was what women did and as far as she was concerned that was what she was. Female. She arched her spine to reveal a miniature pyramid of neat dark curls and looked dispassionately at the modest bud that designated her gender and contradicted her soul. She swept a hand down over her groin and tucked the evidence back between her thighs, crossed her legs and submerged herself in the foam.

Gloria was as critical of her body as any real girl, probably more so. As she stood before the marble framed mirror towelling herself dry, she made an unsentimental appraisal of what her genes had bequeathed her. Thick glossy black hair. Good cheekbones. Delicate chin. Small Adam's apple. Graceful neck. Fine boned shoulders. Adolescent breasts. Exaggerated nipples. Slim waist. Pert bubble butt. Great legs. Small feet, for a guy, size seven. Neat little toes. There was just one addition and one thing missing to make her a girl and not a *gurl*. Otherwise she was perfect.

Gringo's going to find out sooner or later and when he does he will freak. Never be content with just O and A levels. He's going to require the full degree.

Enrique was sympathetic though, supported her, give the old *gato* that. Tío had been overseeing some mines at Muzo when a ten year old contracted assassin had loosed off a dozen rounds from a semi-automatic, half of which had lodged permanently in his back, maiming but not quite managing to kill the old bird. Which was why he moved with an extravagant limp and had earned the nickname of an immortal, old nine lives, *El Cojo*.

Maybe that brush with his Maker had mellowed him. Maybe he desired her. She was the only orphaned child of his brother, victim of a more accurate *sicario*. Her mother died giving birth. Enrique took her in, stopped her from running wild, accepted her androgyny. He had even offered to pay for surgery. But Gloria wasn't interested in any enhancing or realignment. She liked herself just the way she was. Tío's meddling with the gringo was protective, nothing more. He didn't want some ignorant powder punk messing up her head when he realised what kind of girl he was going with. When Rich found out he'd been making it with a chick with a dick, Gloria was pretty sure it wouldn't come as a happy surprise. He would be pissed. Major league.

So what to wear?

Mmm....

Well, when in Spain. She chose an off the shoulder black on red polka dot flamenco calf length dress, strappy heels, combs in her pinned up hair, carmine lippy and a black lace shawl. Strumpet about to be widowed on her second date.

Fuck it. Fuck me, Richly.

Escargot was alternately picking at his teeth with a short plastic stick and spearing the odd plump mussel or prawn from the remains of their overgenerous *paella*. They had agreed on a late lunch, much to the discomfiture of the restaurant kitchen, who were only too familiar with tourists flouting the local conventions. Gloria had swayed them.

It was six-thirty in the evening. The canopy above their heads was no longer snapping in the wind, which had tailed off and the evening air was cool and mild. The last feeble attempts of the sun to penetrate the cloud cover were extinguishing themselves in a purplish haze. Lights in the marina were flicking on.

Rich hailed the waiter. He managed *la cuenta, por favor* and paid up.

'Wanna take a stroll?'

The *tapas* bar fronted onto the third of two dozen finger piers. It was still all first division stuff. Rank upon rank of sleek, shark nosed fibreglass booze barges, bobbing at anchor, a few with riding lights on but the majority darkened. It was mid early season.

Hand in hand they moseyed along *mole* number one where the big boys berthed. Here were immaculately groomed three master sloops, all glinting brass and scrubbed teak. Brutish mega yachts with helicopter pads and dropdown panels in their sides which revealed the usual array of toys, jet skis and subsidiary tenders. Further out, ships of the ocean that had no need to be docked there other than to proclaim themselves and dismiss you as you pondered on their unimaginable cost.

It all seemed so right on to Rich. He had a hot cute coke

connection on his arm. The pink Jag was swaggering right there on the promenade. All he needed was those literary loons with their bundles of dope to get their shit in tow and he was a man ready to be made.

At the far end of the esplanade there rose a squat, conical stone edifice pinpricked with satellite equipment, aerials, and a small conning tower. Around its base spread a concrete yard with a couple of wrought iron benches, a few desultory plantings of palm and yucca and that was it. The Spanish maritime border. They sat down on a bench, snuggled up and gazed out beyond the harbour mouth at the turbulent Med.

'Madre mía! Pobrecitos...'

Gloria was pointing with one exquisite finger out over the mashed up waves toward a small, white, beleaguered boat that appeared to be heading their way. She summed up her disbelief with a weary, heartfelt dismissal of the folly of the world.

'Got to be some kinds of *tontos* to be out in this.'

Rich stood up to get a better look. The vessel was about half a mile off the harbour wall and performing an erratic series of manoeuvres as she fought the current and the waves. He had an abrupt sinking feeling in his gut and immediately regretted those last few prawns. Surely not? It couldn't be. But it was. His immediate instinct was the habitual one. Glide and hide. He turned to Gloria, took her hand and murmured,

'Say we head back to your place. Do a few lines. Check out the sunset?'

The fact that it was already almost dark and what little light remained was no more than a yellowing bruise on the horizon was beside the point. He wanted out of there but he also wanted a view. Gloria's apartment was set back only a few dozen yards from the tower and the customs area. He figured they would have ringside seats from her first floor balcony.

Gloria shrugged and pressed closer to him.

'Sure, let's go inside. *Tengo frío.*'

ARE WE THERE YET?

The final six hours the crew endured aboard the *Mona Gorda* were spent in a monotony of gloom punctuated by despair. Lack of food played a part for there wasn't any and no one had eaten since they left Tetouan. The remains of their provisions were a congealing smear on the cabin bunks below and even if they had had a mind to scrape up the residues, the short passage down the companionway steps might have proved more debilitating than their hunger. So they smoked incessantly, took regular sips from Lúcio's flask and those small poisons sustained them.

Their mood became a mirror of the motion of the boat. When she was up so were they. Each achieved summit of a wave produced the kind of momentary delirium you might have expected if the lookout had halloed *Land Ho*! Instead there was only the dispiriting vista of yet more valleys and hills and a vast empty waste of water. Time played its familiar tricks. The daylight hours seemed to scurry toward darkness, while the minutes in between stretched out interminably.

Shyno was taunted by a phrase from a song - *gimme just a little more time*...but for what? To get there. Before nightfall, before the fuel ran out. Every second was like a finite countdown and the upshot was they needed an answer soon. In their hearts they knew they could hardly afford one single moment longer out on that sea.

Nev never complained once, though the chafing of his

irons as he braced himself against the lurching of the boat had already rubbed his legs raw. Lúcio was absorbed in some private, pre-Queensbury brawl with the storm, a bare knuckle bout with no limit on the rounds. Shyno had entered into a reverie which could only pass for a waking nightmare.

No one spoke much. There was little to say. Occasional gasps as they crested a particularly vicious sea. Murmurs of approval as Lúcio negotiated an awkward turn. Occasional oaths, whether of prayer or blasphemy, then silence again apart from the muffled boom of the maelstrom within the coffin of the wheelhouse.

At around teatime with the autumnal light failing the red bulb of the reserve fuel tank flickered and came on. No one had a precise idea what this indicator meant. No one had bothered to ask. Nor was there a spare can of fuel to hand. For all they knew they were already running on vapour.

This final complicating factor in the already confused mathematics of their lack of progress threatened a short circuit in Shyno's brain. A dull mantra overtook his thoughts.

The slower you go, the less fuel you consume, but the longer it takes to arrive. The more you deviate from the path, the further you must travel.

'I think we're going to have to make a run for it.'

'I do wish you would make up your mind.'

Lúcio was understandably put out.

'First we run *into* it, then *with* it. What are you suggesting now?'

'*Across* it. In a straight line. No more zigzagging. If we don't, it's just a matter of which gives out first. The diesel or daylight.'

'Beam on, as you say? At full throttle? In this?'

'Yes. Not exactly. Eight knots. Maximum fuel efficiency.'

Nev gave him a dubious look and shrugged,

'Alright by me mate, if you're sure?'

Shyno was only sure of one thing. If they didn't change direction they were going to end up out at sea, in the dark, in the middle of the storm, for a second night running, adrift. He was counting on three things in their favour. *Mona Gorda*'s weight, her height and her width. That she was heavy and low and broad enough not to turn turtle, though she would certainly roll. *Just not over* was how he put it to himself.

'It might get a bit hectic. But I can't see any other way.'

Lúcio stepped back from the wheel and let Shyno squeeze through in front of him before taking up position in the middle of the trio. He laid an arm across each of their backs so that they formed the loose knit front row of a rugby scrum and they braced themselves as Shyno took the helm. They were on a heading West propelled by a following sea. He eased the wheel to starboard and the compass swung round to North. They were in a deep wide valley and each of them swivelled eyes right to watch for the incoming feed.

'Hang on!'

Mona Gorda responded like one of those round bottomed dolls, a Polish one, which you try to push over and which always springs back. She leant hard down onto her port side and Shyno could feel the combined weight of the other two pressing him up against the wheelhouse window. They rode like that, canting sideways, as the boat crabbed up the face of the wave and then, as it slid by beneath her rump, she swung over like a pendulum to the other extreme and they dipped back down on the reverse plane. At the base of the swell she righted herself in two short rolls like a dugong, then chugged off along the valley floor at a brisk eight knots. It was not the kind of motion you could wholly trust in. It was not recommended. A degree of sway too far either way and she would roll over. And if she did she would never right herself again. The gang would have found themselves upside down in their own concrete sarcophagus, taking in water, till she sank like the proverbial. Instead *Mona Gorda* barrelled along, rocking and rolling, as if she had been custom built for just such conditions.

The crew were not so well designed. Each swing of the metronome crushed them together, first on one side then on the other. After ten minutes of this Lúcio, who was the filling in the sandwich, reached back behind him and grabbed hold of the four bench cushions. He wedged one down on Shyno's left side, and one on Nev's right, between their shoulders and the wheelhouse bulkheads. The other two he held against his torso and then wormed his way back in between his companions. They now made a snug fit across the front of the cabin and when *Mona Gorda* rolled they rolled with her as if part of the fixtures.

An hour or so passed before they saw what looked like a massed bank of black cloud strung out along the horizon. It was near dusk and in the darkness it appeared as a series of undulating humps that might have been mountains. As they drew closer, two separate swarms of what seemed to be fireflies began flickering like orange embers at the skyline. Then they realised that what they were seeing *were* mountains, not a wall of cloud, and the amber sparks clustered at their foot the first evening lights of human habitation.

It should have been a moment of triumph and relief but they were too exhausted and besides they were still several miles off with the red light on. They could just make out the illuminations of two distinct settlements some distance apart.

'Left or right?' murmured Shyno and without waiting for an answer nudged the helm toward port. It was not easy to restrain the urge to give her more speed. But there was no need. *Mona Gorda* was doing just fine as she was.

They were all focused on the lights of the town as they battered their way in toward the shoreline. It was a town, wasn't it? They screwed up their eyes like viewers of an impressionist painting seen through a bobbing crowd. They couldn't quite make out the detail. There, closer in shore, the seas were even more confused and unpredictable, rebounding from the coast and colliding with the incoming swells. The last dregs of the sunset had sunk into the West and *Mona Gorda* had reverted to her former motion. Pitch and yaw, buck and plunge. Shyno was struggling with the helm. He throttled back to five knots but it made little difference. It was like flying into a night sky full of shooting stars, except that it was land they heading for and no sign of a port. A few hundred yards more and they would have to start thinking about turning away or risk running aground. Shyno steered the boat northwest, parallel to the coast. As he did he glimpsed a green flash ahead, then a red, and rising up behind what appeared to be a squat tower with a beam of sharp white light revolving at its summit.

For the first time in what had been a long spell, especially for Lúcio, he spoke.

'If I am not mistaken, that looks very much to me like Puerto Banus.'

SAFE HARBOUR

Mona Gorda was about a quarter of a mile east of the sea wall that protected the marina and more or less the same distance out from the shore, though it was tricky to judge. The wheelhouse windows were caked with rime and being a truly bare boat there were no windshield wipers to improve the view. It was like peering through semi-frosted glass.

Shyno finally got some sort of fix on the mouth of the port as they shadowed the length of the harbour wall. The entrance was fifty yards wide and marked by the universal green and red beacons. Under fairer conditions it would have seemed more than generous, even for a much larger vessel. But with the prevailing current and contrary wave patterns, he felt like an arthritic tasked with threading string through the eye of a needle. He took aim at a point a hundred yards right of the starboard marker and nursed the boat nearer. It looked an unpromising angle. His idea was to slip slide in until they were nearly square to the aperture, turn her hard over, then give it full power.

To Rich Lee, sitting hunched over the railing of the apartment balcony, it looked as if the driver had got it calamitously wrong, but he was mistaken. A benevolent wave picked up the boat by its broad rump and swept it forward on its crest, then rumbled on, leaving *Mona Gorda* in a trough of slack water. She turned inward and with an unhurried gait, motored the last fifty yards out of the maelstrom into the calm of the channel.

'Looks like they made it, babe,' sighed Gloria, setting down a pair of Piña Coladas and a bowl of lightly toasted macadamia nuts.

'Yeah, for a minute there, I thought those cats were gonna crash.'

On board the *Mona Gorda* no one was talking, they were signing with gestures. Lúcio stroked the underside of his upturned chin with the back of his right hand and flicked his wrist into space. *Va fan culo.* Nev put two fingers to his temple and made an audible click. Shyno dragged a stiff index across his throat and lolled his throbbing head sideways. *It's over...*

But it wasn't yet.

Rich was affecting a nonchalance that he didn't feel. This was not cool. In fact it was what he would have described as *heat* and way too much of it. He took a sip of his coconut shake, scooped a handful of nuts and to distract himself small talked Gloria,

'Uh, Enrique, when's he back in town?'

'A couple of days, *papi*, and what about your friends?'

'Yeah, any time now hon, any time.'

***

Shyno reduced speed to four knots, harbour limit, as they doglegged right out of the main channel into the marina proper. *Mona Gorda* was dwarfed by the thirty foot sea wall on her starboard side. Ahead to port he could see the communications tower and a stretch of brightly lit concrete pier, punctuated by gleaming black iron stanchions noosed with short coils of mooring rope. At intervals along the side of the dock, white painted tractor tyres, slung as fenders. There was

206

a sparsely planted area in front of the tower and behind and beyond, the horseshoe of construction, on going, of low tiered condos. At their base, a curving parade of boutiques, restaurants and a milling crowd, promenading up and down the esplanade, stooping to admire the line of flash motors parked at the heads of the piers.

All this was glimpsed through the salt covered windows of the wheelhouse cabin. A kind of soft focus movie set, with the main players about to be introduced, followed by the supporting cast of boats. Rank upon rank of them, from the simply stellar to the almost mortal, harnessed according to pedigree, in descending size and importance. For an awkward instant their basic craft seemed entirely out of place. As if they were contravening some mercantile dress code that no borrowed suit or tie could gloss over. Shyno felt the same as his co-conspirators. Faintly shabby, unshaven, more than somewhat the worse for wear.

All such niceties were swiftly put by as their new dispensation dawned on them. Safely delivered out of harm's way straight into the beckoning arms of another. Only this time a human one, with a peaked cap and drab olive green uniform, clipboard to hand, waving them on and in; and behind him a pair of Guardias Civiles, semi-automatics at hand, lolling at the foot of the tower, smoking. *Ducados* no doubt. Their very own Spanish Customs welcoming committee.

This way, señores, por favor...

The summons carried across the narrow channel and in through the wheelhouse door, open for the first time in fifteen hours, as Lúcio stepped out into the stern and started untangling a snarl of mooring rope muddled in the corner. The fresh salt air mingled with the fug of sweat, stale smoke and the sour-sweet scent of vomit. The reminder put a new cramp in Shyno's stomach where the adrenaline was already working its acid. He gave a nod to Nev urging him outside and into view. He had acquired a superstitious faith in Neville's power as a totemic force when confronting authority. A conviction that the mere sight of a cripple had the power to disarm and charm. Or if nothing else to provide a distraction.

He tweaked the helm to port, angling toward the dock and was about to throttle back into neutral when the Perkins diesel gave a sudden involuntary hiccupping cough, rattled its dozen tappets and died.

Mona Gorda was still under way, without power, so had no reverse gear. Shyno thought about straightening the helm to avoid a collision but realised the correction would only bring them into line with the exquisitely carved bowsprit of a solid three master jutting out into the channel from the adjacent pier. Instead he aimed for the nearest tractor tyre and bellowed to Lúcio,

'Try to hold us off at the bow!'

Inertia. Momentum. Weight. Velocity.

At the last moment Shyno spun the helm to starboard. *Mona Gorda* came half around. At two knots she rammed into the fender, bounced off and then like a bumper car slammed against the tyre again and stopped. Her hull reverberated with the shock. Nev pitched sideways, but not into the water. Lúcio, bow rope in hand, was propelled over the guard rail and managed an almost dignified landing on the pier. Shyno turned off the ignition and hurried to the stern in time to receive a looping coil of rope from the Customs Officer, which he slipped around a cleat and used to draw the boat in alongside the dock.

Rich observed the landing with a touch of *schadenfreude*. He had been against the plan from the start, in part because it relegated him to a bit player in the proceedings. He thought he knew better where Lúcio's talents lay and it wasn't aboard a concrete barge with a pair of klutzes, messing about with bulk cargo, when a couple of keys of the white stuff could be handled much more discreetly and with almost the same pay out. Still, he was concerned. His prize asset was just ten feet from jeopardy. Nev, almost as valuable, was lying in a sprawl of crutches on the stern deck. Shyno meanwhile appeared to be on the point of licking the customs official's boots.

So it might have looked from above. From below, as he straightened up, tying off the mooring rope, Shyno found himself staring at his own potato faced features in the highly polished domes of the officer's toecaps. He felt a sudden urge to confess. He was not really cut out for this kind of lark. It was a mistake, a mess, a caper gone wrong. He had a plodding, methodical approach to crime and it was not going to plan. Contingencies, even such as this, might have been factored in, but he didn't possess the brio, the improvisatory skills, to handle them. So he looked up the length of the uniform. acknowledging its creases, its leather and steel accoutrements, and an ingrained deferral to authority prompted a subservient smile.

'A fortunate escape. You appear to have the gods on your side.'

The Spaniard made an expansive gesture with his right arm which seemed to encompass all the rigours of the storm and their ignominious arrival. 'Perhaps you should see to your companion?'

Nev was struggling like an overturned insect to right himself. Lúcio stood off to the side, bow rope to hand, holding *Mona Gorda* in to the pier. Immigration. Customs. Anything to declare? Only our stupidity and incompetence, sir.

Shyno was not in the habit of being self critical but on this occasion he felt there was more than reasonable cause. And the reason was rivets. Many dozens of them. Not screwed back into their rivet holes in the aluminium frame which sealed off the hatch to the bilge and the bales.

'Your friend?' the officer repeated, sounding concerned.

Shyno had been abstracted. He snapped straight, just managed to avoid an involuntary salute and about faced. Nev was having trouble getting a purchase with the rubber tips of his crutches on the wet deck. Shyno hauled him to his feet and propped him on the bench in his usual corner. He made a few solicitous enquiries and fussed over him, prolonging the moment before he would have to face the official. He was trying to compose his features into some sort of noncommittal expression, anything to conceal the sense of guilt that he felt sure must be already obvious. As he turned back toward the pier he saw Lúcio tie off the bow line and walk over to the officer, right hand extended.

'Good evening, thank you for assisting us. Not the most propitious moment to run out of fuel. But given the conditions outside, we may have been more than fortunate. By the way I am *Señor* Lúcio, the owner; my driver Shyno and our lucky mascot, Neville. Would you care to come aboard? Or if your office would be more comfortable.'

'No, here will be fine. Jose Murillo. *A su servicio.* Duty Customs Officer. *Con permiso.*'

He was about to place his boot onto the white vinyl bench cushion when he hesitated. There was no other way of boarding apart from jumping straight down onto the deck. Shyno reached into the wheelhouse for a beach towel which he spread out on the seat. Jose stood on it and then stepped down into the stern, his boot tips two inches from the frame around the hatch. Before he had time to sit, Shyno used the towel to wipe any moisture from the bench.

'*Muy amable.*'

It was a minor courtesy but clearly not the kind the official was accustomed to. No doubt he was more familiar with the barely disguised impatience of the vulgar foreign rich, treating him as some minor irritant. A tiresome mosquito whom they tolerated and would have squashed were it not for his office. Politeness, respect, consideration? Rarely. In truth, he was nothing more than a low paid civil servant, a rubber-stamper. And though these visitors appeared far from wealthy they were behaving, well, like *caballeros*.

'Gentlemen. A few brief formalities. Your passports. Travel itinerary.'

'Shyno, would you mind? In my briefcase.'

José Murillo was a well upholstered, unassuming, middle aged pen pusher. His one concession to contemporary modes was a faintly preposterous pair of Zapata-like moustaches and a set of jaw length, carefully trimmed sideburns. When he removed his cap he revealed a smooth bowling ball skull with a monkish fringe of close cropped salted black hair above and behind his ears, which were tiny. He was perspiring although the evening was cool. Shyno handed him the passports and sat down beside Nev.

The last time a foursome had sat around the stern benches was in Ceuta and The Mechanic had been dealing. Now Jose found himself in the same position. Nev opposite, Lúcio to his left side, Shyno across at an angle. There was a game in play but only three of them knew the stakes. The hatch had become their table and each had his feet close to the chips. Shyno thought of Lord Jim, fixated on a patch of rust, trying to calculate if this was the moment to jump. He willed himself to maintain eye contact with their guest and not draw his gaze downward. Jose made his opening gambit. He was not so much suspicious as baffled, embarrassed to state the obvious. So he didn't.

'What was your last port of call?'

'Nerja.' Lúcio replied.

Shyno passed, as did Nev.

'Date of departure?'

'Three days ago, around noon as I recall, yes?'

Shyno and Nev nodded, wondering where this was going.

'Two hundred miles and three days. Not *all at sea*, I presume?' Murillo appeared dubious.

'Oh far from it. We are rank amateurs when it comes to any sort of boat business. Nothing so bold. We put in at a couple of small *calas* overnight. Day trippers. Coastal hugging and all that.' Lúcio called.

'Date of arrival in Spain? Ah, here it is, Palma, September 21st. Visas? Yes, all in order. Three months leave of stay.'

Jos'e was flicking through the pages of their passports, occasionally looking up and glancing at the crew, offhandedly it seemed, but to Shyno it was the gaze of a bluffing inquisitor. He had nothing but he thought that they did. A certain fastidiousness that went with his sharply pressed creases and shiny toecaps and pursey mouth. He was playing the Fool. Next thing you knew he would be saying *naughty night to be out in, nuncle.*

'We made a mistake!' Shyno blurted out and appeared to fold.

Lúcio gave him a cool look. Nev fiddled with his braces. José clicked his boot heels together.

'We moored up in a bay forty miles west of here, yesterday. We heard the weather was deteriorating and thought we could ride it out. We set two anchors. It should have been enough. Then the storm broke. The hooks were dragging. There was no choice. We had to go to sea. We would have been wrecked on the shore otherwise.'

'And where was this precisely?'

'There's no name on the chart. See? It was just a stopover.'

'Why didn't you radio the coastguard? Send out a mayday. We have no record of a distress call. *Perdóname*. I know you must be exhausted. No one would choose to be caught out in that.'

Shyno appeared to suffer a brainstorm.

'This is a bare boat. *Desnudo! Comprende?* There's nothing on it. Nothing at all. Take a look around. No bloody dinghy, no auxiliary motor, no navigation system, no radar, we more or less steer by the stars when you can see them. That's why we stuck to the coast. I'm just a hired hand. As for piloting this *puta de piedra*, it's like driving a stone. *Disculpe*. We have been eighteen hours stuck out in this filthy storm and I am tired, sick to my stomach. I thought we weren't going to make it. So if you have any more questions, ask the owner. I need to lie down.'

José was taken aback. He hadn't expected this outburst. Nev looked distracted. What was the skipper playing at? Lúcio assumed it was a diversionary tactic, unscripted. Or Shyno had finally lost it. He plumped for the former, before his companion got carried away and started believing his story. But he knew he could use it to their advantage.

'Now now, Shyno.' Lúcio tried to mollify him and made a gesture of apology toward Murillo. 'We are out of danger. No need to upset yourself further.'

'Danger? Danger! Well if that's the case, perhaps this officer will just put us out of our misery and then we can all take a shower, get some food and rest. I'm all in and about ready to resign.' With which Shyno stood up, appeared to stifle a retch, covered his mouth with his hand and shuffled off through the wheelhouse and down into the cabin.

The sarcasm was not lost on José Murillo. The outburst was reminiscent of many other encounters with spoilt, over-indulged prima donnas on the verge of hysteria, but different. The fellow seemed tormented, somehow haunted.

'Please excuse him,' said Lúcio. 'It has been a very long rope and I believe he is at the end of it. He takes his responsibility for all this much too seriously. He is young and not that experienced.'

Nev caught the drift of the play and started drawing attention to himself as only he could. He reached down to his right knee and started fumbling with the mechanism of the calliper beneath the fabric of his trousers. He snapped open the lock and used both hands to bend and re-straighten his leg as if stretching it. Then he reversed the procedure and started on his left limb without looking up, self absorbed and unselfconscious. This time he pulled up his trouser leg to examine the brace and in so doing revealed a glimpse of the damage done by the many hours of chaffing. He rolled the trouser back down. Grasping his two crutches he attempted to lever himself into a more upright comfortable position on the bench, then gave up, unsuccessful. He sighed, lifted his right thigh, crossed it over his left, folded his arms and gazed at José with an expression of stoic humility.

It was a masterstroke. Murillo's plump features flushed with shame. He had been caught staring.

Lúcio cleared his throat. 'Sir, you are more than welcome

to look us over. As you can imagine this has been something of an ordeal.'

José reacted as though he had been invited to take a tour, then refreshment, in some indigent's hovel.

'No, no thank you. I think I have seen all I need.'

Lúcio, ever the punisher, wasn't going to let this rotund soul get off quite so easily.

'You were asking about our itinerary?'

Shyno lay on the sticky cabin bunk listening to the discourse of the master as he dallied with the customs official, reeling him in every time he threatened to escape. What he told him does not matter. *Se non è vero è ben trovato.* And of course the officer discovered everything about them but uncovered nothing.

***

Rich watched the dumb show unfold much in the way he looked upon life in general. As a movie in which he saw himself auditioning for a more prominent part. For the moment however he was content to remain in the stalls, munching on costly nuts and slurping on his slushy, which Gloria replenished at regular intervals puzzled at the gringo's fascination for such a commonplace event.

She had lost count of the bumbling tyros who fouled mooring lines, snagged anchors, scraped hulls, made wake in the marina, cursed their crews, got drunk and fell overboard. Messing about in boats. It was everyday stuff and it used to amuse her. Not any more. At least it was keeping the *tooter* occupied, which suited her fine. She hadn't yet thought of a way to break the news of her deception and wasn't sure she could handle any sudden discovery. The only real hold she had over him was powder and the connection with Enrique. She wasn't sure if she could trust him on that score either. Maybe when the *socio* showed up she would know better. Meantime she had to keep him out of her pants and entertained and the scene down below was doing just that.

After about twenty minutes the official stood up, shook hands with Lúcio and Neville and hailed the two *Guardias Civiles*. They stubbed out their butts and strolled over to the Mona Gorda. There was a brief guttural confab in Spanish, a bit of shoulder rolling, then each of them took hold of a mooring rope and began dragging the Mona Gorda along the dockside in an easterly direction. José conducted operations and Lúcio monitored their own fenders to keep her off between the gaps in the tractor tyres. The boat wasn't exactly dead weight but she was twelve and a bit tons so the cops had to work at it. What Nev would later describe in a stoned apotheosis as,

'A pair of Spanish pigs, mate, like dray horses, except it wasn't beer they were hauling, but our dope.'

It wasn't far to go. A hundred feet down the dock stood the dispensary, diesel and regular. Jose unlocked the siphon and Lúcio gave her a good long glug. He proffered a bundle of notes which Murillo counted before peeling off the requisite. Gesturing ahead into the marina he made a circular pointing movement with his arm and then the three uniforms headed back to the tower. More shrugging, head scratching, trouser hitching, cigarettes offered and lit. The general consensus: *bufones, turistas.*

Shyno reappeared in the wheelhouse, saw that their lines were clear and turned the ignition key. She fired first time.

'Pier number 3, skipper. Berth toward the end on the east side, no wake if you please.' Lúcio was in mocking mode.

'Just give us your instructions, crew standing by. All hands Nev, let's make a decent show of it. No fumbling now.'

Shyno eased her away from the fuel dock, gave the three master a wide margin, chugged past piers one and two, turned in, spotted their slot, eased off the throttle, spun her slowly round and reversed into the gap between two fifty foot gin-joints taking pains not to trouble their fenders. They tied up, slung out their own plastic bumpers, cut the Perkins and then the three of them sat down in the stern deck to check on their neighbours. They were either out or away. The crew slumped into a reverie, stunned by the effrontery of the whole charade.

'Fancy a pint and bite to eat? I'm starving.' Nev was the first to venture.

'Perhaps we should spruce up a bit first,' said Lúcio.

'We are pretty rank.' said Shyno. 'I'll hook up the power and water. Who's first in the shower?' Lúcio, of course.

An hour later, at eight o'clock, the trio emerged onto the catwalk. Nev had contrived a pirate look with a colourful silk kerchief tied round his temples and knotted at the side. He hadn't shaved and was naturally swarthy. A pair of skull rings on both thumbs, *Obatala*'s necklace, a white cotton waistcoat unbuttoned at his chest and the obligatory crutches added to the effect. All he lacked was a parrot. Shyno went androgynous. Sunshine smile singlet, bare midriff, black suede hipsters. He was barefoot. He still wore Yemanja's string of beads. With his long auburn hair, blue eyes and high cheekbones, he looked like a tall, flat chested girl trying to pass for a guy. Lúcio opted for the tried and trusted. Just the two piece rumpled linen suit, no shirt, burgundy leather buckled slip ons, matching briefcase. Elegua's chain in black and red round his throat. Silver marquisate ring on his left pinky.

All the almost-young dudes.

They sauntered down the finger pier in their finery, stopping here and there to deprecate a particularly vulgar stinkpot or admire the rare example of craftsmanship, lovingly cared for, of some proper wooden boat. As they neared the promenade, drawn on by a waft of grilling seafood, they spotted, amid a lineup of criminally expensive wheels, the sleek pink contours of their own Jaguar.

'I thought I told that idiot to be discrete.'

'Perhaps he's trying to blend in.' Shyno made a gesture toward the line of limos, sports cars and recreational vehicles that adorned the harbour front. An orange Lamborghini, a yellow Ferrari, a sky-blue 450SL and an incandescent Pontiac Firebird were just a selection of the Jag's near or immediate neighbours.

'That's not the point and you know it. It's bad enough us having landed up here, at least Bizarre had the choice.'

'Well, no one seems to be paying us much mind. We might as well be invisible.'

This was not exactly true, for Nev was a curio in any context, even amidst the circus of Puerto Banus. And Rich was clocking their every move from the apartment balcony.

'Bit like South Beach, but without the beach,' said Nev.

'Or the architecture.'

Lúcio had an unabashed fondness for the rundown Art Deco district of lower Miami, having spent several months holed up on the shabby fringes of the Cuban enclave, pursuing both business and pleasure.

'Food's probably better here, though. A chap can only stomach so many beans. Shall we give *El Cabrón* a try?'

It seemed the obvious choice. The handwritten chalkboard of daily specials made enticing promises, the Jag was in plain view and they could look straight back up the dock to where the boat was berthed. The evening had turned almost balmy and apart from the regular muffled boom, followed by silvery sheets of foam flung into the distant air against the harbour wall, the storm was something that was taking place elsewhere, not there under the blue canvas that stirred above their heads as they sat down two tables away from Rich's earlier tryst. Nev couldn't resist. In a passable imitation of the gringo he said,

'Gee, guess I'm gonna have to go for the *escargots.*'

Shyno thought that he might just manage some bread and a bowl of soup.

*

Rich was sitting on the balcony wondering how to make an early exit without seeming rude. Gloria was inside the apartment having the same dilemma. Rich settled on the truth, improbable as it seemed. He was both drunk and yet still suffering from a sinister *guayabo* and he had an incipient gurgling gyp in his gut. A bad mollusc or a case of the frights. Gloria was sympathetic. He was more than understanding when she confessed it was her time of the month. She laid out a few fat lines on the rose granite table and they rubbed noses for a while. Just when they thought they might change their minds and rub something else, Rich butted out and saw himself to the door.

Nev, alert as ever, clocked his inventor swaying on pier number 1, trying to appear nonchalant but looking shifty, just as the waiter set down a plate of sizzling snails, burgundy style, in front of him. He leant forward and sniffed.

'Mmm, garlic with gristle and a baker's dozen to boot.' He looked over to Lúcio and nodded in the direction of the yank. Lúcio stood up, beckoned to Escargot and asked the waiter if he would kindly set another place and bring a menu. Rich made a pretence of appearing not to see them. A long appraisal of some towelhead's gilded barge, a lingering peruse of a boutique's window dressing, before he sidled through the maze of diners at the *tapas* bar and greeted the crew like newmade acquaintance.

'So guys, how was the trip?'

'Breezy,' said Shyno.

'Too right,' added Nev. 'Want a taste?' He winkled a bogey out of its shell. Rich hesitated and declined.

'I was there you know, at the marina, waiting on you guys, but you didn't show. No phone call. Nothing. And this frigged storm just blew up out of nowhere. I didn't figure you would try it on in this. Thought maybe you'd holed up somewhere to wait it out, you know?'

'And where might that have been? said Lúcio. He gave Rich an arch look and studied the menu.

'Well, sure, I get you. But you must have had a fall-back, you always do.' Rich was fumbling. 'Anyways, you made it. Some deal you guys pulled. I mean you did, didn't you? Is it safe?' He flashed a pearly grin.

'I'm not entirely certain.' said Lúcio. 'Das Booty is *aus den augen*, but not *aus dem sinn*, if you catch my drift.'

Shyno hated this toying with Rich, he was such a willing victim.

'It's pretty cool,' said Nev.

'Well yes, I suppose so,' said Lúcio. 'Although we *are* moored up fifty yards from Spanish Customs and Excise, in plain view, with that pink pussy on display and about as obvious as a tic on a cat's pucker. Do have a snail.' Lúcio could lay it on with relish when he had a mind to. 'We will need to sleep on board tonight and work out some sort of transfer in the morning. You may as well park up where you are now. If nothing else we can always engage a porter. Now this villa, Nova isn't it? Adequate I hope.'

Rich was not easily deterred.

'Well, it's pretty funky. Shower's primitive, yard's a jungle. Private though. Air con's wacked out, you got mosquitoes. Garage is neat. Nice pool. What can I tell you?'

Lúcio cut short the forthcoming inventory. By half-nine the crew had worked their way through a repertoire of *tapas* and were on their third bottle of *Rioja*. Nev, under the influence of several *sols,* was loosening up. Lúcio had dropped his initial antagonism, largely on the basis of Rich's revelation about his new squeeze and the Colombian connection.

'So what's she like?' said Nev. 'Your usual. Blonde and brainy?'

Rich got a mite huffed. 'Brunette, if you really want to know, and sharp. Latina type.' He glanced over at Lúcio. 'She's got a condo overlooking the tower. I saw the whole show from the balcony. The pad belongs to her uncle Enrique. An Old Boy out of Muzo. Some kind of para-military overseer at the mines. Drinks a lot. Traffics green gold. I saw the stones. Quality. Has to be some white stuff there as well. He wants to meet.'

Rich had a gift for précis when it came to marching powder.

'Well we have a more pressing, or should I say, pressed matter in hand. But no harm in a *tête à tête*, if the occasion presents'.

They all had a chuckle at that. Lúcio had begun to mellow

with the aid of a few Spanish brandies. He liked a bit of banter with Rich. He preferred a show of spunk to the usual craven obsequiousness. After a while he began to regale him with exaggerated tales of their more inglorious escapades. Rich struggled to take on board the sum of their folly. His eyes blanked over at their sea trials. He could not fathom if they were a gang of crazies winging it or simply inspired. All he knew was that he was dog tired and when he could no longer endure the revelations, he made his excuses. He stood up, bootheeled the ten paces to the Jag, ducked inside, fired up and made off to Villa Nova. The boat buggers drank, reminisced and smoked a little while, then decamped up the pier to the *Mona Gorda* and their bunks.

BOARDWALK

'Don't you think it's a little bit obvious?' said Shyno.

Lúcio had just proposed that the two of them grab a bale each, stroll the fifty yard stretch down the finger pier and deposit the dope in the boot of the waiting Jaguar.

'I doubt anyone will be paying much attention and if they are they won't have the least idea what they are looking at. Nothing particularly remarkable about a couple of chaps off a boat lugging their dirty linen to the Laundromat. Besides, there's hardly anyone about. Just the odd Fred and Ethel enjoying their *ensaimadas* over a game of Scrabble. Just be natural, nod and smile, no need to get into any chit chat about the weather.'

Shyno glanced back inside the wheelhouse and pondered the two bundles, unrecognisable in their new packaging. One they had stuffed inside Nev's sleeping bag. The other was wrapped in a turquoise beach towel. On top of each was a jumble of soiled t-shirts, shorts, sheets and underwear. As with many of Lúcio's stratagems it seemed all too plausible.

'What about the tower?' Nev pointed a crutch in the direction of customs control.

'I think you'll find that we are out of their sightlines.'

Shyno wanted to make sure. He scrambled up onto the pier. All he could see was a porcupine of aerials and the quarter moon of the radar scanner. The body of the tower and the courtyard offices were hidden by the flying bridge of the cruiser moored in the berth opposite. He panned down the length of the dock. An unbroken rank of identikit craft stretched to the promenade. He could see the Jag waiting, parked adjacent to the *tapas* bar and Rich sitting at a table drinking something. It was ten in the morning. Shyno stepped back down into the stern, gave Lúcio a nod and went into the wheelhouse. He was still thinking. Fifty yards at a casual stroll, pausing for pleasantries, might take two minutes. Each parcel weighed thirty pounds, plus the trimmings. Ever practical he stooped, hauled up a bale and set himself a time trial.

The pack was too big to sling under his shoulder and unless they went African porter style there was no option but to take the brunt of the weight on his upturned forearms. Shyno started counting slowly. At sixty he began to tremble. At eighty his shoulders caught fire. One hundred and he felt his heart ticking like an overwound chronometer ready to pop a cog. One twenty and he dumped the bale onto the wheelhouse floor cursing in a lather. The other two were watching from the stern deck, grins on their mugs.

'Looks like we might need a breather on the way after all.'

Lúcio was flexing his biceps, striking boxer poses. It seemed preposterous that someone so slight could be so powerful. He was no more than five foot eight and ten stone, a flyweight, yet Shyno had never seen him bested in an arm wrestle. Even with Nev it always ended in stalemate. The story went as follows, that the ulna and the radius in Lúcio's right arm were fused together from birth. A rod of bone. He said it accounted for his knockout punch, which he delivered with an abrupt, twisting action. He had trophies and the scars to prove it. One eyebrow was slightly lower on his forehead and the break in his nose, though expertly repaired, was still visible. It was one of those assertions you either accepted on faith or dismissed as a fiction. Shyno had no real reason to doubt it. As for Nev, if he'd had the legs, he could have toted both bales, no bother.

'You wait and see, this shit is heavy duty.'

They sent Nev on ahead. He swung his way down the dock at an easy pace, garnering a few surreptitious stares. Rich was ready with the passenger door, acting as chauffeur. Shyno made a last recce of the *Mona Gorda*. The aluminium frame to the stern hatch was sealed tight, all the rivets in place. He had done it before dawn after retrieving the dope. He unplugged the fridge and set the door ajar, took the keys from the console and locked the wheelhouse. They wouldn't be back for six weeks or more. They hefted their loads onto the pier and took a look around.

'Do you know Ruben Razzo?' asked Lúcio.

'Fetch and haul?'

'Back of pot.'

'Carry that weight.'

'Mule is as mule does.'

They bent to pick up their burdens and set off down the dock. Lúcio went at a steady rate, delivering the odd nod to the few occupants they passed on their way. There were a couple of crews doing a spot of hosing down and pair of expats who looked up momentarily from their tabloids, but that was the sum of it. Shyno managed a fixed grin and strode out ahead. Rich was ready with the boot open and watched them advancing down the pier. Lúcio appeared cool, well in control. Shyno looked like he was about to hit a wall. Rich stepped up just in time to relieve him of his bundle. He gave a grunt as he hefted it to the boot. Lúcio was not long behind, barely breaking sweat as he deposited his load on top. Rich shut the lid and the three of them slipped into the bubble of the Jag and they all just sat there inwardly digesting. No one spoke and no one seemed quite sure exactly what they were waiting for. Some kind of siren perhaps, sounding the all clear. None was forthcoming. Instead there was a sharp rap on the driver's side window and the frame filled with the features of a blue uniformed tourist policeman. Rich went a shade whiter and lowered the glass.

'It appears you have forgotten something, *señor.*'

The voice was only mildly supercilious. Rich looked flummoxed, glanced around him and then saw in the rear view mirror the waiter from *El Cabron* waving a strip of paper. Richly flushed, fumbled in his jeans and extracted a 500 peseta note, twice what he owed. With admirable *élan,* not to say relief, he proffered it to the bluebottle saying,

'Tell Manuel there to keep the change, *grassyass.'*

The crew just managed to smother a collective smirk. Rich started up the motor and eased out onto the main drag. He idled down the strip, making way for the few early morning strollers and late night stragglers. There was a brief hold up at the barrier where security were quizzing two longhairs in a dented Fiat and then they were through, out onto the coastal highway. Rich cruised well below the speed limit. As they began the short and winding climb up into the hills the gang had time to look back down on the marina and out over the sea. At each bend in the switchback, the picture became more static, less threatening, a miniature. Only memory kept it immediate. At 500 feet they thought they could almost make out the coast of Africa, but it was probably an illusion, a trick of cloud and light. In the end it didn't matter. All they knew was that they couldn't quite credit how they had made it this far.

Rich swept through the village and turned off into the

gravel drive of Villa Nova. He pulled up in front of the garage and hit the remote. Shyno got out and secured the gate. Lúcio disembarked and strolled about, sniffing the rampant oleanders. Nev grabbed his crutches and swung off to explore the patio area and the pool. Rich eased the cat into its cage and put down the shutter. There was a high whoop followed by a splash and pretty soon they had all joined Neville in the warm chlorine. It was their first freshwater bath in four weeks and they revelled in it. Despite Nev's best efforts to sink him, Rich just managed to keep his hair above water.

Lúcio was first out of the pool and went in to inspect the kitchen. There was a typically batch lack of provisions. The fridge furnished a quartet of *sols*, a punnet of parched olives and some unintentional yoghurt. Nothing else. A swift examination of the cupboards disclosed no more than basic condiments. He was puzzled by the half empty bottle of vegetable oil. On the sideboard stood a wooden fruit bowl stacked with windfalls from the garden. Bonus. He bit through the skin of a plump orange and strolled back out onto the patio, juice dripping from his jaw. The rest of the crew were splayed out on the poolside deckchairs in various attitudes of supplication as if willing the sun to appear. So far no answer to their prayer. Watery low cloud and no breeze to shift it. The aftermath of a freak storm still lingering in the air and the battered participants effecting repairs.

Lúcio commandeered Shyno for a run to Malaga, to stock up on food and collect the rest of their gear from the boat. Shyno was eager. It was his first chance to try out the Jag on foreign roads, see how she handled. He had only done a few turns around Oxford prior to the voyage and was looking at fifteen hundred miles driving and three borders fully loaded. He dragged on a pair of shorts, t-shirt, and unloaded the bales from the boot of the car. The soiled linen went into the top loader and he set it to boil wash. By the time he had backed out the car, Lúcio was waiting at the end of the drive with the gate unhitched. Shyno shuffled through Rich's tapes and selected the one least likely to provoke a headache. As Lúcio climbed aboard the first sad strains of *Madame George* filled the interior.

'Could you turn that down a bit?'

Shyno ignored the request. Lúcio had brought with him as his desert island treat the entire opus of Sibelius. He reckoned he would have more than a nodding acquaintance of the Finn by the time they reached Dover.

'Market first, then Banus.'

'Buckle up, just in case. Should be a smooth ride.'

And it was. The contrast with *Mona Gorda* seemed almost shameful. Here was power and response, a reverse gear that worked properly, comfort, luxury. He felt a tug of nostalgia for the lumbering hull that had borne them across the straits. The Jag ate up the switchback, dipping into the curves and by the time they hit the coast road Shyno was purring.

Lúcio had the same indifference to the workings of motor vehicles as he once had to boats. Fill-ups elicited a frown. Traffic flow was a mystery he chose not to examine. Speed limits he took as a personal affront. Such niceties as map reading or chatting to help the driver stay awake on a night journey simply passed him by. Any reference to mechanical frailty was met with incomprehension. Shyno had a fair idea of what kind of a copilot he might prove on the passage home. Less than cooperative. Possibly testy.

Banus passed them by on their right hand side and twenty minutes later they were in the petticoats of the town. It was not a lovely sight. The latest rash of development was spreading like an STD on both sides of the road. The coastal flank was a march of tawdry neon. Burger bars, cheap eateries, slot joints targeting the invaders, the Brits and Jerries. *Fish y Chips* was a frequent offender. *Cerveza Halle* completed the mockery. Inland, a mushroom canker of half built bunkers, concrete and girder, cranes, innumerable cranes, like locusts stalking the low hills and onetime orchards.

'Rifraff.' Lúcio sighed, as if he could put the whole lot down.

Shyno followed the signs for *centro ciudad* and before he knew it was lost in a maze of pinched cobbled streets, strung out with drying laundry. Lúcio had withdrawn into his customary trance. Eyes closed, slumped against the door jamb, he could have passed for comatose were it not for the irregular drumming of his fingers against the dashboard. He was composing. It always baffled Shyno that Lúcio could make poetry amid the least propitious circumstances. He gave him a nudge and the bard surfaced.

'Yes, yes, left, left, right.' Lúcio knew the town of old, another of his former haunts. Five minutes later they were in the *plaza mayor* where the first of the market stalls were already being dismantled. Shyno pulled over and Lúcio ducked out to do the shopping. He was brisk about the business, not bothering to haggle. Markets were his *metier*. He came back with fistfuls of plastic bags and dumped them on the back seat. He was gnawing on a stub of blood red *chorizo* and handed Shyno a greasy *empanada*.

'Right. Right, right, left, *andiamo*.'

Twenty minutes later they pulled into the marina. Lúcio suggested they park a little way past their pier and have a coffee, take a look around, see how the land and the lubbers lay. Shyno found a spot thirty yards beyond the *tapas* bar and slotted in. They wandered back, sat at the same table as before, ordered and took in the scene. Nothing to report. No change. *Mona Gorda* still bobbing in her berth, serene and unmolested. But the port was hotting up.

It was as though they had swapped one market for another, except this one was mostly meat and still on the hoof. It was a lurid display, red through orange, with several splendid cuts of rare Brit, pink and blistered from the summer's barbecue. Big hair was the order of the day and thongs were the thing, stringing up cuts of slack rump. Ankle bracelets, slave chains, fly shades, chunks of gold, and that was just the men. The women were mostly mannequins. They could have walked straight out of the bijou boutiques and probably did. Some gook had decreed that cork heeled platforms were *de rigeur* for the season. The upshot was a parade of tottering totty.

Shyno spooned the froth from his *cappuccino* and Lúcio, with an expression of mild disgust, stirred his *tinto*.

Gloria was on the apartment balcony painting her toenails when the Jag pulled in. *Nearly Nude* said the label on the bottle. It was a rude pink. She picked up her pearl-handled opera glasses and zoned in on the poets. From that distance the blond could have been Rich. But leaner, better looking, more delicate. Almost effeminate. The *copain* was a pocket Latin with a languid demeanour. Gloria giggled and wiggled her toes, urging them to dry. Time to have some fun at the gringo's expense.

Shyno saw her first, strolling down the promenade. On anyone else the outfit would have looked merely vulgar. All white, too little of it, and what there was, topped off by a wide brimmed straw hat above bugeye sunglasses. Shoulder length black hair for contrast and fluorescent toenails as highlights. To Shyno she looked like an extra out of *la dolce vita*. To Lúcio she seemed not exactly right.

'Unicorn?' he murmured.

Whatever kind of creature she was, she was clearly a feature of the port. As she sashayed down the walkway there were *hi babes* from the crews swabbing down their decks, *saludos* from the waiters setting up tables, a few cat calls, but most of it respectful, nothing too ribald. Gloria acknowledged yet somehow managed to ignore it all. She cruised by the bar and swung right, along number three pier. As she tacked up the dock, Shyno had his first long look at a rear view every inch as enigmatic as her front. It took him a while to work it out, so Lúcio gave a hint.

'Remember that one in the club off the *Damrak*, who asked you to dance? Same story. Only this one is eminently passable.'

Shyno recalled another occasion. Drinks at the Regency Bar in Piccadilly. Talk about picking a dill. An impossibly elegant woman of indeterminate years had sat down at their table and introduced herself as April Ashley. Shyno was bowled over and out when she enclosed his hand in her larger, exquisitely manicured grip and murmured in what he took for a smoker's husk,

'Sweety.'

Gloria reached the end of the pier, paused, came about and when she arrived at the *Mona Gorda* slowed and gave the old girl a good once over. She now had the poets' full attention. Lúcio had his espresso to his lips but wasn't sipping. Shyno was sucking on his spoon like a lollipop. She turned and walked straight back towards them. As she approached their table she took off her sunglasses and perched them on the brim of her floppy sombrero.

'*Hola! Me llamo Gloria.* A friend of your friend, Rich? You must be the *socio*. Lucy? And you?'

Shyno muttered something incomprehensible while appearing to haruspicate the coffee grounds at the bottom of his cup. He was smitten. It was that simple and that immediate.

ISOSCELES TRAPEZIUMS

'She's a guy, you know.'

Rich must have misheard. Shyno had one of those indeterminate mid ocean accents that was often mistaken for
South African.

'A gay? You mean *lesbo*? Nah, she's really into men.'

Rich wasn't really paying attention. He was too busy
wrestling with the lug nuts on the Jag's rear tyre, one eye on
the jack in case it slipped. As soon as the wheel was off,
Shyno shoved a breeze block under the sill and slid a piece of
2x4 on top to protect the metal. Rich winched the chassis
down until it was resting firm, cranked the jack an inch or
two further and freed it. On to the front tyre and the same
procedure.

Shyno stepped away and went back to work on the tool he
was improvising. A broom handle with an odd shaped block
of marine plywood nailed to one end. The rest of his kit consisted of a Stanley knife, a twelve inch metal ruler, a small
Phillips screwdriver, a pencil torch and a roll of duct tape.
Rich got the second wheel off. They blocked her up and the
Jaguar sat there at a rakish angle like she was cornering too
fast.

Shyno sat on the front tyre and scraped the mud and
blacking off the sill cap. He went at it like a cautious archae-
ologist. Alan had welded two small metal flanges to the lid
and fixed them with tiny screws. Shyno undid them and
prised out the cover. Then he went to the rear wheel arch and

repeated the operation.

Sill. A six foot long hollow metal tube running the length of the chassis on either side of the car beneath the door jambs, in the shape of an inverted rhomboid. A beheaded, upside down pyramid, three inches wide at the base, six across the top, each equilateral side five inches high.

Shyno flicked on his torch and peered down the cavity. He could see Escargot's nose twitching at the far end. The tube was dry and rust free. Just to be sure, he wrapped a linen dish cloth around the block on the end of his pole and pushed it through the barrel as if he were cleaning a rifle. Rich saw it coming just in time and barked his scalp on the wheel arch as he pulled away.

Geometry. Volume.

Each slab of hash was twelve inches long, six wide, one thick. Shyno tried to figure out how many cuts he would have to make, how many chances to slice a finger. Only one whole block could fit the width of the tube. The rest would have to be trimmed, assembled to shape and then taped together. There would be a great many offcuts to deal with as well.

It took him half an hour to construct the first brick and when he looked at the ragged projectile he winced. Sure, it fitted, but it was such a laborious process, such a waste of precious space. He went for a template next, using the ruler to measure the width of the tube at one inch intervals. After twenty minutes fiddling about, jotting down numbers, he thought he had a method. Rich was already bored and made his excuses. It was nearly four o'clock and Shyno had finished only two of the six packs required. There was still the other side to fill, plus the cavity beneath the rear seats.

Cutting through pressed resin, even with a new Stanley blade, was like hacking through an inch of stiff leather. Too much pressure on the scalpel and it dug in. Too little and it barely scored the surface. It took repeated precise slicing. Shyno sent Rich in search of a candle to heat the blade. Meantime he made do with a lighter, blistering his fingers. No joy. Rich came back shrugging and empty-handed, then filtered away. Nev clunked in to provide some company, but mostly to smoke up the odd offcut or two. Lúcio was cooking oxtail. He said it would be ready around eight. The aroma drifted through from the kitchen and despite the open utility room door it was hot in the breezeblock garage with the shutter down and the fluorescents humming overhead.

'Fancy a smoke?' said Nev, who was propped up on the floor against the rear tyre.

'Maybe later. This thing is lethal.' He waved the Stanley in the air and shook his head. He had a thing about knives.

'What do you make of Gloria? Showing up like that, doing her own intro?'

'Brassy. Rich didn't seem to mind much. I reckon she did him a favour. You know that he wants to put some extra luggage in the hold?' Shyno snapped off the edge of the slab he was working on and pointed at the sill. Nev licked a paper, put the finish to his number and sparked it.

'Who says the Uncle is going to front up anyways?'

'And if he does, do we want it? Serious, Nev. We're packing sixty pounds of hash here. If we get done by the polis, it's a fuck stretch, years of it. And then there's what's sitting in the boat. If they find that, *kaput*. Put a bag of powder on top and you might as well ditch the key. Down and out. Ten to twenty.'

'In for a pound...yeah, not pretty.'

'Pass me that.'

Shyno reached for the joint. *To do is to be. To be is to do.*

Frankie says doo-be-doo-be-doo. He took several deep tokes, smoked up a lungful, and coughed till he blew it all out.

'Let me tell you how I see it. First, we've got this load to flog. Lúcio thinks we might off it in Amsterdam, if Jan rates the quality. If not, it's back to Albion and Al gets to parcel it out. Could take a couple of months. That's one trip. First of five. Meantime we sit around and wait. Then there's Larry to square. We still owe him for the boat. Ten grand. Our rental at the villa is up in three days. We've got to be packed and long gone before then. Get flights for you and Rich. Think of moving the boat up the coast, somewhere discrete. It costs a packet to moor at Banus. You can see where the money's going. Be lucky if we get anything out of the first run. So, if we did have some blow to shift, it would help with the cash flow.'

Shyno tore off a strip of duct tape and wrapped it around the third block he had constructed, inserted it into the tube and ramrodded the wad down the muzzle of the barrel.

'That's assuming the Uncle is forthcoming.' Nev added. 'I mean, Rich said his business was emeralds. Even if he does have a side line, no guarantee he's going to sub to a bunch of strangers.'

'I wouldn't worry about that. Lúcio's a *loro*. Talk him into anything. Anyway, I guess we'll find out soon enough. Didn't Loose tell you? Rich is angling for a meet and greet, tomorrow night at the marina. Parlay.'

Nev chuckled. 'Yeah, I heard. Finally get to see the Glory girl. Is she for real?'

Shyno pulled another slab from the bale and laid it on a wooden cutting board purloined from the kitchen. 'Oh, she's the business alright. Only Rich doesn't know the half of it. Shit, I'm going to be here all night packing this mother. Good grief.'

Nev shuffled the skinny bones of his butt against the concrete floor and sucked on the roach.

'Rather you, mate. Still, if you want some help chopping?'

Shyno was tempted. His fingers were raw and sticky with resin. He had a crimp in his spine from hunching over which he couldn't shift. His eyes were pink rimmed and itching from the pollen he had rubbed into them, trying to keep the sweat off his face. Nev did this kind of thing as a hobby, to supplement state benefits, for pin money, dicing chunks of press, accurately, without the need for scales. It came naturally.

'Nice. But we've only got one knife.'

'No worries, man. Just pass me a blade and show me the widths that you want.'

'Ok. Split that in half. See how it goes.' Shyno slipped him the board, the steel rule and a two inch wide offcut.

Nev's palms and fingertips were calloused with layers of built up skin, accrued over years from wielding his weight against the handles of his NHS crutches. Nothing elaborate or designed for comfort. Functional. Just like his callipers. Your basic tools. He gripped the blade between his right thumb and middle digit and placed his forefinger along the angled front edge of the stainless steel scalpel. Shyno had a minor epiphany. The blade was a perfect miniature of the shape of the sill. Nev lined up the ruler in the middle of the strip of dope and with two quick strokes ran the razor down the length of it. Grasping it in both hands he blew on the incision then snapped it in half like a biscuit, or a tile he'd run through a cutter. The edges were virtually smooth, but just to be sure, he pared the blade along the side of each one, making a small pile of shavings. He scraped them into a mound, moistened a finger, dipped it in the sherbert and stuck it in his mouth. With the remainder he began assembling another joint.

'Any good?'

Shyno sat back on his tyre and exhaled.

'Ace. Look, if I mark the widths you could cut the strips and we can use the next set as templates. It's easier if you use the whole knife.'

By eight, when Rich came to call them to eat, they had the first sill packed and the tube caps screwed back in place. It took ten minutes to rebolt the wheels. Shyno opened the garage shutter and reversed the Jag out and then back in, so they had the wide side to the right where the bales were and could work freely.

They could hear Lúcio singing in Italian as he prepared the dinner and the smell wafted through from the kitchen into the garage. It was a caramelised, herby, tomato based aroma that promised a treat. Lúcio was, on his own admission, something of a gourmet and a terrific cook when he chose. He claimed to have elicited secrets from a handful of select chefs on his world travels and these he cherry-picked and rearranged to his own personal delectation. He rarely cooked for anyone other than himself. He ate mostly in silence, more like a gourmand, almost a glutton, inhaling from his plate like a man starving. It was the one social act in which he was entirely unselfconscious or showed any lack of grace. He simply fed his face. So the gang followed suit, got stuck into the fork meat, sucked out the melted marrows, crunched through a tart green salad and lined their bellies with some crusty bread to mop up the juices. They washed it all down with an aged *Sangre de Toro,* two bottles. And when Nev got Rich to fetch a few *sols* from the fridge, Shyno could almost hear Lúcio mutter,

'Beer after wine...*das is für schweine.*'

There were two main topics of conversation in between mouthfuls; the proposed meet with Enrique and updates on their progress with the packing. Shyno reckoned they would have the job done by mid-afternoon the next day. Lúcio proposed they aim for an evening rendezvous. Rich said he would take care of the diary, see about ordering a taxi. It was near ten when Lúcio yawned and made ready to retire. Rich got lumbered with the pot wash and the havoc of the kitchen. The packers stretched and went back out to the garage. They made good time working together and just past midnight had the second sill stuffed, the wheels back on and the Jag jacked down. Shyno offered to clear up and Nev swung off to the third bedroom taking with him a slice that would make several numbers. Shyno switched off the garage lights and was heading to his own berth in the main bedroom where Lúcio was no doubt still awake, when he changed course and went through the patio doors and stood by the pool.

The underwater lights were on and they shot the palest of emerald beams through the crystalline liquid which was as still as any block of stone. He stripped and made a flat dive in at the shallow end. He swam two lengths beneath the surface, eyes wide open, letting the chlorine rinse his pollinated sockets. At the third he turn he slowed, kicked and blew out a stream of bubbles. He could feel the pressure in his lungs and relaxed. He knew he was capable of a hundred and fifty feet. Five laps of the pool. It was different when free diving down after a fish. Forty was his limit. You had to swim like a turtle with a lazy stroke, conserving oxygen.

When he surfaced his vision was blurred, but no more so than the stars pricking the high thin cloud. He swam over to the side of the pool and hauled himself onto one of the rubber rafts and lay there gazing up at the night sky. He fell asleep, rocking to his body's slight motions and dreamed that he was waving and not drowning. It was dawn when he woke and the sudden movement made him slip off the float and into the lukewarm water. He hauled himself out, towelled off, took a look in on Lúcio who was still deep, brewed some coffee, and then went back to the garage to see what Alan had done with the Jag's interior.

CULO LIBRE

Enrique was prone on his recliner, mask in place, breathing with difficulty, but complacent nonetheless. Schipol had gone as smoothly as anticipated. The business with Joost, the broker, better than expected. When Tío produced the first few stones the Belgian had shrugged, but when he saw the postage stamp *Princess* he murmured,

'You have more like this?'

'Many. In theory.'

'I should like to see.'

Enrique went away with fifty thousand dollars in hand, a hundred on spec and irritable piles from passing the product through his bowels. He placed the bulk of the cash in his private box at Swiss Credit and caught an evening flight out to Malaga. That night he slept in snatches dreaming of *Muzo* and woke before dawn. He limped to his couch and dozed off again until Gloria woke him around nine.

The two bodyguards were sipping coffee out on the balcony. Gloria brought in a breakfast tray of fresh pomegranate juice, honey, yoghurt and a shot of *crystal*. She knew that his throat would be sore. He often had difficulty swallowing anything solid after a business trip. Uncle sat half up and perused the medicaments. He coughed, took a sip of juice and downed the chaser.

'This gringo, do you trust him?'

'He is straight, *Tío*.'

'Yes, I know, but for business.'

'You should talk with the *socio*.'

'Agreed. Arrange it if you can. Invite them here. And tell the *muchachos* to take the evening off, they won't be needed.

SEATING ROOM ONLY

Shyno levered out the leather banquette that served as the Jag's back seat and scrutinised the fawn carpet beneath. No sign of tampering, the pile smooth, the fabric unmarked, as if straight from the manufacturer. Alan had told him it was only spot glued, but to ease it off gently. Shyno peeled back the carpet to reveal the hollow metal seat base and two eighteen-by-six inch rectangular panels, either side of the hump of the drive shaft, cut into the fascia of the box and fixed with the familiar flanges. They were obvious cuts, no disguising them. Alan had used an angle grinder to create the openings in the metal and there was a two millimetre gap around the traps. It wasn't crude, but neither was it subtle. Still he thought, if it comes to uniforms ripping up carpets we're probably rumbled.

He used the Phillips to unscrew the panels. The space inside was ample. No trouble fitting the remainder of the dope and with minimal cutting. He got to work. It was a hand job, feeling his way into the interiors, fisting whole blocks up into the cavity. And still there was room. So he went on packing. Soon it was down to the offcuts which he taped together in slender ingots and wedged into the gaps. Then it was slivers mostly, individually wrapped in cling film and pushed into crevices. And suddenly all of the dope was gone, bar a few oddments. Enough to keep the crew mellow for a couple of days.

Shyno was on the point of screwing the dummy plates

back into place and gluing down the carpets when he stopped. Sod's law, if he sealed it all up there would be some last minute packing to do. So he half screwed the panels, rolled back the carpet without sticking it down and replaced the seat. He was sweeping up the crumbs and shreds of wrapping when Nev swung in through the utility door.

'This should keep you rolling. Afraid it's all that's left.' Shyno held up a fistfull of fragments, probably a good half ounce. 'Would you do the honours, I'm dying for a smoke.'

Rich was hatching something with eggs in the kitchen. Lúcio was still asleep. It was around ten in the morning and a low sun had begun to burn off the haze. It looked like a fine day for lolling round the pool and catching some rays. Escargot had already been on the blower, first to Iberia to make bookings for their flights, then to Gloria to firm up the diary. Drinks at 7. Informal. She would be sending a car.

'So who's on the guest list?' Nev asked.

Rich dropped an egg and in the silence that followed looked awkward.

'Well, I guess...she just said bring your friends.'

'Good. I'm friendly.' And that was that settled. They would be going mob handed.

There wasn't a whole lot to do for the rest of the day. Hit the pool, bask on a deck chair, smoke, quaff a few *sols*, rustle up lunch, score a *siesta*. Lúcio made brief appearances but spent most of the hours in bed, studying his Ephemeris, consulting the Ching, revising *The Stranger on His Sand,* eating whatever was brought to him. Shyno had a quick chat about moving the boat but in the end they decided against it. Neither had the heart for another day out on the water. They would just swallow the cost and take the risk. Maybe see about a cheaper berth down at the minnow end of the mari-

244

na. Note. *Remember to pay mooring fees at the office, two months in advance.* Besides, they had slipped beneath the radar. Where better to store their haul than right under the toes of Customs and Excise?

SALUDOS

The cab came on time and by half seven they were back at Banus. Rich led them to the condo elevator and Gloria buzzed them up to the first floor. She was casual, no makeup or accessories, when she opened the door. Enrique was prone on his recliner, taking in air. He didn't get up. He raised a palm in greeting and gestured to the sofa. He wasn't expecting Nev, nor was Gloria.

Neville swung into the apartment, planted his crutches on the marble floor and stood there swaying. When Enrique saw him he jerked half upright and reached for his cane. It was as if some sense of honour had been challenged that he couldn't ignore. Gloria hovered over him and he waved her away. He levered himself to his feet and limped across the room to greet this strange familiar. Nev met him halfway and they both stood there examining each other. From the expression on their faces they might as well have been staring into the distorting glass of a funfair mirror. They could have shaken hands but that would have called for unnecessary complications. Instead, Enrique raised his emerald tipped cane, Nev his aluminium crutch, and they crossed swords smiling.

'*Hermano*. Welcome.'

'Pleasure, Bro...'

Everyone relaxed. Enrique made a half bow to Lúcio, nodded to Rich, planted a dry kiss on Shyno's forehead and bade them sit. He seemed reanimated, almost jocose. Gloria steered Rich in the direction of the kitchen to fetch the refreshments and the crew settled on the sofa.

It was a long liquid session from which Escargot desisted as best he could. Lúcio kept pace with El Cojo. Nev made the odd pilgrimage to the balcony and Shyno joined him for the joints. Gloria set a lump of flake on the granite top, ground it with her rose quartz stone and produced a tiny silver spoon so they could dip into the powder as if it were caviar. All the while there was *Crystal* and *chicharrones,* green mango slivers and *ballenato* or *cumbia* on the stereo. Happy days. Lúcio hit it off with Enrique right away. Rich beamed. Shyno flirted with Gloria. Nev rolled and shone. Around midnight, with the stone well on, Enrique started to undress.

Nobody blinked as he slipped off his sharkskin jacket and began unbuttoning his shirt. He swivelled and lifted up the linen fabric to reveal a hairless torso studded with bullet marks. They were like black berries imbedded in his back, six of them, ranged close round his spine. As if someone had repeatedly jabbed a thick lead pencil into the flesh, breaking off the tip at each new stab.

Lúcio made a murmur of commendation and stripped to the waist. He had a beautiful back, a living bronze, but if you looked closer there were weals and scars, dozens of them, crisscrossing the flesh in a haphazard mesh. They were the result of a dare, a boyhood one. He and a friend had fashioned a whip from nettle stems, braiding them into a vicious scourge. They took it by turns to lay it on and see who would yield first. Long after the bout was won Lúcio had his friend administer a further dozen lashes. He described it as being chastised by fire.

The others looked on, baffled and embarrassed, not sure if they were voyeurs at some masochistic bonding ritual or witnesses to *macho* bragging rights. For one shameful moment it looked as if Nev might feel obliged to trump them, but he simply shrugged and smiled. His wounds were on permanent display and besides they weren't invited or provoked.

After that the two Latins talked business and drank. They spoke in Spanish. Most of it was lost on Nev and Escargot. Shyno grasped the basics. Gloria listened as though she had heard it before. Enrique talked in a sardonic, clipped manner from the side of his mouth, like a best man delivering a speech rehearsed many times and which has become so familiar he no longer feels obliged to amuse or explain.

'What other men do with other men is none of my concern. I make no judgements. Neither condone nor condemn. Each to his necessity. Business is business. It is not a question of morality, for the *mores* change, according to our masters. What was prohibited once is now permissible. Therefore I acknowledge no manmade rule. I am an outlaw. Show me a trade that does not bring its measure of pain. These pills I swallow, some rat suffered for them. This suit, which flatters my vanity, no doubt the product of a child's indenture. Where there is traffic there will always be casualties. I leave the numbers to the clerks, adjust them as they will. I speak of the manufacturers. Of arms, chemicals, fuel, tobacco, alcohol. *Salud!* All poisons. All sanctioned. All taxable. Which brings me to this powder. For three thousand years or more the poor of my country have brewed or chewed on the *coca* leaf to suppress their hunger. To march over mountains. Marching powder, as the *gringos* call it, which they sniff to satisfy their own hunger. Better it were made legal. Cut out the cartels. Prevent the war that will be waged against our people. It is a cash crop. Our second coffee, which wakes to kill. Meat? Meat is murder. Forests felled to graze cattle.

Poppies. Opium. Junk for the masses. Goods for sale. Goods? What is good? Life is the only drug. *The drug of living and the drug of dreams*, as your poet says. I see harm in everything. There are no blameless merchants. Only those with the mark of the beast can buy and sell. And God is far.'

'Fuck,' thought Shyno, 'the Old Boy's on a downer.'

But Enrique wasn't finished yet. He stuck out his thumbs which had thick, ragged white scars circling their bases where they joined his hands. He coughed and swallowed down the phlegm with a throaty rattle.

'My enemies, they hung me up by these once, to make me talk. Now I ask you, should you find yourself in a similar predicament, would you give me up? To be precise, can I trust you, should you get caught? I only enquire because I have no wish to spend my twilight years behind bars, spitting out the remains of my lungs in some cockroach pit in Bucuramanga. Do I make myself clear?'

Lúcio had not the least intention of being caught. The very idea was foreign to his imagination. The possibility simply did not occur to him. But he knew that Enrique was unlikely to be fobbed off with blithe reassurances about integrity or the favourable auguries of the household gods. So he played his high card.

'I have a Vatican Passport. Diplomatic immunity.'

Enrique's emerald eyes flickered and widened a fraction. Shyno smiled inside. It was only the second time that he had heard Lúcio make this claim. The first was to Rich, who swallowed it whole. It was an outrageous bluff but *Tío* didn't know that and appeared unwilling to call. Of course Lúcio possessed no such document and the only immunity he enjoyed was the one he conferred on himself.

Enrique gestured at the pile of *perrica* on the table and

simply upped the stakes.

'*Bueno*. How many kilos can you handle? Five? Ten?'

Lúcio had never sold a gram of cocaine in his life. He had made two mule runs for Rich, who handled distribution. Mostly to friends, in small amounts, over a period of months.

'Our main market is California. We would take two to start with and build up the business gradually. It's safer that way. Our last contact flew in a planeload via Morgan's Bluff in the Bahamas and insisted on wholesale. A quick turnover. Naturally, I advised against it. He made an arrangement for fifty kilos with a new buyer. Dismissed me as small fry. He phoned me from Los Angeles County jail two weeks later, begging for help. He said they were raping him. It turned out that his client was the DEA.'

Enrique slapped his palm against a bony thigh and cackled.

' A *bobo*! You must come and see me in Muzo next time you visit our country. I will show you how these things are done. We have a canning factory, exporting pet food for yankee dogs. Alas, what is here in Spain is for our guests' amusement only. I am sorry to disappoint, please explain to your American friend.'

So that was the flop. Rich was going to have to wait see how it turned on the river. The result? A no score draw. All to play for at some future fixture, down the road, away. Lúcio wasn't fazed. His stock was up. He'd made the connection and he was patient, methodical. He had the mindset of an angler who feels a strike. Enrique was a big fin and his first aim was to set the hook, then reel him in, no matter how long it took.

Shyno was relieved. They had made the leap from small time dope dealers to bulk importers almost by accident and the whole business had been nothing but a succession of cockups. It was Lúcio's approach that shredded his nerves. *The visible, the untrue.* What was that supposed to mean? It seemed to him like a gang planning a bank caper and taking no account of alarm systems, security, combination locks or getaway cars. Contingencies.

Things happen. And always fall apart.

Meanwhile they were on a green light from the planets and all that was required was blind faith. It galled him. He felt like some bumptious, obstreperous clerk, assured of certain certainties which were constantly being subverted and thrown back in his face.

Enrique exploded into a *cantata* of wracking coughs. It sounded like he was hawking up gravel from deep in his lungs. Had he spat out the green mucus it would have surprised none of them to see the odd unpolished gem glistening in the sputum. But then they were all pretty stoned. Gloria got the old man onto the recliner and laid him out without protest. She applied his mask and turned on the oxygen. The party was over.

Shyno went out onto the balcony for his own breath of air and lent over the rail. He tried to make out *Mona Gorda*, but she was hidden from view. What was it Jones had said? Something about Conrad and boats. Something sexual. Gloria appeared at his side.

'I have called a cab. *Tío* is tired.'

Shyno dipped into a habitual reverie. He was ever dreaming of some perfect escape. From the daily grind of dealing with his gender. The exhausting business of not being quite himself. The long littleness of life.

Gloria said,

'I know you like me and accept me as I am. We are not so

different.'

She pressed up against him and he could feel her desire. He still hadn't managed to direct a single word to her all evening. As if reading his despair she placed a fingertip against his lips and murmured,

'Next time. I'll be here.' And then as an afterthought, 'I'll keep an eye on your boat'. She gave him a quick darting kiss and went back inside. Shyno thought she tasted like extract of malt, sweet and dark.

HEADS OUT ON THE HIGHWAY

The next day was a flurry. Rich and Nev packed and cabbed to the airport. The agent swung by, assessed no damage and said,

'Drop off the keys at the *inmobiliaria* or leave them underneath the pot with the yucca. I hope you enjoyed your stay. Check out is midday.'

Shyno screwed the plates tight, glued down the carpet under the rear seat, stowed their bags in the boot and by noon they were gone.

It was weird driving back into Puerto Banus. Shyno parked in the public slots and they went to the tower to pay their dues. Murillo was there, round and damp, fanning himself with a palm frond. Yes, there was a berth, down on number eleven, at a more modest rate. How many weeks? *Tal y tal*. Lúcio fronted up and they strolled to the boat. It was a faultless performance for once. Untie, back out, chug down, reverse in, moor up, check fenders, cut engine, lock and leave. A pretty fat girl with a four-fifths full belly.

They had decided on a scenic route. Motor inland towards the Alhambra, catch the first snows glinting off the Sierras and pitch up at a *parador*. Dine on milkfed baby kid, sip a *Rioja Reserva* and sleep in a four poster bed. Onward, North over the dry quixotic plateau, bypass Madrid, post at Burgos. Cross borders at San Sebastián, coast hug and likely get soaked in Biarritz. Northeast then to *Collonges*, sample the miracles of Paul Bocuse. Replete, rested, take the *péages* all

253

the way to Paris. Negotiate the perils of the *périphérique*, then eyes down to Belgium. Overnight in Bruges, overlooking the canal. More rich food and a quick morning visit to the Mauritshuis to gaze at Vermeer. *Girl with a Pearl Earring,* a particular favourite. Point toward Amsterdam and Jan. To buy or not to buy? If no, onto Ostende. Catch a ferry to Dover and complete the last leg back to Oxford.

Lúcio slotted a cassette into the player. It was the Karelia Suite. As the intro of jaunty trombone notes parped through the speakers, the Jag rolled over the first of three sleeping policemen en route to the exit barrier. When the car met the hump it let off a silent fart, rich and resinous, which filled the interior with the unmistakeable odour of freshly pressed pollen.

Shyno's first instinct was to brake hard but he was overcome by a fit of sneezing and hit the accelerator instead. The Jag surged forward and he could see the guard at the barrier waving them on. Lúcio jabbed twice at the button on the console and the front windows slid down. The sudden inrush of air seemed to dilute the smell, but they were fast approaching the second sleeper. Shyno shifted to low and slowed to a crawl. He eased the cat over the bump, ever so gentle and she farted again. The interior was swamped. Lúcio hit the button for the rear windows this time and fumbled in the dash. He pulled out a *Cohiba*, bit off the tip and punched the lighter. They were twenty yards from the barrier. For a moment Shyno deluded himself that the guard might recognise the car and wave them through. But he was raising his hand and that meant, well it was obvious. Lúcio worked the windows again and sealed the interior. He was sucking hard on his cigar and blowing out plumes of smoke. They rolled over the third hump. The Jag blew off and came to a halt. There was a rap on the driver's side glass and Shyno eased it a crack.

'*Abre.*'

Shyno wasn't sure if he meant the window or something else but he lowered it anyway. The guard flinched as a waft of Cuban leaf assaulted his nose. He gave a perfunctory look at the empty rear seat and said,

'*El maletero.*'

Shyno got out, popped the boot and the stroppy little *Francoista* strutted and muttered a bit before he remembered his station. Tourists. Trade. He pursed up an obsequious fixed smile and clicked his heels.

'Ok. *Buen viaje.*'

Shyno wasn't having it. Some jumped up stripe had put him through the fear. He looked the provo over. A measly pair of *bigotes* straddling a weak chin, the odd pluke pimpling the beaky nose, jittery eyes. He felt a demonic urge. He was shocked how quickly his fright had turned into rage. He was tempted to go nuclear. Tear the little fuckwit off a strip. Then the insanity passed. The fellow was simply doing his job and not very well and for that Shyno should have been unutterably grateful.

'*No hay problema.* '

He got back in the car and they waited for the barrier as security waved them through. At the first layby on the coast road he pulled over. Lúcio was frowning as he stubbed out his cigar.

'Any ideas?'

Shyno had a pretty good one but he wished he'd come up with it earlier.

'It's not the sills, they're airtight and outside the car. It's coming from under the back seat. There are gaps around the panels. Every time we hit a bump it pushes out the air inside the cavity. If I'd realised I could have sealed them with mastic, but it never occurred to me. It's not too late, but I'd need to take out the seat, pull up the carpet. It would have to be somewhere discrete.' He tailed off. He tried to imagine the scenario. A country road, a public car park late at night, but all that he could think of was a lyric by Tommy James and the Shondells.

I think we're alone now.

There doesn't seem to be anyone around.

Meanwhile the traffic droned past and they were stranded in the reeking cockpit of the car. Shyno ran his fingers through his hair and came up with more than the usual few strands. Christ, I'm going bald. He rubbed the thinning patch at the back of his skull. It was one thing to blag their way through a checkpoint at a marina, another to finesse a border frontier. He felt close to despair. Lúcio looked serious for the first time in a while.

'It worked once. I can't see why it shouldn't again. There are only two borders, France, Belgium. Holland is a drive through. Three if Jan proves uncooperative. The approach roads should be fairly flat. We can always pull over a mile or so before each crossing. Fumigate the car. People smoke in cars and cigars are particularly pungent.'

Shyno submitted to the logic. He felt out of control, committed, manic.

'Always get one of those dangly pine scented things, hang it on the rear view, slap on some poove juice, Brut maybe, light a few joss sticks, Patchouli.'

Lúcio gave him a wry glance.

'We don't want to appear too obvious.'

BAEDEKER

The first stage of the tour went to plan. They arrived at their stop at around sunset, in time to see a spectacular lightshow colouring the peaks below the *parador* which managed to be both austere and decadent. A paradox resolved by the fact that it was a former monastery, refurbished at lavish cost.

It perched high in the *Nevada* and as they hurried out of the near freezing night air, they found themselves in a small arched vestibule dominated by an open hearth the height of a man. Yard long trunks of flaming pine hissed and spat in the grate. They were escorted to a bedroom that seemed more like a boudoir, except for the bare stone walls and tiny mullioned windows. Centre stage stood a rosewood four poster, smothered in pillows, and some kind of fur coverlet that might have been ocelot. The floors were worn flagstone, heated from beneath and strewn with rugs. The bathroom was vast, marble and mirrored on one entire side, with a tub they could completely submerge in. The corridor that led to the dining room was lit by sconces with thick church candles and there was a kind of holy hush about the entire place.

Shyno half expected Lúcio to address the waiter in Latin. There was another enormous blazing fireplace in the restaurant and a dozen immaculate wide spaced tables. They were the only diners and the only guests at church that night. They gorged on tender three month old baby goat, drank a rust red ancient *tempranillo* and just managed a memorable egg flan called simply *pudding*. At nine, stuffed and exhausted they withdrew and wallowed in a cedar scented bubble bath before slipping between crisp linen and duck down pillows. Despite all the delightful stimulants the *copains* were far too shagged to do anything but sleep.

Meanwhile Rich and Nev endured a seven hour delay at Malaga Airport. The Aircon was on the blink, the urinals blocked. They shared the limited facilities with a peevish assortment of torched Brits, mewling brats in tow. When they finally took off it was seven thirty. An hour into the flight, prodding with a plastic fork at a congealed stew in a dented tin tray, Escargot would have been green-eyed at the feast unfolding thirty thousand feet below; except the only green was in his gills, as the plane experienced moderate to severe turbulence most of the way across the Bay of Biscay.

HUGGER MUGGER

The next leg was more arduous. Their target was Burgos and a converted castle renowned for its way with a roasted haunch of boar. But it was three hundred miles up the road which, according to the map, was rarely straight until the high plateau. So they breakfasted in bed and by eight they were under way.

For an hour or so the Jag seemed to have cured itself of flatulence, but coming down a mountain the first of many silent emissions filled the cabin with its odour. Shyno didn't bother voicing his deductions since Lúcio was either napping, or composing to the subterranean chords of the Finn's sixth symphony. The freezing overnight cold had hardened the blocks, but as the interior of the car warmed up so did they, releasing their perfume. The slabs were packed either side and above the drive shaft which was conducting heat. And the twin exhaust pipes were adding their complement of therms. It was precisely the same effect you get when flame is applied to a chunk of hash. It softens and starts to smell.

Lúcio affected to ignore the matter. Rather as one might an antique, incontinent, crapulous relative on their annual Christmas visit from the old folks home. But it irked Shyno. He felt a mixture of dispiriting sensations. Guilty for not having foreseen the problem. Incompetent for not being able to provide the remedy. Ridiculous for having gone to such lengths to conceal their business only to advertise it so fragrantly. Unlike the aged aunt who would be leaving after lunch, they were stuck with this old girl. And she was getting on. Four years is not long in the life of a luxury car but the farmer had worked her hard. There was a towbar still in place at the rear and eighty thousand on the dial, assuming it hadn't been clocked. Why anyone would choose to use a highly tuned thoroughbred to do a donkey's work was beyond him. But then maybe what they were doing was not so different.

So they ascended to the land of tilting windmills, knights errant, ugly women, and the drowned voice of reason. There was the usual long littleness of any journey. Lúcio worked the windows and smoked a yard of tobacco. At nine, red eyed and exhausted they scrunched to a halt in the gravel courtyard of what looked like a miniature Spanish bastille. It was squat and brutal, but there were torches guttering in front of the raised portcullis and liveried youths to usher them in. The wild pig was commendable. The bed big. They only had a leisurely half day drive to the border so they opted for a lie in and a late breakfast.

GOODBYE HELLO

They delayed their departure as long as they could. Checkout was noon, so they called on room service for coffee and *churros* and dipping chocolate. Shyno kept half an eye on the clock but kept dozing off. When he surfaced around eleven he could hear Lúcio's voice from the bathroom. He appeared to be talking to himself in the mirror.

'There will be two check points. One leaving Spain, one entering France. As agreed, we will have to clear the air before we cross. I will do the talking. Present our passports. Right hand drive means when we pull up I will be facing the immigration officer. You are my chauffeur. We have been on visit to Malaga where I rent a villa and we are returning home. No, we have nothing to declare.'

It was like being programmed by one of those tapes that teach you a foreign language or persuade you to quit smoking while you sleep. Somehow the mantra seemed to work. For the first time in weeks he felt relaxed, focused, free of fear. If you can't do the time, don't do the crime. Lúcio seemed almost debonair and it was infectious. They rolled down the road to San Sebastián ready for whatever awaited them as if they didn't have a care.

On the Spanish side it was a bored, indolent time-server who greeted Lúcio's Havana breeze with his own pungent gust of unfiltered black tobacco. He cast a desultory look over their passports and a more lingering one at the driver. He seemed on the point of making some kind of gambit but glanced back at the queue of cars behind the Jaguar and waved them through. Fifty yards ahead was the French barrier. Shyno eased forward with the windows still lowered and pulled up at the booth. A lean, officious looking head bent to the passenger door. This one was also reeking but of garlic and Gitanes and a powerful aftershave which barely masked his unnatural odour. Shyno wondered. Does everybody smoke? Does nobody wash? The Gendarme was neither bored nor in a hurry. There were a few brief exchanges at which point the frog took exception to Lúcio's immaculate French.

'Brésilien?'

It was one thing not to speak the native language, quite another to speak it better than the native. The guard withdrew into his cabin and fingered their documents. It was a delaying tactic. There were no computers back then, no databases, no joined up police work, no sniffing dogs. He was looking for a reaction. He came back out, walked around the Jag from front to rear, then knelt down at the driver's side wheel examining the tyre. He got up, shook his head, then stuck it in the frame of Shyno's window.

'Vous parlez francais, monsieur?'

Shyno took a short drag on his Rothman's, exhaled and replied with the truth.

'Un petit peu.'

The cheese monkey launched into a lecture of which Shyno grasped only the occasional word. After a minute of vaunting, he handed back their passports and motioned them through. Show over. As they pulled away he could see in his rear view mirror the next unfortunate victims pulling up to the booth. An elderly couple with a caravan in tow.

'What the fuck was that all about?'

Lúcio was more than amused.

'You have two millimetres of spare tread on your front right tyre before it needs replacing. Your headlamps are occluded, covered in insects. You are required to fit deflectors on your high beams when travelling at night. Observe our speed limits. Penalties for any breach are immediate and severe. Get a haircut! Chauffeur? Merde. Actually I made that one up. Come on, let's get out of here. We're through.'

It was more or less the same all the way to Amsterdam. They walked on the beach in Biarritz and got duly soaked. Empty emerald waves careened in and exploded on the shore but there were no surfers. Bocuse produced a five-course series of marvels at Lyon and they slept fitfully. There was a relapse in Paris where the frenetic *périphérique* got the better of the driver and they went around twice. They stayed in a faded hotel on the Île Saint-Louis and listened to the antique plumbing gurgle and the wheezing of the lift. It all seemed like some minor miracle or magic trick or simple good luck. Something had to give.

AMSTERDAMNED

Jan was one of Alan's connections. A mixed race Dutch youth of Asian extraction who had set himself up as a connoisseur and dealer of Moroccan hash. In this he was unusual. Most of the dope pedalled in those days was from the subcontinent. Any colour you liked as long as it was black. It was heavy handed stuff, knockout, like a hammer on the head. Top Rocky was different. It actually got you high.

Jan occupied an apartment overlooking the canal and he knew their predicament. They wanted to offload, avoid the gauntlet of Dover. They talked prices, quality, market forces, but in the end he wanted a sample. As if to show them what they were up against he produced a chunk of his own, rolled a thin number and invited them to smoke. It was heady stuff.

An hour later they wandered back to the Sofitel. The hotel had an underground car park with several levels. Shyno took the Jag down to the bottom circle. It was past midnight and deserted. If ever he performed a frantic, furtive manoeuvre, that was it. Under the dull sodium flares, Lúcio standing watch, he undid the work on the rear seat, removed a sliver and then rearranged the furniture. They got a taxi over to Jan's place and put up with his rigmarole. He sniffed the taster, applied heat, crumbled it, mixed in some shag, rolled, fired up, inhaled, ruminated a while and pronounced judgement.

'Yeah, it's ok. How much do you need to move?

'Sixty pounds. And there is more, as you know.'

'My problem is I am holding already. Twenty keys of this.'
He picked up his piece of hash. 'I can help you out, but not immediately. I can do 350 a pound but I will need six weeks.'

He leant back, stubbed out the half smoked joint and shrugged as if to say, you went to all that hassle for this? In common modern parlance it was a deliberate diss.

Shyno was working the numbers. It was outrageous. A blatant rip off.

Lúcio smiled. It wasn't friendly.

'It seems to me you are running a retail outfit here, which is not what I was led to believe. Pity. I already have a set up on similar lines back in England. True, prices are marginally higher, but that merely reflects the higher risk of getting it there. So this is my proposal. Five hundred pounds a pound, cash up front. You can still make three on margin and take your time. Unfortunately our time is pressing.'

Jan ran a hand through his hair and made a petulant gesture.

'That's thirty grand.'

'Have you got a pipe? Anything to drink? Aquavit?'

Jan, somewhat uneasy, produced a stained meerschaum and passed it over. He had slid down into his bean bag and had to haul himself upright to get to the fridge. He came back with a bottle of *poire* William. Lúcio relieved him of the flask and tipped it up to his mouth. He gargled, swallowed and passed it to the Dutchy.

'*Sabroso. Toma su trago.*'

It was more a command than an invitation. Lúcio leant forward and broke off a pebble sized lump of Mustapha's labour and jammed it in the pipe.

'Light?'

Shyno rasped a Swan Vesta and held it over the bowl

while Lúcio puffed and passed over the glowing brazier.

'Have a proper smoke. No need to stand on ceremony. Take your time. It's all yours.'

Jan sucked, blew, deep throated and eventually started to cough. Lúcio kept thrusting the bottle at him, taking big swigs before he passed it over. He recharged the pipe and dared him to refuse the offer. Shyno was mesmerised. It was all too familiar. Can you take it, you fucker? Faker? Well, I can. It only took an hour to wreak the damage. Jan was gagging, blasted horizontal on his bean bag, flagging surrender. Lúcio had the whip in hand. Take that. Then he gave him his load.

'I have not come all this way to be buggered about. I am less desperate and more serious than you can hope to imagine. Leave it at that. You strike me as a time waster. A picture collector. Do you take me for a novice?'

They left the fly Dutchman wrecked on his floor. It was all down to Dover.

RELAY

'You probably think I was harsh?'

Lúcio was in reflective mode. They were en route back into Belgium heading for the port at Ostende. It was one of those now all too obvious diversions which in those days still counted for something. Arrive from Holland and you raised suspicion. Arrive from neighbouring Belgium with its shared open border and you did not. It was the infancy of smuggling.

'I've met a few Jans already in this game. I doubt if he had two ounces let alone twenty kilos to sell. He was main chancing. More than likely Alan put him up to it. If he was holding that much he would have simply said no, not interested, and spent six months ouncing out his stuff to extract every guilder. Mind you, it was pretty decent, but so is ours. I assume the mechanic was in for a fifty-fifty split if we had handed it over. Sit back and let the dope do the donkey work. It will be different back home. We are out of the retail business. It's not just a matter of numbers. I will set a bulk price and a reasonable time frame. If he chooses to sit on the stuff and parcel it out that's up to him. There's always some smart Al trying to chisel or cheat you. It's rarely an honourable arrangement.'

Shyno nodded and drove. It was a relief to hear Lúcio explain things in rational terms.

They were on the motorway heading to the coast. The Jag was behaving better but not perfectly. The odd blast of fresh air and occasional cigar did their work. At teatime they found themselves in a moderate queue, tickets purchased, waiting to board the ferry. They nosed forward, obedient to traffic control, waving them on and in. It was drizzling and overcast, but no wind. It promised a smooth crossing. They were about fifth in line. Shyno could see the metal ramp ahead leading to the car bay and the brief glow as each vehicle going in put on its lamps. He turned the key in the ignition and idled in neutral as the car in front nudged forward a few yards. He slipped the automatic to drive, touched the accelerator and the Jag juddered and stalled. Ok. No problem. Back to park, fire up, engage gear and go. Nothing. No? Ok, give it a moment. Don't panic. Check the gauges on the dash. Fuel? Three quarters full. Oil? Oil is fine. Water temperature, normal. No flashing red lights. Nothing out of the usual. Meanwhile they had become the front of the queue and were going nowhere. Shyno tried a third time. The Jag ignited, trundled forward five yards and died. The controller waved them on but it was no use. The big cat had inexplicably gone on strike. Shyno depressed the hazard button and slumped into the leather. Of all times to choose this not to start. The Belgian in his yellow waterproofs came over. Shyno rolled down the window and dredged up some French.

'La voiture ne marche pas. Je ne sais pourquoi.'

No one else did either. They sat there in the gloom while the waiting trail of vehicles detoured around them, until only they were left. The ramp was retracted and the ferry departed. Various officials came and went. The Jag's bonnet was raised and her innards examined. No one had the least idea, least of all the occupants. At first it was simply embarrassing, but underneath it all was the knowledge of their situation and that was frankly dire. Talk about putting on a show. It looked farcical but felt tragic. They sat there like fat ducks in the line of fire, just waiting for a hunter who wasn't fitted with blinkers. For the first and only time in a long liaison Lúcio seemed at a loss for words. Lost in the incontrovertible contingent world.

Shyno hated to break into the mystery that had propelled them this far.

'Can't see any alternative but to call out the AA. At least we have 5 star cover.' He couldn't even take credit for that. It was obligatory under French law. So he went to find a phone and after an hour the rescue service arrived. Their man did a few preliminary checks but couldn't fathom the problem. Shyno stood at his shoulder making encouraging noises while the mechanic made discouraging ones.

'Might be your head gasket. Or the starter motor. Transmission maybe. Not easy to tell, not without stripping her down. Liquid levels look ok. Plugs are fine. Not much I can do here gents. Looks as if you're going to need a tow. Might need more than that. She's automatic so she'll have to go backwards. Not really recommended over long distance. Top speed is fifty so it'll take a while. Let me see if I can get them to send out a flatbed. Better all round. Oh, off the record mind, I'm contracted to drive you to your destination, but I can't leave till morning. It's up to you if you want to go on ahead, but they won't cover your costs. Have a think while I make a call.'

Shyno got back in the car and relayed the news. For twenty minutes they discussed the cons. There weren't many pros. Meanwhile another line of vehicles was forming at their rear. Shyno switched the hazards on again and they sat there growing colder as dusk settled in. There were lights in his rear mirror and the queue behind them began to snake its way around the obstacle and onto the six o'clock ferry. There was a rubberneck in every motor. Some indignant, but in the main, pitying. Glad it wasn't them. Little did they know. Their mechanic reappeared on cue and delivered an update.

'Can't get a vehicle out till tomorrow. I'll have to tow you to the depot.'

Shyno told him that they had decided to travel on ahead. Breakdown man nodded.

'Wise choice, in my opinion. Now, where do you want the vehicle taken. Is there a dealer in Oxford? You might want the Jaguar people to have a look see.'

The last thing Shyno wanted was an expert poking around in the car.

'If not, it's the garage of your choice or your home address.'

Shyno could just see the low loader pulling up outside Alan's lockup with a posse of unmarked police cars in tow. He had already resigned himself to getting busted, it seemed inevitable. Alan would simply give the know-nothing nod and sooner rather than later the drug squad would be knocking on their door. Shyno felt an immense lassitude overcome him as he gave the AA their home address. He still had enough resilience to torture himself with a favourite quote. *A long loneliness limps in front of me. A mortally weary, death intoxicated sadness, which speaks with a yawn.*

The AA man took possession of the keys and the kilos, wrote down their details and promised a next day delivery.

'Any idea when, roughly?'

'Around sundown. All depends on the chaps at Dover. The paperwork.'

The poets took the next ferry on foot, arrived at said port, walked through, caught a stopping train to Victoria, tubed to

Paddington, napped back to Oxford, indulged in a cab to Kingston Road and crashed, oblivious to every consequence.

NOWHERE TO RUN TO

Nowhere to hide. Shyno woke with a thumping headache and that lyric going round in his brain like a stuck record. He looked at his watch and grimaced. He'd only been asleep for three hours and it wasn't yet dawn. He could hear music coming from downstairs and the smell of incense burning. Clearly Lúcio hadn't been able to sleep either. Nerves? Unlikely, the fellow was incapable. Probably writing. Or up to some juju.

Shyno kept returning to the question that had been nagging at him ever since they boarded the ferry. Should they have stayed with the car? Of course it was a pointless exercise in speculation but it occupied his mind nonetheless. At the time he had been persuaded that an AA man going about his job would attract little attention from the officials at Dover. Just another professional in a uniform doing a day's work. But if they had been there then they could have acted as some sort of distraction, played for the sympathy vote. Shyno had kept his own counsel throughout the journey. Lúcio had no truck with second-guessing. Once a decision had been taken that was it. If ever Shyno indulged in what Lúcio called *extra-gesis*, he would quote Eliot on 'anxious worried women' and call him The Amplifier. And he meant it literally, as if by turning up the volume on an idea you might actually bring it about.

'Thoughts are things, you should know that by now.'

Shyno wondered if he thought long and loud enough he

could bring about their freedom. He pulled on an absurd dressing gown that Lúcio had given him, a heavy black silk number with a Chinese dragon in gold embroidery on the back, and wandered downstairs. The dining room table looked like a wizard's drawing board.

Guttering candle, mouse skull, Ephemeris. I-Ching open at chapter 64, three thrupenny bits. A piece of rose crystal on a short string for dowsing. A small heap of grains of white rice. A jar of honey. Pierced cowrie shells. Coral bead necklaces. An incense cone smoking.

Lúcio was crouched down in the kitchen in his cotton pyjamas, chef's hat on his head, talking to Elegua.

The small stained god was in the corner on the black and red Victorian tiles near the back door. There was a saucer in front of it, a smouldering cigar and a miniature gourd half filled with firewater. Had there been a farm nearby no doubt that diminutive altar would have been furnished with a headless cockerel and some fresh blood to boot. Meantime Lúcio was chanting, over and over, a Yoruba praise song, which sounded like the nearest thing to poetry in a barbarous tongue.

Shyno backed off and went into the downstairs front room that overlooked the street. There was a gap on the other side of the road where he tried to imagine the Jag safely home and parked. The full moon above the terrace opposite was doing something he had never seen before. It must have been an effect of the mist but it was spectral nonetheless. There was an air of relaxation, of true ease, about the planet. It was laid back in every sense. There was the familiar defused torchlight effect, fading into black. But around the cone two distinct circles, one a shade of purple, one indigo, circled the beam like thick static smoke rings. It was mesmerising, like looking at the cool white tip of a glowing cigar. Shyno bathed in the ghostly light for what became hours as the vision drifted above the rooftops and then faded in the dawn.

So what does a sober sailor do, standing on the plank?

Nothing. Just waits and accepts his fate.

The day crept by. Shyno spent part of it watching from the upstairs window. He went out and did a furtive scout of the nearby streets searching for advance forces. He had moments of paranoia. He made up and then retracted a confession. At noon they walked to the corner store and got in some food. They ate crumpets, drank tea and fell asleep around four. It was already dark when they were roused by the banging on the front door knocker.

Lúcio rolled over.

'You go.'

Shyno stumbled out of bed and into some clothes. As he came out onto the top landing he glanced right towards the upstairs sitting room and saw through the sash windows the metronomic flashes of a warning light from the street below. Fuck, this is them now.

Except it wasn't them. It was him, Keith, their mechanic and the flashing light just the warm yellow beacon of the low loader with the Jag perched on top. Shyno couldn't accept what he saw. He gave a furtive glance left and right down the road expecting a trap. He felt a compelling urge to relieve himself and might have done so had not Keith spoken and snapped him out of his funk.

'Are you alright, mate? Got your motor here. No fears. Had a good run up from the coast. The lads are on short time at Dover. Union dispute. The port was clogged. They were waving us through.' He was and almost certainly had been speeding.

Shyno nearly fell into his arms. Lúcio was in the hallway standing behind ready to sign the paperwork. Keith found a triple slot further up the road, tilted the flatbed, slipped the Jag off and was gone: on to the next one.

Lúcio went back inside to phone Alan. Keys in hand, Shyno walked a hundred yards up the street, turned around and walked back, all the while anticipating the feel of his collar. On a whim he opened up the car, got in, reached for the ignition and turned the key in its slot. It fired first time and the motor stayed running. He selected drive and eased forward. Still running. He pulled out into the road and took a short spin around the block, came back and parked. The motor kept on running. Shyno switched off the engine and sniffed the air. The dope was still there. He sensed that he was on the brink of madness and that if he wasn't very careful he was headed for his own kind of breakdown.

THE OTHER AA

Alan turned up around ten with Lenny in tow. They arrived in a peeling Morris Traveller. Lenny was a gaunt, dedicated smoker and the mechanic's main distributor for the Thames valley area. He had been Lúcio's first choice of driver both for the boat and the car. Shyno had sampled a taste of his road philosophy on a stretch of winding tarmac between Pangbourne and Newbury. They were stuck in a tailback caused by a tractor when Lenny simply pulled out across the double whites and overtook three cars, just managing to force his way back into a non-existent gap and avoid being totalled by a Transit coming the opposite way around a blind corner. Turning his tar-stained, snag toothed grin toward a petrified Shyno he proclaimed,

'It's only a white line, mate, not a fuckin' wall.'

The poets had already agreed not to dwell on the mystery of the Jag's misbehaviour. Alan would take it to his lockup, unload and vacuum it out before returning the car. Lenny would bring the bulk of the dope back to Oxford for them to sit on, bar a few slabs which he would keep to prime and test the market. Lúcio proposed five hundred a pound. Alan swallowed it. Shyno gave a précis of their mishap with the motor. The Mechanic listened with occasional grunts.

'More than likely a block in the fuel line. Happens with that foreign muck. Could be a circuit coil. I'll check it out.' Then he got on to the business with YaYa. He didn't amplify there either.

Bad luck, worse timing, what with the storm and all that. Banged up, but he won't talk. Hardly get a word out of him anyway. Nothing on him. Not even a passport. That's why they done him. Main thing is, keep Lucy sweet so she doesn't freak out. Consul's on the job, but it takes time.

Case dismissed.

They left around midnight. The poets crashed and were awake early to receive their delivery. And that, with a few minor variations, was how it went. They kept the slabs of dope in the basement. Lenny made regular visits, bringing wads of soiled notes and retrieving the next batch of smoke. It was going well. The punters were loving it. Easy money as the press would have it, but it was far from that. Nev ventured round occasionally. He had bought himself some new boots and a set of custom made crutches with proper padded handles. He admitted he was having trouble getting used to them. That he was using again – not much you know but you know how it is. Rich steered clear, went back to LA. Waiting for the word on the Tío. Alan pitched up a couple of times in a late model Transit to give the low down on Dave and his prospects for release. He played down the danger of word getting back, but he acted shifty. He didn't hang about. Lúcio carried on composing as if nothing was untoward. Shyno hunched up and hunkered down for the long haul, taking it all on board, porter and night watchman rolled into one.

ENOUGH IS NOT ENOUGH

Over the next nine months and during four subsequent trips down to the boat and back, Shyno endured many small things and learned one big one. There was nothing glamorous about the business they were in. It was an exercise in monotony punctuated by outbreaks of fear.

Of course there was money, loads of it, but it went as it came, in tranches. The first run produced almost 30k. The second the same. Ten went to Larry, ten to Nev, ten to Escargot. Ten went via Lucy to a Moroccan lawyer to sort out YaYa. Ten seemed to be the going rate.

They decided to use a different car for each trip in case they were spotted. Four decent secondhand Jags at around, yes, ten a pop. Once they had been cut and shut, Alan sold them for scrap. *Can't take the risk mate*, though Shyno doubted it. Lúcio bought the house they were renting in a distress sale. They were sitting tenants and the owner wanted to emigrate. It was a steal at eleven. Then there were the overheads, the running costs: mooring fees, fuel, villas, hotels and restaurants, most of them starred.

For the second run they drove a discrete brown Daimler with same set up as before, sills and interior. Alan agreed that a thin seal of mastic would prevent any smell. Back at Banus, José Murillo seemed relieved when they entered his office since they were two weeks overdue with their bill. While Lúcio explained that they were moving up the coast, Shyno went and rang the bell to the apartment. There was no answer and the blinds were closed. As they drove to the public car park, Lúcio handed him an envelope. It was empty except for Enrique's business card with a hand initialled G in the bottom right corner.

The trip up the coast was uneventful. A six hour chug on a calm sea on a clear day. They took their prepaid allotted berth next to the two cruisers Rich had described, still wrapped in their tarps, no sign of the owners. It was a twenty minute walk to the town, an hour back by cab to Banus to pick up the car and the same for the return journey. The house they had rented was pretty much like Villa Nova, high on a hill above the marina, secluded, good garage, only newer and with decent showers. It was the same drill as before, except they could park ten feet from the stern of the *Mona Gorda* and there was no one about. Two more bales, three days of cutting and packing. No Nev this time so it was a solo effort. Lúcio ate, drank, composed and slept. They took the east coast route for a change and crossed at Perpignan. No further mishaps on the way home. No smell. No drama. Almost routine.

In late January after the run, Lúcio began shopping in earnest. The house first, then furniture, then furs. True it was a fierce winter. He became an habitué of several antique dealers in North Oxford. Acquired an 18th century mahogany gate legged dining table and matching chairs; a reupholstered dropdown Regency sofa in dove coloured velvet and two Rococo plaster Italianate mirrors. It was a small two up two down but he managed to stuff it with treasures. He dropped another ten on four full length fur coats. A matching pair of grey and black opossums, improbably thick and heavy, with high Russian collars and ludicrous suede belts. A brown bear pelt with fur as deep as your wrist. And to top it all an ankle length mink. Fedoras to go with them he picked up in Paris.

Shyno had no say in these purchases, they simply appeared. As did the two bottles of 1927 Château D'Yquem which they downed at a sitting. Meanwhile there was a salon to support, with first growth wines, uncut coke, caviar, ribs of beef and poetry, which cost something. Lúcio continued to write in any of the five languages he chose. Shyno made wry faces or struck a pose. He was stuck in the middle. It was all about women, the lack of them, what to do with them, and how to live without. It had been seven years. And the same went for money.

Lúcio had always been inventive with the truth but he started to lie for the fun of it. When confronted he claimed that he only lied to those who wished to be deceived. He became his own mythmaker, the *mythomane* of later years. It was compulsive and completely unnecessary. Instead of having two narratives to keep up, Shyno had several to maintain. Schroders, copper, pork belly futures, property, inward and outward investment. It was one thing to be evasive about the source of their income another to parade it. Besides, no one was asking. Anyone entering his sphere took it as given that he was independently rich. It all seemed reckless and undignified but Lúcio wouldn't be told. In private Shyno became the Official Leader of the Opposition. In public he nodded and toed the lines.

It was on the road, somewhere in the deserts of Murcia, on their fourth run home that Shyno asked outright for his share of the loot. Lúcio gave him a contemptuous glare.

'Aren't you farting rather higher than your arse?'

It was a calculated insult, designed to remind him of his place. As kept minion, chauffeur, domestic skivvy, and for some while now no longer the inspiration for Lúcio's poetry or willing participant in bed.

Shyno lashed out and caught him with the back of his half clenched fist on the side of the mouth. It produced an immediate welt and later some bruising. It almost certainly hurt. But it was the mixture of rapture and disdain in Lúcio's gaze that hurt the most.

'Well, if you insist, you can have the boat.'

Sometimes it is not common to explain. Shyno could do nothing with *Mona Gorda*. Could not afford her. Neither the fuel, nor the fees, nor her upkeep. So he kept his counsel. There was a coolness between them on the long trip home which took weeks to thaw.

THE ART OF LOSING

Is not hard to master. Try losing further, faster.

It was nine months of hard labour since YaYa mooted the idea of a boat and the first day of his release back in England. He spent it with his family and as Alan relayed, wasn't really up for a meet, not yet anyways. It turned out Dave's keepers had bashed him about, for being rowdy. He'd lost a fair bit of weight. Admitted talking but couldn't be certain what he'd said. Tired, just needed time to get himself right. And money. Money was tight.

It was an unsubtle threat and Lúcio paid him his share. More than fair. What with the lawyers and Lucy his cut came to twenty.

YaYa. Dear dim Dave, skulking somewhere on the boulevards of Milton Keynes. They never saw his light again. Put out that candle.

Meanwhile the last of the dope was in. *Mona Gorda* lay empty and clean, lapping at the dockside in an obscure marina somewhere near Nerja.

Shyno pursued his claim and Lúcio knew he was onto a loser, losing the only game that really mattered to him.

'Fifteen thousand pounds then. You can buy the corner shop. Be your own boss. Newspapers, sweets, stamps.'

It was a calculated dismissal. Take it and leave. For your little life without me.

'I'll think about it.'

And what he thought about was this. First the insult. As a

divorce settlement, which in essence it was, or as a share of the spoils, it was derisory. As an estimate of his worth, it seemed worse. Pride. Vanity. Greed. Three unwise counselors told him there would be a bigger payout down the road; that he deserved better, that he was owed. For services rendered. As for women, there would be time, opportunities would present themselves. It was all deluded nonsense of course. He was mostly afraid of having to invent himself on his own. It seemed easier to exist as the invention of someone else.

Six years later when he finally abandoned their project there was nothing left to leave, or leave with. But that is a different tale.

'Thou hast committed fornication. But that was in another country and besides, the wench is dead.'

In short, Shyno stayed.

LAST ORDERS

On August 18th, 1979, the day before his twenty seventh birthday, Shyno picked his way down the wooden stairs to the cellar. It was damp, cool like a larder, but not dripping wet. After all Thelma, one of Lúcio's muses, had slept six months down there, painting ethereal still lives, fending off the chill with a small blow heater. Just dry enough, short term, to store the hash.

It was a bare whitewashed room with a concrete floor, littered with scraps of cellophane wrapping and the residues of *Mona Gorda*'s haul. Lenny had come for the last few blocks and off cuts a few days before. Shyno took with him a dustpan and brush, a black bag and the hoover. In the end there wasn't much left over – Lenny had been pretty thorough, as a scavenger should – and what there was, unsmokeable. A mixture of dust, dirt, debris and plastic. Shyno swept it all up, vacuumed the floor and later burnt the detritus in the back garden. He opened the tiny sash window that gave onto the bin bay, lit a tealight and left it to burn.

Lúcio was in the upstairs room. He spent much of his time there reading, composing at night, listening to music, sometimes venturing to the shared bed. They had established a kind of truce, a temporary peace, though as he put it in an English poem,

'Peace is not always clear. It is opaque, full of splinters.'

Whenever the opposite threatened to break out they would quote to eachother a lyric from the one incontrovertibly great poet alive in England whose words had helped keep them from war.

'Lion and lioness, the mild
Inflammable beasts,
At their precise peril kept
Distance and repose.'

Or Tomlinson and 'Hawks'.

Lindesay and 'Salome'.

'I need an ocean's plunging silences
to bless my undiscovered face – to drown.'

Hart Crane. Bespoke voyages. Cruises to the bottom of the sea.

TSE. 'Marina':

'What seas, what shores?'

'Dover Beach':

'Its melancholy, long, withdrawing roar.'

Names. Names.

Poetry.

'For poetry makes nothing happen.'

But for them it was their mask and metier and it held them together. Meantime the subtext was money and dope talk, to a backbeat of white lines chopped out on mirrors.

THE POLICE IN DIFFERENT VOICES

'No, you go.'

'I suppose I'd better.'

There were three more emphatic blows with the brass knocker followed by a thump that rattled the front door, then a bellow:

'Open up! Now!'

It was the dark hour before dawn and being midsummer about four in the morning. KNOCK KNOCK KNOCK. No need to wonder *who's there,* not with that infernal racket. Lúcio rolled out of bed straightening his chef's hat. He was wearing old fashioned striped pyjamas with the top button of his jacket done up. It was one of his foibles. He slipped on his loafers and padded off down the stairs. Shyno pulled on jeans and went barefoot to the upstairs sitting room. As he knelt on the sofa to peer out he had the distinct sensation that he was watching a police procedural on the television so familiar was the detail. Two squad cars at opposing angles blocking the road, blue lights flashing. A white Transit in the middle with all the dinky decals, the driver in his seat holding a walkie talkie. No sirens of course. No advance warning. The contents of the van and cars numbered nine. A bit over the top he thought. He leant forward and could see the front path right up to the arch which sheltered their doorstep. The troops were in a double line, each of them bulked up with protective jackets. No helmets, no firearms, at least not un-holstered, just batons. This was North Oxford after all, not

Brixton.

'Open the fucking door or we'll break it down!'

Bang. Bang. Bang. Lights going on in the house opposite, a furtive twitching of net curtains. What on earth was Lúcio doing? Taking so long. One of the raiders glanced up and caught Shyno staring out.

'Oi! You! Don't you bloody move!' The others looked up and started pointing and shouting. Shyno pulled back from the window. It was as if he had poked a stick into a hornets nest. He went back along the corridor and down the stairs. Lúcio emerged from the dining room with a mug of tea in his hand.

Thump. Thump. Thump. A gloved fist on the Victorian wood panelling.

'Right! You've had your last warning. We're coming in.'

Lúcio was almost at the door. Shyno had seen the officer with the short metal battering ram practising his moves in the front garden. The Yale lock was ancient and flimsy. There were no deadbolts, metal plates, steel cages. A shoulder charge or short arm jab was all that was required, but nothing was required as Lúcio was opening up. If they were expecting armed resistance they were deceived. There was only one weapon to hand and that was wit and to that they were impervious.

'What seems to be the trouble, officer?'

It was like the starting pistol at the National. A big bloke waving a bit of paper barked,

'Warrant to search the premises, on suspicion of...'

The rest was lost in the thunder of boots rushing past, clumping up the stairs and throughout the house. Melee at Melling Road, doors banged open, whinnying cries, a good deal of intimidatory swearing, before they all settled down and got into their stride.

'You, in here!'

'You, upstairs.'

They were truly a pumped up bunch of plods. Takes some nerve to burst in on a pair of desperadoes, mob-handed, putting a bit of stick about, never know what you might encounter. In some gesture towards politically correct PCs, one of them was female. She was a gem, a real find. A sour faced bottle blonde specimen fizzing with hostility.

'Fuckin' poofs!'

It occurred to Shyno that the force was recruiting from more or less the same strata of society as the criminals it pursued. The dregs pitched against their kin. Only legal. Power, if granted strength, equals pigs.

So they rooted about, turned the turf over, nosed in among private places, snuffled and sniffed and came up empty handed. Each suspect was required to accompany a pair of officers as they conducted their search. To bear witness.

Cellar? Empty.

Kitchen? Cupboards full. Each jar and container shaken out and shaken down. *Nada*. Front room downstairs, ditto. Ditto the dining room. Then they missed a bit. A free standing bookcase in the upstairs sitting room. A chest high mahogany glass fronted cabinet, its shelves stacked with poetry. They weren't to know. That the top lifted off and underneath there were wooden cross struts where Lúcio had stuffed maybe twenty grand, tied up with rubber bands. It was all that was left.

Things got a tad grubby when missy worked over the bedroom. She was poking about in a chest of drawers when she found Lúcio's collection of Tom of Finland cartoons and a novelty toy, impossible to use. A yard long double headed pink monstrosity of improbable dimensions, for amusement only. She didn't find it funny.

'Take a look at this! Fucking queers, fudge packers.'

It was as though their mere existence were some affront to her gender.

'I think the words you are looking for are homosexual and sodomy, madam,' said Lúcio. That got her tits. Two red patches flared on her cheeks and she made as if to spit.

There were the polaroids as well. At the dock in Puerto Andratx. Of *Laurene* before they painted out her name; Larry with a gin; a grinning Wilhelm; Lúcio, Nev, Shyno. The other officer jabbed a finger at their lucky mascot.

'This one looks familiar.'

'Unmistakeable,' said Lúcio.

Shyno was beginning to share his disdain.

'Is this your boat?

'Yes?'

'Do you own a pink Jaguar?'

'No.'

'Do you currently own a vehicle?'

'No. We scrapped our last car several weeks ago, it was unreliable. We now rely on public transport and the kindness of strangers.'

'Right. Get dressed. You're both coming down to the station.'

'Are we under arrest?'

'Helping with enquiries.'

Lúcio fixed the goon in charge with his most winning smile.

'It would appear that you are in need of some assistance.'

The gorilla didn't like that, he didn't like any of it. Come barging in on the back of some useless information, expecting a major bust, and all he had got for his trouble was a yard of paperwork. Nine hours and nine months too late. He would have had a fit if he'd known that.

'Listen matey, don't push your luck.'

By the time they got downstairs the van had departed. They were handled not bundled into the waiting squad cars. Ten minutes later they were passing Christchurch on their way to the lockup and the sun was burning off the morning dew on the meadow. They were neither fingerprinted nor charged, though they were taken to separate cells, freshly painted in cream and pink like a confection from Walls. At around eleven breakfast was served. A yellow sponge of scrambled egg in a puddle of water, soggy toast and tea. No one came with any further questions or enquiries. They were left to stew. Around noon Lúcio began singing, Shyno could hear it down the corridor. A negro spiritual, then a rendition of Kumbaya in a fine baritone. A fist banged on the nearby cell door.

'Quieten down in there!'

Of course Lúcio didn't. He chanted until the sergeant let them out, some twenty minutes later.

'Alright, you're free to go.'

They wandered out on to Speedwell Street, strolled up past Tom Quad and down St Aldates. At Pusey House, Lúcio popped in to have a word with the priests. He was booked to give a talk there in a week or so on 'The Folly Of Redemption'. Then they were heading back to Jericho. As they passed Sunshine Records *'It's just a kiss away, kiss away'* was ricocheting through the open door.

'So, what now?'

Shyno had paused outside the Phoenix Cinema. It was

showing Gimme Shelter.

'Maybe a spell in South Beach. Head down to Bogotá and visit Muzo. Drop in on Enrique. Say hi to Gloria?'

Hell. It was his birthday. They were in the clear. Ok. Deal.

'Better have a word with Jade.'

'I agree.'

APPENDIX

OBITUARY

The Brazilian poet Bruno Tolentino, who died this summer, was a personage far stranger than fiction. He won the Premio Revelacao de autor for his first book, Anulação e outros reparos (1963). Moving to Europe to translate Ungaretti, he apparently worked as an interpreter for the then EEC before publishing the very fine French volume Le Vrai Le Vain (1971). It is a graceful meditation on phenomenology as experience.

He subsequently worked at Bristol University teaching Portuguese before moving to Oxford, where he published a striking but incompletely successful volume in English, About the Hunt (1978) under the imprint of Oxford Poetry Now.

When I met him in Oxford, he lived a life of Epicurean leisure and claimed acquaintance with the cream of Europe's literary figures. How much of this was true I never knew; most of it, I suspect. I know he was friends with Yves Bonnefoy and Eugenio de Andrade, and knew Charles Tomlinson and Michael Hamburger. His then aisance was explained some years later when he was convicted of cocaine smuggling.

He served his sentence partly in Dartmoor and was deported to Brazil, where he published As Horas de Katerina (Premio Jabuti, 1995) and A balada do carcere (Premio

Abgar Renault, 1997). He won a second Jabuti in 2003 for
O mundo como Idéia and a third posthumously in 2007 for
A Imitação do Amanhacer.

Short, slight and handsome in appearance, vain, garru-
lous, and charming in person, Bruno was a man of prodi-
gious talents. Fluent in French, Spanish, Italian, German
and English, he could quote from these at the drop of a hat:
Rilke, Machado, Montale, Calderón and Bonnefoy might be
followed by Agrippa d'Aubigné or Luis de León. Bandeira,
Drummond de Andrade, Cecília Meireles and Adélia Prado
were often on his tongue. When quoting Ungaretti ('Questi
cretini Svedesi') in relation to Quasimodo's Nobel, he ac-
quired Ungaretti's features.

His company was always disconcerting since he was a
pathological liar. Nothing he said could be assumed to be
true. He claimed descent from Il Condottiere Tolentino and
did indeed strongly resemble the figure in the National Gal-
lery's section of the Battle of San Romano. But he might
equally produce bottles of Sainsbury's Beaume de Venise,
announcing airily: 'From my college.' His charm and aston-
ishment when his lies were questioned meant that increduli-
ty generally went unspoken.

I would describe his belief-system as 'cosmological hypo-
chondria': he combined a vestigial Catholicism with voodoo
observances, astrology and almost any other available
practice. Promiscuously bisexual, he entertained a coterie of
bright young things from the University and a number of
moronic hangers-on who seemed only there to allow him to
continue talking. This he would do even after one had left
the room, reeling one back into the room on interminable
sentences.

For my undergraduate self, meeting this cosmopolitan

figure felt like an amazing privilege. After graduating, I would often turn up at the door of his Kingston Road house and join the talk that went on into the early hours. He was invariably flattering company, assuming one's acquaintance with world literature, interested in one's opinion, and purveying fine wines and drugs. Here was a notion of civilisation rather remote from my experience of Oxford classics and analytical philosophy. He broadened my horizons considerably and introduced me to many abiding literary influences. Later, having apparently fallen on harder times, he came to live in the house I was sharing on Walton Street, and was occasionally visited by mysterious persons bearing cash in brown-paper bags. He would rise at two in the afternoon and breakfast daily on roast rib of beef and tinned potatoes, sometimes wearing a white-paper voodoo hat for the day. Even in this house-share context, his air of distinction (in which one was assumed to share) was all-encompassing.

I had no contact with him after his deportation. The nature of the remunerative investments he had been offering made clear by his conviction. He was by then a desperate man. But the advent of the web meant that I could tune in to his activities from time to time. He seemed true to form, inveighing against the cultural decline of Brazil and the fallible linguistic knowledge of his contemporaries.

The web also showed that he had 'taught at Oxford University'; that About the Hunt had been published by OUP; that Dartmoor Prison was known in England as 'Devil's Island'; that he had been both 'pardoned' by the British Government and 'acknowledged to have been the victim of an injustice' (see the obituary in O Globo online). His works and lies survive him.

De mortuis nil nisi bonum. But that would hardly do justice to Bruno. It is not often that one meets a drug-smuggling poet of distinction. And Bruno was a poet of distinction, one of the few twentieth-century poets to have accomplished the feat of writing well in more than one language. Flawed, infuriating, brilliant, he marked my life and I cherish his memory.

Chris Miller

ACKNOWLEDGEMENTS AND THANKS

To Chris Miller for permission to reprint his Obituary which first appeared in PN Review 2008 and for his unflagging enthusiasm and editorial support. Ben Steiner who urged me to write the story and encouraged me to finish it. Fabienne Pagnier for her generous help in formatting the text. Matthew Astley for designing the cover. Hamish Pringle for permission to use his photograph of Bruno Tolentino, copyright 1972. Lastly to all those who read the manuscript in draft and without whose encouragement DAS BOOTY might well have sunk without trace. Too many to name but you know who you are.

Author's note
DAS BOOTY is a true story but it is not reportage. It is an imaginative recreation of actual events and I have employed a degree of poetic licence in telling the tale.

Lightning Source UK Ltd.
Milton Keynes UK
UKOW02f0746071114

241258UK00001B/7/P